T0168186

ARCHAEOLOGICAL INVESTIGATIONS IN WEST-CENTRAL ARIZONA:

THE CYPRUS-BAGDAD PROJECT

Prepared for

The Cyprus-Bagdad Copper Company

By

Laurance D. Linford

with Revisions by

David A. Phillips, Jr.
Richard G. Ervin

Edited by

John F. Robertson

Submitted by

Cultural Resource Management Section
Arizona State Museum
The University of Arizona

June 1979

Archaeological Series No. 136

ABSTRACT

For ten weeks during the late spring and summer of 1976, the Arizona State Museum conducted data recovery operations at seven archaeological sites as part of the Cyprus-Bagdad Project. These sites were located within the right-of-way of a pipeline to be built by the Cyprus-Bagdad Copper Company, and were investigated in an effort to mitigate adverse impacts from pipeline construction.

Research conducted within the project was directed primarily toward problems involving prehistoric adaptation to the local environment. The analyzed data were applied to the testing of hypotheses regarding the relationship of site locations to local availability of water and to the locations of economically significant resources. Also tested were hypotheses intended to assess the importance of agriculture as a mode of subsistence for the area's prehistoric inhabitants.

The data were also used to determine the functions of individual project sites. Analysis indicates that these sites represent differing functions ranging from specialized activities such as lithic raw material procurement and wild plant food procurement and processing to long-term habitation. At least one site possessed material remains that indicated its inhabitants practiced agriculture. Evidence from the project sites also suggests that the availability of water was perhaps the primary consideration of the area's prehistoric inhabitants in determining site location.

The history of previous anthropological research and the culture history of the project area are briefly discussed. All seven project sites are described in terms of their condition when discovered; morphology; environment; architectural and agricultural features; and chipped stone, ground stone, and ceramic assemblages. The appendices to this report discuss the criteria used in evaluating the various artifact assemblages and the location and composition of local source areas of lithic raw material.

TABLE OF CONTENTS

LIST OF FIGURES

LIST OF TABLES

CHAPTER 1

INTRODUCTION

Recent federal legislation, particularly the National Environmental Policy Act of 1969 and the National Historic Preservation Act of 1966, has heightened the awareness of government agencies and the public concerning the irreversible effects of technology upon our nation's cultural resources. The Cyprus-Bagdad Project is the result of a combined effort by the Cyprus Mines Corporation and the Bureau of Land Management (BLM) to meet the requirements of these laws.

The National Environmental Policy Act of 1969 states that it is the "continuing responsibility of the Federal Government to use all practicable means...to improve and coordinate Federal plans, functions, programs, and resources to the end that the Nation may... preserve important historic, cultural, and natural aspects of our cultural heritage" (as quoted in McGimsey 1972: 119). The Historic Preservation Act of 1966 further directs that "any Federal department or independent agency having authority to license any undertaking shall prior to...the issuance of any license...take into account the effect of the undertaking" (as quoted in McGimsey 1972: 113).

Over half of the Cyprus-Bagdad pipeline right-of-way affects land administered by the Bureau of Land Management. In order to comply with federal legislation, the BLM requested as a provision of their pipeline permit (A-8876) that the Cyprus-Bagdad Copper Company conduct archaeological studies of the pipeline right-of-way in order to locate and to mitigate the effects of construction on any archeological remains in areas of direct and indirect impact.

Project History

In October of 1975, a week-long archaeological survey was conducted for the Cyprus-Bagdad Copper Company by the Cultural Resource Management Section of the Arizona State Museum along 58 km (36 miles) of a proposed pipeline right-of-way. The surveyed right-of-way, 15.24 m (50 feet) wide, was for installation of a 61-cm (24-inch) pipeline to bring water from wells north of Wikieup to Bagdad as part of the expansion of the Cyprus-Bagdad Copper Mine.

This survey identified six archaeological sites within the proposed corridor. All sites were located in the eastern portion of

1

2

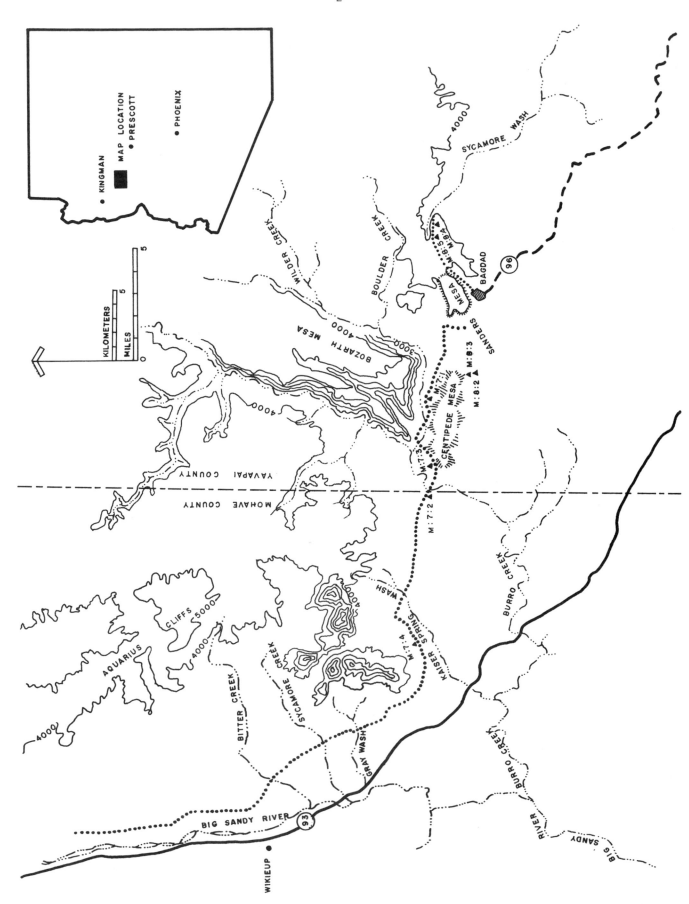

Figure 1. Location of the Cyprus-Bagdad pipeline right-of-way

the pipeline route (Hammack 1975) (Figure 1). Hammack recommended
that Cyprus-Bagdad mark the site boundaries with flagging tape and
avoid the sites in the course of building the pipeline. However, the
company determined that avoidance was not feasible, and requested
that the Arizona State Museum develop a research strategy to mitigate
the adverse effects of construction upon the cultural remains.

Phase I

Phase I of the project consisted of a one-week testing phase
carried out in April 1976 to identify the research potential, subsurface extent, and most appropriate research strategy for each site.
During this testing, one site identified in the survey proved to be
a deposit of erosional material; this site, AZ M:7:1, was omitted
from the research design. In addition, the Cyprus-Bagdad Copper Company had decided to avoid two other sites (AZ M:8:2 and AZ M:8:3).
However, subsequent inspection of these sites by the archaeological
field crew showed that they were still in danger of at least indirect
impact due to the large amount of construction associated with other
aspects of the mine expansion. Accordingly, permission was obtained
for limited data recovery from these sites.

Phases II and III

Phase II research, comprising an eight-week field season for
data recovery, was begun in May 1976 with a crew of six. During this
excavation phase, additional survey work was requested by the sponsor.
Under provisions of the Phase II contractual agreement, a single
right-of-way for both a transmission line and a second, shorter pipeline also associated with the mine expansion was surveyed. The
right-of-way, which was approximately 3.2 km (2 miles) long and 100 m
(300 feet) wide, extended from a newly drilled well to a mobile home
park about 5.6 km (3.5 miles) northeast of Bagdad along Sycamore
Creek. These utilities had been installed one year previously without benefit of an archaeological survey. Survey work was subsequently
required, however, since the lines crossed BLM land. Consequently, a
"post facto" survey was performed, and two sites (AZ M:8:4 and
AZ M:8:5) were found to have been disturbed by the pipeline and by
construction of an access road. Furthermore, both sites were subject
to additional secondary impact due to increased recreational and off-
road vehicular use following the opening of the access road. Therefore, two additional weeks of study (Phase III) were undertaken to
recover any remaining cultural data.

In addition to this work, two small surveys were conducted
during Phases II and III. The Cyprus-Bagdad Copper Company chose to
use sand and gravel deposits in Kaiser Spring Wash and Gray Wash in

the construction of the pipeline. Surveys were performed in and around the perimeters of these proposed borrow areas, the first just south of the juncture of Burro Creek Road and Kaiser Spring Wash, and the second in Gray Wash, due east of the Arizona Public Service 345 kV Mead to Liberty transmission line. Each surveyed area was approximately 656 m (2000 feet) by 65 m (200 feet). A single, small lithic scatter (AZ M:7:5) was found next to Gray Wash. It was well outside the impact zone, and though observations of site content were made, no collections were taken.

The Data Base

The Cyprus-Bagdad Project data recovery phases dealt with a total of seven sites (Table 1):

Table 1. Archaeological site types from Cyprus-Bagdad Project

Number of Sites	Types of Sites
1	Habitation (AZ M:7:2)
1	Lithic procurement and agriculture (AZ M:7:3)
1	Lithic manufacture (AZ M:8:2)
2	Extensive sherd and lithic scatters (AZ M:7:4 and AZ M:8:3)
2	Small sherd and lithic scatters (AZ M:8:4 and AZ M:8:5)

Seven sites along a narrow corridor constitute a limited data base for a regional research approach. However, the multisite framework which the project used allows an examination of these data within a fairly broad perspective. As Goodyear points out (1975: 12-14), transects are valuable in a number of interpretive functions. Given proper consideration of cultural and natural formation processes (Goodyear 1975: 12; Schiffer 1972, 1975a), the reconstruction of past activities relating to a particular locus can be accomplished through the use of behavioral chain analysis (see Chapter 2). Furthermore,

Schiffer (1975b: 1) asserts that under the proper conditions "there is no site that cannot provide relevant information for some substantive, technical, methodological or theoretical problem of interest in archaeology. Once the data have been compiled, the "relevant information" from the various sites can be used in addressing broader, regional problems relating to such topics as cultural ecology, settlement, and subsistence (Goodyear 1975: 12, 13). Linear transects of the nature of the Cyprus-Bagdad Project extend for miles and traverse numerous biotic zones; it should be possible to make observations concerning human adaptation within each zone. Admittedly, a 50-foot wide corridor allows only a limited sample of each biotic zone, and thus cannot serve as a basis for establishing exhaustive schemes concerning such adaptations. However, it is possible (if not imperative) to apply newly acquired information in the support of or in comparison with previously established data and observations (Goodyear 1975:13). Accordingly, the archaeologist should not hesitate to point out broader patterns of behavior suggested by data from linear transects. As long as these observations are presented in the form of suggestions rather than confirmed fact, they may prove useful to subsequent projects of regional scope.

Rather than discuss the results of this project only in terms of quantitative studies on a site-by-site basis, the data recovered from the Cyprus-Bagdad Project have been augmented by data from both archaeological and ethnographic studies previously undertaken in the same area. In a very broad sense, the project's findings suggest general patterns of settlement and subsistence that are supported in most cases by the supplemental data. It must be emphasized, however, that the outlined research provides only suggestions. In some instances, the data from the Cyprus-Bagdad Project are too limited to accomplish some of the goals outlined below. However, presentation of the data applicable to those goals is here viewed as a "first step", in the hope that information from subsequent projects in this area will be considered in relation to the data presented here. Whether our findings are supported or refuted by later research, the result can only mean advancement of the understanding of the prehistory of this region.

A Regional Perspective

A basic goal of the Cyprus-Bagdad Project is to apply the data recovered to a broader, regional scope (see Chapter 2). The first step in this process is a description of the project area. The project is concerned with three concepts of space: 1) the project zone, 2) the physiographic region, and 3) the "culture area."

The Project Zone

The project zone has already been described as a linear
corridor extending from a point 3.2 km (2 miles) northeast of Bagdad,
Arizona, to a point on the Big Sandy River 17 km (10.5 miles) north
of Wikieup, Arizona. The corridor is about 58 km (36 miles) long
(Figure 1 above). The project zone also lies within the Bureau of
Land Management Aquarius Planning Unit, an archaeological overview of
which was prepared by Andrews (1975). The boundaries of this unit
are arbitrarily defined; they fail to take into account archaeological
or anthropological considerations and do not follow topographic features. However, since this planning unit is used by at least one
federal agency (the BLM), it provides a convenient if arbitrary set
of boundaries defining the second spatial concept to be considered,
the physiographic region.

The Physiographic Region

The Aquarius unit is bounded on the west by the Big Sandy
River from a point 16 km (10 miles) north of Wikieup, south until it
joins the Santa Maria River, the unit's southern boundary. Its
eastern line runs northward from the Santa Maria to include Bozarth
Mesa, while the unit is bounded on the north by the Mohon Mountains,
paralleling Route 66 (I-40) (Andrews 1975: 5) (Figure 1).

Topography. The route of the Cyprus-Bagdad water pipeline lies
in the Basin and Range Physiographic Province and is located in the
Mountain Region Subdivision of the province as defined by Ransome
(1903) and employed by Wilson (1962).

To the northwest of the project area lie the Hualapai Mountains,
reaching an elevation of 8266 feet at Hualapai Peak (Andrews 1975).
These mountains, approximately 30 km (18.5 miles) from the westernmost archaeological site within the project zone, represent the most
prominent topographic feature in the area. The Hualapais, however,
are only one mountain range of three (the Hualapais, the White Hills,
and the Cerbats) that combine to form "a nearly continuous range, east
of, and parallel to the Black mountains. This range is granitic in
composition, and true sierra in form" (Kniffen 1935: 27). This
impressive range is also composed of intrusive volcanics (Wilson 1962),
a trait common to the project area.

To the north of the project area is located a series of mesas,
while to the northwest, the Mohon Mountains represent the westernmost
escarpment of the Colorado Plateau (Kniffen 1935). Bozarth Mesa, at
approximately 4300 feet average elevation, is the largest and closest
mesa, 2 km (1.25 miles) north of the project area. It is actually a
large basalt flow encompassed by low mountains of granitic and

gneissic composition (Andrews 1975). Separating Bozarth Mesa and Centipede Mesa is Boulder Creek, a tributary of Burro Creek. Bozarth Mesa is bounded on the west by Burro Creek, which drains to the southwest and skirts Centipede Mesa after its confluence with Boulder Creek.

The immediate southern portion of the project area is taken up by Centipede Mesa, also of granitic and volcanic composition. As one proceeds south beyond Centipede Mesa, the elevation decreases (as in the Mulholland Basin), and other diagnostic features of the Basin and Range Province are seen. Smaller and more defined ranges and mountains are common to this area, and abrupt geologic formations appear. These topographic features blend into the lower, more open basins. Kniffen (1935: 27) describes these intervening areas as "broad expanses, fairly flat-lying, with floors composed of materials derived from the bordering ranges." The region to the east of the project area ascends toward mesas cut by large impermanent drainages and eventually to the mountainous Transition Zone Physiographic Province.

For additional geological and topographic considerations, see Appendix C.

Drainages. Drainages within the BLM Aquarius Planning Unit are partly situated within two contiguous watersheds, the Santa Maria and Big Sandy river basins, which form part of the larger Bill Williams River Basin. This region contains eight streams characterized by interrupted perennial flow and occasional pools along some portions of their lengths (U.S.BLM 1976). Two of these streams, Boulder Creek and Burro Creek, are within the immediate project area and will be discussed further in view of their proximity to the archaeological sites. All but two of the sites investigated lie in the Burro Creek drainage, two along the Creek itself, the others along its tributaries.

Drainages in this region generally flow southwest to the Bill Williams River, which empties into the Colorado River. Of the drainages in the greater Bill Williams River Basin, only the Big Sandy and Bill Williams rivers flow year-round. However, on the basis of observations by the field crews, Burro Creek probably flows nearly continually and may be more of a permanent stream than is generally thought. The flow from Boulder Creek, on the other hand, is restricted to impermanent runoff; however, the sites located along Boulder Creek in the project area are only 8 km (5 miles) from its confluence with Burro Creek. For further discussion of streams and other water resources, see Chapter 6.

Climate. Elevation determines much of the variability in temperature and climate for this region. Elevations in the project zone range from a low of 2400 feet near Wikieup to approximately 4000 feet northeast of Bagdad.

Precipitation and temperatures for the Bagdad area from 1931 to present are reported by Sellers and Hill (1974). This region "has a climate intermediate between that of the desert to the southwest and that of the highland regions to the northeast" (1974: 88). For most of the sites, precipitation comes in winter and summer, with spring and fall normally dry. Precipitation averages 9.4 to 13.4 inches per year, increasing in direct relation to elevation.

During the summer months, "afternoon showers and thunder-showers develop when moist air, advancing into Arizona from the Gulf of Mexico, is heated over the warm ground and forced to ascend over the rugged terrain of the central and southern sections of the state" (Sellers and Hill 1974: 88). The area receives additional summer precipitation from weak tropical storms moving northward from the Pacific Ocean.

Winter rainfall is generally more extensive and of greater duration. Storms originate in the northern Pacific Ocean and reach the state usually by a southeasterly movement. Snow in the Bagdad vicinity "is not especially common", and accounts for "only a small fraction of the total winter precipitation" (Sellers and Hill 1974: 88).

To illustrate the precipitation and temperature range of both desert and mountain regions of the project area (under 4500 feet in elevation), a graph (Figure 2) produced by the BLM for the pipeline project area is provided (U.S.BLM 1974: 12).

Documented temperatures (from 1931-present) show an average monthly temperature of 17.2 degrees C (62.8 degrees F). In winter, temperatures range from lows of -3 to -2 degrees C (26 - 28 degrees F) to highs of 13 - 20 degrees C (55 - 68 degrees F) during the day; sum-mer temperatures range from lows of 14 - 16 degrees C (57 - 60 degrees F) to highs of 44 - 47 degrees C (110 - 115 degrees F) from June through August. The mean high temperature for the summer is 36.1 degrees C (97.6 degrees F) and the mean low temperature for the winter is -0.1 degree C (31.8 degrees F) (Sellers and Hill 1974: 88, 90, 556).

Vegetation. The project area's diversity of vegetation, a result of changing elevation, reflects characteristics of both Upper and Lower Sonoran life zones (Lowe 1964). Furthermore, the boundaries of the Mohave Desert to the west and north lightly mesh with the Sonoran Desert in this general area, resulting in additional changes in vegeta-tion distribution, though not enough to warrant a classification of

AVERAGE TEMPERATURE

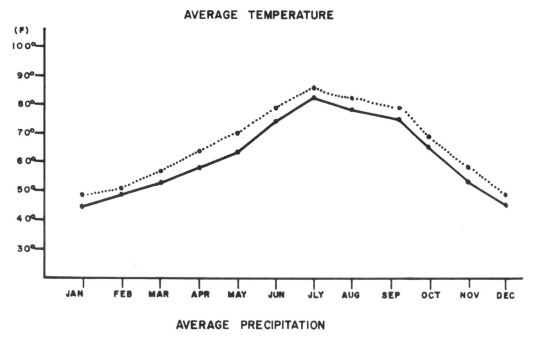

AVERAGE PRECIPITATION

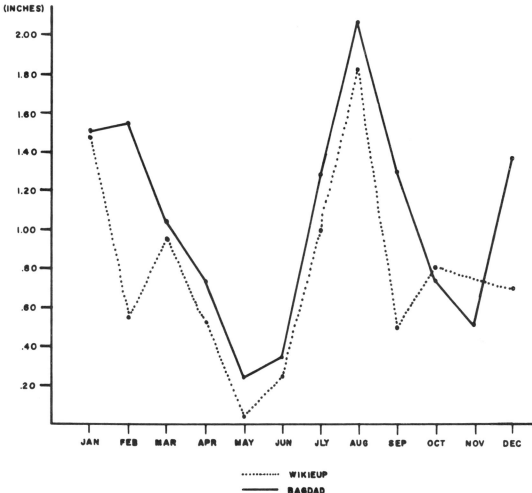

Figure 2. Precipitation and temperature ranges in the Cyprus-Bagdad project area

the region as a Mohave Desert vegetative type (U.S.BLM 1976). In some instances, archaeological sites were located in ecotonal settings with impressive plant diversity close at hand.

Desertscrub, grassland, and chaparral (as defined by Lowe 1964) are the three plant formations occurring in the project area, and were identified in areas ranging in elevation from 2550 to 4000 feet.

Within the desertscrub association, palo-verde--saguaro, one of the most characteristic of Lower Sonoran plant communities, is encountered at the following sites: AZ M:7:4 (elevation 2950 feet), AZ M:7:3 (elevation 2600 feet), and AZ M:7:2 (elevation 2800 feet). Except for its perimeters, AZ M:7:3 is actually located in a wide, shallow basin dominated primarily by creosote-bush.

At higher elevations, the vegetation association found at sites AZ M:8:2 and AZ M:8:3 (elevation 3800 feet) closely resembles desert grassland and chaparral of the Upper Sonoran Life Zone. Various grasses abound, as do yucca, agave, and ocotillo. Here, also, the increased incidence of juniper trees indicates an ecotonal shift.

At sites AZ M:8:4 and AZ M:8:5 (elevation 4000 feet), the vegetation closely approximates the chaparral and oak-woodland associations of the Upper Sonoran Life Zone (Lowe 1964: 50-51). Scrub oak is the dominant cover on the mesa slopes, with juniper, prickly-pear, yucca, and agave also occurring.

A fourth vegetation community occurs in riparian environments in the immediate vicinity of all the project sites, with the possible exceptions of AZ M:8:2 and AZ M:8:3. At these latter sites, the original topography has been substantially altered by mining activities; the headwaters of Copper Creek provide the closest water and riparian growth today. In general, these communities are heavily dominated at lower elevations by thick stands of mesquite. Cottonwood and willow abound in Burro Creek near AZ M:7:2, and cottonwood, willow, sycamore, and oak were observed in Sycamore Wash near AZ M:8:4 and AZ M:8:5. A more detailed discussion of vegetation associated with each site will be presented in Chapter 6.

Of course, the plant species observable today in the project zone do not necessarily conform to those of the past. Instead, the present environment should be considered as only a general indicator of past environment. Prehistoric availability of economically useful plant species may be suggested by this kind of data but cannot be confirmed. For example, overgrazing has caused considerable disturbance in the project area. The area has long been used as range land for cattle, and wild burros also inhabit the same region. These activities have reduced the number of grass species and correspondingly increased the number and kinds of disturbance plants. Such considerations take on significance when one notes, for example, that the use of wild grasses is thought to have been an important aspect of prehistoric subsistence strategies in the area.

The Culture Area

A "culture area" designates that space occupied and/or used in subsistence activities by individuals from one or more distinct cultural traditions, regardless of time. Ideally, then, a particular "culture area" has more or less specific geographical boundaries. The Cyprus-Bagdad project zone, however, lies in an area of archaeologically documented cultural overlap and has been recognized as a frontier area during prehistoric and historic times. Accordingly, the concept of "culture area" can be applied here only to a limited degree, and the culture area encompassing the project zone will not be assigned any precise geographical boundaries.

The area which includes the project's sites was once used by the prehistoric Cerbat and historic Hualapai, along with western groups of the prehistoric Prescott and historic Yavapai (see Figure 3). Both prehistoric groups are considered branches of the Patayan "root" (Colton 1939), and both historic groups are Yuman speakers. Continuity from Cerbat to Hualapai and from Prescott to Yavapai has not been demonstrated, but similarities in material culture, settlement, and subsistence modes suggest that this may be the case.

Admittedly, the data recovered from the project zone provide a very small sample of the larger culture area. Nonetheless, the relevance of these data lies in their relationship to general cultural processes of which they are part. Site data can accordingly be properly interpeted only when viewed in the context of the broader scheme offered by the culture area.

12

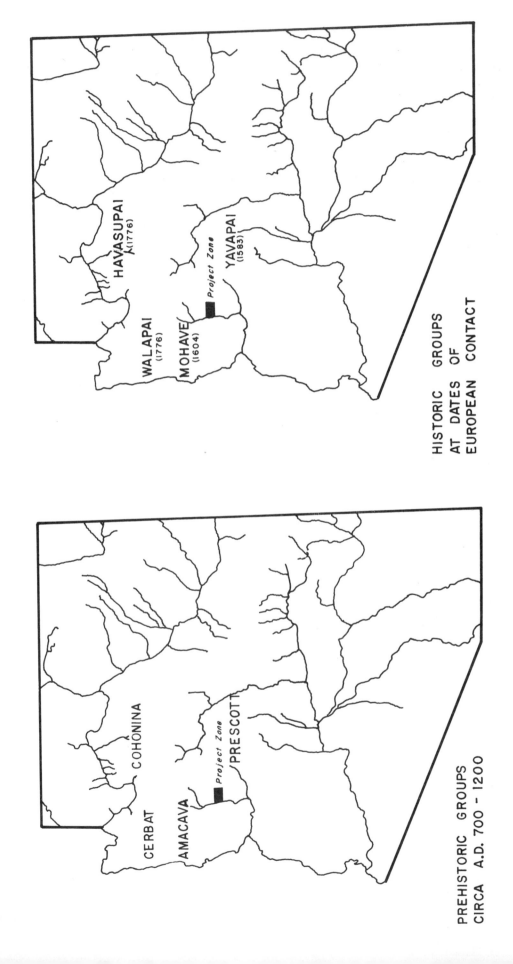

Figure 3. Areas used by prehistoric and early historic inhabitants of Cyprus-Bagdad project zone

CHAPTER 2

THE RESEARCH DESIGN

The research design for the Cyprus-Bagdad Project reflects the
multistage approach suggested by Redman (1973, 1975) and Binford
(1964). Since the project's inception, the design has undergone a
number of changes. The original survey (Hammack 1975) was carried
out without the benefit of a research design. Survey goals were to
locate archaeological remains in the path of the proposed pipeline
and to recommend avoidance wherever possible or data recovery where
avoidance was not possible.

Field work began in April, 1976, when each site was tested.
Three weeks before, a survey of the literature had been undertaken to
assess the research potential of the six sites located in the pipeline
corridor. This assessment, which outlined a number of potential
research problems for the area (Linford, n.d.a.), served as a general
research design for the testing phase and was the basis for subsequent
research designs.

The Assessment

The three broad "problem areas" considered in the assessment
were: chronology and culture history, cultural ecology, and band
structure; the choice of these problems represents an approach similar
to that of Matson (1971, 1974). Within each problem area a number of
specific research questions were defined, although the project was
never expected to be able to deal with all of them. The list presented
below incorporates a number of research problems of interest to the
author which deserve attention in the region as a whole. It was
expected that by selecting such a broad range of questions, the data,
no matter how limited, could be directed toward at least a portion of
them. The problem areas under consideration when the testing phase
began were:

I.   Chronology and Culture History
      A.   Sequence of occupation
           1.   Paleo-Indian: date of earliest human arrival in the
                region.
           2.   Archaic complexes
                a.   Span of occupation

    b. Culture or cultures present
     (1) San Dieguito
     (2) Amargosa
     (3) Cochise
     (4) Other, unspecified
   3. Prehistoric cultures post-A.D. 1
    a. Cerbat
    b. Prescott
    c. Cohonina
    d. Hohokam
    e. Yavapai
    f. Hualapai
 B. Culture history and culture process
   1. Origins of prehistoric peoples
    a. Intrusive population
    b. Continuity of indigenous populations
   2. Chronology
   3. Culture change
   4. Prehistoric/historic continuum
   5. Cultural interaction
    a. Frontiers
    b. Competition

II. Ecological Adaptations
 A. Hunting and gathering vs. agriculture as modes of
   subsistence
   1. Influence from external sources
   2. Causes of indigenous change
 B. Subsistence/settlement system
   1. Settlement type
    a. Winter base camp: village located near permanent
     water sources; evidence of hunting, maintenance
     activities, and habitation structures
    b. Short-term procurement camps: located near
     specific sets of resources; evidence of special-
     ized activities
   2. Subsistence scheduling
    a. Spring (April, May): leave base camp--agave
     harvest
    b. Late spring, early summer (June-July): grass
     seeds on the plains
    c. Late summer (August-early September): banana yucca,
     cholla, acorns from the upper woodland
    d. Early autumn (late September-early October):
     pinyon nuts in the foothills
    e. Late autumn and winter (November through March):
     dried, gathered foods--return to base camp

III. Band Structure: a model for identifying patrilineality
    (Matson 1971)
    A. Four causative factors of patrilineality
        1. Population density: one person or less per square
           mile
        2. Environment: as stimulus to hunting and gathering
           technology
        3. Limited transportation: human carriers only
        4. Cultural-psychological fact of exogamy (Steward
           1955: 135)
    B. Patrilocality of patrilineal bands (Service 1962: 135)
    C. Model for patrilocality (Deetz 1967: 95)
        1. Intrasite comparisons of artifact distribution
           (Deetz 1967: 95)
        2. Interregional comparisons of patterns noted on a
           band level (Matson 1971)

The Research Design

The test excavations were carried out with these areas of
investigation in mind. The purpose of these tests was to determine
the extent and nature of the cultural remains, thereby enabling an
evaluation of the suitability of the data to be recovered as well as
an estimate of the time needed to complete the project. On the basis
of the information recovered in this and successive stages of excavation, a research design was evolved to incorporate those problems
best suited to the data; other problems (notably the question of band
structure among the sites' inhabitants) were rejected. A series of
hypotheses, test implications, and data recovery techniques were
formulated to approach the research objectives.

The evaluation of the test excavations likewise led to a
redefining of the research design. As outlined below, this redefini-
tion reflects both the nature and limitations of the recoverable
data.

I. Patterns of Exploitation
    A. Settlement patterns
    B. Subsistence economies
    C. Trade

II. Demography
    A. Repeated occupations
        1. Same culture: seasonal migration
        2. Different cultures: population interactions
    B. Single occupations

The research design also considers various environmental factors as they relate to the inhabitants of the region.

I. Climate

II. Geology
    A. Formations
    B. Resources and their locations

III. Hydrology
    A. Permanent water sources
    B. Intermittent water sources

IV. Biology
    A. Exploitable flora
        1. Wild
        2. Domesticated
    B. Exploitable fauna

The Research Focus

The goals of the project are oriented towards investigating problems of human ecology. The research focus was altered to determine the manner in which occupants of the region interacted with the "effective environment" through their use of natural resources.

> The term "effective environment"...designates those parts of the total environment which are in regular or cyclical articulation with the unit under study. Changes in the effective environment will produce changes not only in the boundaries of the ecological community but also in the internal organization of the community (Binford 1968: 323).

The chronological framework for the occupations was deemphasized due to the nature of the data recovered. At present, such a framework would at best be speculative. Certain evidence leads one to suspect contemporaneity between AZ M:8:2 and AZ M:8:3 and between AZ M:7:2 and AZ M:7:3. However, the existence of such relationships between these or any other project sites cannot be proven conclusively.

The primary emphasis of the research design is to identify the function of each site through the analysis of a number of criteria. Site location as it relates to natural resources is an essential part of this approach. The activities performed at particular sites were to be identified through the analysis of artifact assemblages. This process would include identification of wear patterns and of other traits indicative of specific activities. Within the context of the behavioral chain model (Schiffer 1972), this approach can determine how extensively the site was used, and perhaps whether it was used for a single activity or a set of related activities.

Behavioral chain analysis is based on the assumption that every object ("element") used by humans passes through a sequence of distinct stages between its procurement and discard. Schiffer (1972: 157) divides "elements" into two categories, durables and consumables. Within the lifespan of a durable element, Schiffer sees five stages or processes: 1) procurement, 2) manufacture, 3) use, 4) maintenance, and 5) discard (Schiffer 1972: 158). However, these stages can be complicated by the introduction of multiple use, recycling, and other factors, which merely adds loops to what is otherwise a consecutive ordering of events. Consumable elements, according to Schiffer, pass through fewer stages or processes: 1) procurement, 2) preparation, 3) consumption, and 4) discard (Schiffer 1972: 158). Presumably, in this ordering, there would be no added loops, but simply a linear progression from procurement to discard. A site's artifact assemblage may then, as suggested by Matson (1971, 1974) be analyzed in terms of the extraction of natural resources near the site.

Another factor considered was the possibility of agriculture at the various sites, as evidenced by features such as terraces, check dams, and storage cysts; by the presence of agricultural tools, such as hoes; or even by the presence of pollen or charred plant remains.

All of the archaeological remains were to be interpreted wherever possible through comparison with ethnographic evidence. Drucker (1941), Kroeber (1935), Dobyns (1957), Euler (1958), Dobyns and Euler (1956, 1960a, 1960b), and Euler and Dobyns (1956) provide ample information on the lifeways of the historic occupants of the region. These lifeways possibly characterized the earliest occupations of the region as well.

Hypotheses and Test Implications

The following hypotheses and test implications have largely been drawn from the previous research design, although some changes have been implemented in order to produce a better problem-data fit.

Hypothesis I: The availability of water was the primary determinant for the location of settlement sites (base camps), and was instrumental in the location of all other types of sites.

Test Implications (The hypothesis will be considered supported if):

T1:   All sites with habitation structures are located near permanent or semipermanent water sources.

T2a: Those sites with or without habitation structures, but with evidence of numerous and varied activities, are located near permanent or semipermanent water sources.

T2b: Sites not located near such water sources are loci of special, limited activity.

T3a: The strongest evidence for prolonged or repeated occupations is derived from sites located near such water sources.

T3b: Sites immediately adjacent to permanent or semipermanent water sources exhibit the most complete chronological sequence from the earliest cultural occupations to the latest.

Hypothesis II: Given that the availability of water was the primary determinant of settlement location, all sites were also functionally related to other biotic and abiotic resource locations.

Test Implications (The hypothesis will be considered supported if):

T1:   Along permanent or semipermanent water courses (which cross a variety of biotic zones), sites are located primarily within zones with a potential for intensive biotic exploitation (as determined by ethnographic data).

T2a: For those sites near impermanent sources of water, there is a direct correlation between the season of plant resource availability and the availability of water.

T2b: The artifact assemblage (tool kit) at each food-processing site reflects activities directly related to the procurement and use of available biotic resources.

T3:   Sites not related to biotic resources are directly related to an abiotic resource location.

Hypothesis III: Agriculture was an important method of subsistence for the prehistoric inhabitants of this area.

Test Implications (The hypothesis will be considered supported if):

T1:   Agricultural features (such as terraces, check dams, or irrigation ditches) are discovered, indicating that a sizable amount of time was invested in preparation of plots for horticulture.

T2:   Agricultural fields are situated in areas amenable to natural watering (through runoff or channel overflow), but in areas protected from violent floods which would wash the seeds or young plants away.

T3a: Sites nearest the identifiable agricultural fields were occupied during the growing season to facilitate cultivation.

T3b: Crops were processed at nearby sites, rather than at the location of their growth and maturity.

T3c: Agricultural and food-processing tools (hoes and picks, manos and metates) are found at nearby habitation sites.

Data Recovery Techniques

1. Mapping of site locations in relation to water sources

2. Identification of habitation structures

3. Identification of agricultural features

4. Mapping of agricultural features in relation to water sources and to nearest habitation sites

5. Determination (on the basis of observation and informant data) of season(s) of water availability at individual sources

6. Identification of wild plant foods (correlated with ethnographic data) and their season of maximum productivity

7. Identification of activities and tools required to procure and process the above resources (based on ethnographic data)

8. Functional analysis of artifacts and assemblages in order to determine the activities occurring at individual sites

9. Collection of pollen samples from the surface of, or directly beneath, grinding implements and large potsherds to determine plant association and season of occupation.

10. Collection of pollen samples at suspected agricultural features to identify crops grown

11. Analysis of stratigraphy at sites with cultural deposition in order to reconstruct multiple or prolonged occupations

12. Dating of sites

13. Collection of pollen samples from stratigraphic columns at sites with cultural deposition in order to detect changes in the environment

14.   Ascertaining of abiotic (lithic, clay) raw material source
       locations and correlations with artifact assemblages (particu-
       larly material types and stage of manufacture)

       The results of the excavations will be discussed in terms of
this design in Chapter 8.

Problems Encountered

       Difficulties encountered during this project were resolved with
varying levels of success. In some cases, the problems led to further
revisions in the research design.

       A fundamental problem was the lack of recent published litera-
ture dealing with the project area. Most of the published works are
at least two decades old, and fail to measure up to current archaeological standards. Most of the earlier research focused on single
sites, which reduced its applicability to the findings of the Cyprus-
Bagdad Project.

       The distinct lack of geographical and geological publications
on the area made it more difficult to pinpoint the source locations
for various lithic and ceramic raw materials. The most detailed USGS
map for parts of the project area is on a scale of 1:250,000, nearly
useless for locating other recorded sites for settlement pattern
analysis.

       The identification of pottery in order to determine cultural
affiliations must be considered tenuous. The guidelines set up by
Colton (1939, 1958) are of little use in discerning Tizon Brown Ware
from Prescott Gray Ware, and of even less use in trying to identify
the subtypes of each ware. This problem is underscored by the fact
that, 23 years after Colton's original 1939 description of Prescott
Gray Ware's various subtypes, Euler and Dobyns (1962: 76-77) concluded
that: "Verde Gray, Verde Black-on-gray, Prescott Black-on-brown,
Aquarious Black-on-gray, Aquarious Gray, Aquarious Black-on-orange,
and Aquarious Orange are in reality all of one type, or two types if
one distinguishes as one should between the painted and unpainted
sherds."

       Michael Waters (personal communication) has recently completed
a study of Yuman pottery and has reached a similar conclusion concerning the subtypes of Tizon Brown Ware. Many of the surface sherds
recovered during the Cyprus-Bagdad excavations were so extensively
weathered that temper often remained the only reliable criterion for
identifying the pottery. The intergradation of temper between the
two major wares in this area, especially between Aquarius Brown and

Aquarius Orange (Euler and Dobyns 1962: 74), usually rendered this final method of distinction ineffective. Furthermore, there is only a weak association between the above pottery types and given cultural groups which makes the ceramics almost useless as a dating mechanism. For instance, if one accepts the supposition of Dobyns and Euler that Cerbat Brown was manufactured up until about A.D. 1900, it has a range of at least 1100 years with no diagnostic changes known.

The remainder of the difficulties encountered were site-specific. Among these was the lack of datable materials. Two closely associated samples of carbonized wood were retrieved from one site (AZ M:7:2) for Carbon-14 processing (see Chapter 6). The remaining six sites cannot be dated to within more than 200 years of their occupation. This increases the difficulty of ascertaining cultural affiliations or site relationships. Sites that may have been occupied hundreds of years apart may nonetheless exhibit virtually identical assemblages. By the same token, the data cannot inform us as to whether a site was occupied once by 100 persons or ten times by ten persons.

Lack of definable stratigraphy at six of the seven sites intensified this problem. Repeated occupations are almost impossible to prove at sites with only surface remains, and interaction between populations cannot be demonstrated. The presence of mixed cultural remains at a site could result from the mingling of individuals from different cultures, from two or more separate occupations decades or centuries apart, or simply from trade.

There are virtually no data available on the prehistoric environment of the area due to a lack of early plant remains or tree-ring data. The problem is compounded by the lack of stratigraphic excavations. Under such circumstances, the validity of the ethno-graphic comparisons drawn in this volume may be questionable.

Perhaps the greatest problem encountered by the Cyprus-Bagdad field crew was the fact that all the sites investigated had suffered some degree of contemporary disturbance. Some of this disturbance had been inflicted several years previously as an unintended result of other activities. For example, AZ M:7:4 was found to be traversed by: 1) a graded road, 2) a Southern Union Gas pipeline, 3) the Arizona Public Service Meade-Liberty 345 kV transmission line, 4) a fence line, and 5) two jeep trails.

Three distinct areas had been bulldozed at AZ M:7:2. More recent damage had been caused by the Cyprus-Bagdad Mine operations. AZ M:8:3 was bisected by a bulldozed road connecting two construction sites at the mine. Further damage accrued when pipeline workers ignored flagging and drove bulldozers and pickup trucks across AZ M:7:3.

Just as frustrating was disturbance caused by "pot hunters" or amateur collectors. At the time the sites were first recorded (Hammack 1975), most of them were in good condition with very little disturbance. Once flagged, however, they became the targets of week-end relic hunts. Hammack (1975: 18 and personal communications) describes the cultural remains at AZ M:8:3 as including fragments of shell bracelets, slate mescal knives, large (6+inch) potsherds, and slate knife fragments. When the testing phase began, no shell fragments were to be found, and the largest potsherds were about the size of a quarter.

In discussions with the more talkative collectors, it became clear that a pattern was emerging in this damage. Apparently the items most sought by such collectors are bifacially retouched, symmetrical chipped stone artifacts; whole ground stone artifacts; larger, painted potsherds; and ornamental objects (bracelets, beads, pendants). In an analysis such as that applied in this report, this kind of selective collecting undoubtedly skews the data in ways which cannot be controlled for without further studies specific to this problem.

CHAPTER 3

HISTORY OF ANTHROPOLOGICAL RESEARCH IN WEST-CENTRAL ARIZONA

Although very little anthropological research has been carried
out in the project zone itself, a review of the available literature
shows that a surprising amount and variety of research has been performed within the culture area as a whole. A study of this literature
provides an outline of the culture history and human adaptation to the
project zone itself. Therefore, the discussions of previous archaeological work will incorporate not only research within the project
zone, but also major treatments of the culture area and its peripheries.

Archaeological Research

The culture area as a whole is poorly understood archeological-
ly. Compared with other parts of the American Southwest, the area
has seen relatively little archaeological research. Fuller (1975: 11)
has suggested that the reasons for this are obvious: the sites offer
little in the way of architectural remains, deep middens, or aesthetic,
artistic elements, unlike settlements of the Hohokam to the south and
the Anasazi to the north and east.

Most of the work accomplished in the area has consisted of
surveys, published reports for which are generally lacking. The few
reports dealing with excavation are often limited to a single site or
a small cluster of related sites, with no attempt to relate the data
from the excavations to a broader, regional scheme.

The Project Area

The earliest studies in the project area were large-scale,
problem-oriented surveys. Frank Mitalsky (also known as Frank Midvale)
of the Gila Pueblo Archaeological Foundation was the first professional
archaeologist to survey this territory in 1929. His work was part of a
search for the northern and western limits of the Hohokam culture
(Gladwin and Gladwin 1930; Fuller 1975). In 1932, J. W. Simmons surveyed the eastern portion of the region for Gila Pueblo, whose records
indicate that at least 112 sites were found within the project area.
Of the 45 sites discovered in the desert lowlands in the central and
western portions of the region, 42 percent were identified as camp-
sites and 36 percent as rock shelters. Fifty-one percent of these

sites were found near permanent sources of water and 20 percent near
intermittent sources; for 13 percent of the sites, the presence or
absence of local water sources was not specified. Thus, only 16 to
29 percent of the sites had no nearby sources of water.

Malcolm Rogers may have preceded both Gila Pueblo surveyors,
as he surveyed in western Arizona and southeastern California throughout the 1920s and 1930s. However, it is unclear when he was working
in each area, and how many sites he found. Fuller (1975) states that
Rogers discovered three to 12 sites in the area, depending on how
one deciphers Rogers' numbering system. However, according to Rogers'
map (1966: 176), as many as 17 or more sites were located in this
region.

Rogers' goal was to determine the origins and prehistory of
the Yumans and to define their relationships to various southern
California Indian groups (Rogers 1939, 1945). Although a number of
the sites found by Rogers were of San Dieguito or Amargosa affiliation, the majority seem to have been used by Cerbat or Amacava people
(Rogers 1966: 173; Fuller 1975: 13). All appear to be surface
scatters of artifacts, or rock shelters with no architecture.

In connection with dam construction on the Colorado River, the
National Park Service conducted an intensive survey along both banks
of the river during the 1930s. A number of sites were also located
east of the river near Kingman (Fuller 1975: 9).

The earliest known professional excavations in the region were
carried out by Edward Spicer at King's Ruin and Louis Caywood at Fitz-
maurice Ruin, both in the Prescott area (Spicer 1936; Caywood 1936).
These excavations were organized by Byron Cummings, who had previously
found evidence of the Prescott Branch in this area.

In 1938, a linear survey was conducted by the Museum of Northern
Arizona through the approximate center of this region. This survey,
performed under the direction of Harold S. Colton, and in conjunction
with the Santa Fe Railroad, resulted in the original definition of the
Cerbat Branch and Tizon Brown Ware (Colton 1939).

Schroeder (1961) carried out test excavations at Willow Beach
on the Colorado River in 1950. His report also describes previous
excavations conducted in the 1930s and 1940s. Five stages of occupation were defined, including the earliest and westernmost evidence of
the Cerbat Branch.

Between 1952 and 1955, Henry Dobyns (then a graduate student at
the University of Arizona) and Robert Euler (Arizona State College)
surveyed extensive areas from Kingman to the Bill Williams River. A
large number of sites were located, a few of which were excavated by

Euler (Dobyns 1956; Euler 1958). This project used archaeological remains to document the territorial range of the Hualapai Indians in prereservation times. The resulting data were used for a land claims case brought against the federal government by the Hualapai Tribe.

In 1957 and 1958, the Museum of Northern Arizona conducted a survey in connection with the construction of a natural gas pipeline across the region and located a number of sites near Sitgreaves Pass in the Cerbat Mountains (Fuller 1975: 10).

Also in the late 1950s, Paul V. Long located a few sites south of Kingman in the Hualapai Mountains, including Boulder Springs Rock Shelter (Andrews 1975: 12). Michael J. Harner, of the University of California, excavated a number of sites found 25 years earlier by Rogers in the vicinity of Bouse, Arizona.

A joint archaeological-paleontological survey conducted by the Arizona State Museum and the National Park Service in 1963 located a number of sites along 8 miles of the Bill Williams River, 5 miles of the Santa Maria River, and 4.5 miles of the Big Sandy River. This survey was undertaken in conjunction with the Alamo Reservoir Project (Wasley and Vivian 1965).

From 1965 to 1967, Franklin Barnett (1970) conducted survey and excavation operations in the Williamson Valley on Matli Ranch properties. A total of five sites was recorded and excavated.

In 1966, the Arizona State Museum conducted Highway Salvage surveys along the newly proposed route of Interstate 40, running across the midsection of the region. A number of sites were recorded (Fuller 1975: 10).

In the following year, the Museum of Northern Arizona surveyed the proposed route of a power transmission line across the northern portion of the region, and discovered (but did not excavate) three sites (Jennings 1971).

During that same year, Prescott College contracted with the Bureau of Reclamation to survey portions of the Granite Reef Aqueduct, part of the Central Arizona Project. More intensive surveys were recommended on the basis of these initial studies (Euler 1968).

In 1969, Richard G. Matson of the University of California at Davis conducted what Fuller (1975: 10) has called "the most sophisticated inquiry into the archaeological remains of this region." Matson carried out a stratified sampling survey of a portion of the Cerbat Mountains in a project with two goals. The first of these was to examine a number of sampling strategies. The second was to test hypotheses concerning Hualapai subsistence and settlement patterns by using statistical techniques to delineate relationships between sampling units and observed data (Matson 1971, 1974).

A proposed power transmission line route from Bagdad to Prescott was surveyed by Prescott College in 1971. In addition, a preliminary biological survey was conducted earlier that year along Burro Creek northwest of Bagdad by Prescott College students. This survey also recorded archaeological remains (Andrews 1975: 12).

In 1972, following Euler's (1968) recommendations, the Arizona State Museum contracted with the Bureau of Reclamation to conduct more intensive surveys of the Granite Reef Aqueduct from the Buckskin Mountains to a point near Phoenix. A few sherd and lithic scatters were discovered just north of the Bouse Hills, and isolated artifacts were noted in the Cunningham Wash area (Kemrer and others 1972).

In 1973 a few sites described as limited-activity loci were recorded by the Arizona State Museum in the Harcuvar Mountains (Andrews 1975: 11).

Working for the Museum of Northern Arizona, McPherson and Pilles carried out in 1974 a survey around the Cyprus-Bagdad open-pit copper mine at Bagdad, Arizona in conjunction with the mine's proposed expansion. Four sites were located but not excavated (McPherson and Pilles 1975).

In 1975, Cyprus-Bagdad contracted with the Arizona State Museum to survey a proposed water pipeline route from Bagdad to Wikieup in conjunction with the same expansion program (Hammack 1975). It was this survey which led to the mitigation project reported here.

Additional information has been accumulated through the efforts of various individuals. D. L. True, of the University of California at Davis, has been surveying and conducting test excavations in the area sporadically since 1943. The results of his work are unknown at this time (Fuller 1975: 10).

Mr. Ken Austin of Prescott, acting as an Associate of the Museum of Northern Arizona, has been surveying in the mountain regions between Prescott and Bagdad for a number of years. Primarily interested in hilltop "defensive sites", Austin has only recently begun surveying the valleys and streams in the area. So far he claims to have mapped more than 850 sites in this region. The information is being passed on to the Museum of Northern Arizona (Ken Austin, personal communication).

Work continues in the region. The Museum of Northern Arizona is currently conducting a power line survey from Bagdad to Wickenburg. In addition, the Bureau of Land Management is supervising a one-percent survey of the entire region in order to produce an initial inventory of the cultural resources. Also in connection with the Bureau of Land Management, Jean Fryman, of Arizona State University and working through the Museum of Northern Arizona, is conducting an overview of the region encompassed by the Cerbat Mountains and Black Mountains BLM planning units.

Ethnographic Research

The ethnographic projects conducted in the area, though less numerous than the archaeological projects, seem more comprehensive in that they take into consideration an entire culture, rather than a single village or family.

The study perhaps most relevant to the Cyprus-Bagdad Project is that headed by Kroeber (1935). The papers compiled in Walapai Ethnography were produced by a number of collaborators who, under the sponsorship of the Laboratory of Anthropology, conducted archaeological, ethnological, and physical anthropological studies among the Hualapai in 1929. In the same year and continuing until 1932, E. W. Gifford studied the neighboring Yavapai. Two volumes resulted from these studies, one on the Southeastern Yavapai (1932), and the other on the Western and Northeastern Yavapai (1936).

Somewhat more removed from the present study is Spier's (1928) ethnography of the Havasupai, who, Dobyns and Euler have argued, came from the same ethnic stock as the Hualapai.

Drucker (1941) devised trait lists for the Hualapai and Yavapai as well as for other lower Colorado River cultures. The previously cited work of Dobyns and Euler in the 1950s, in conjunction with the Indian lands claims case of the Hualapai, involved more than archaeological surveys and excavations. In the course of their research, they were compelled to undertake ethnographic studies in order to formulate hypotheses concerning prehistoric land use (Dobyns 1956; Dobyns and Euler 1960b; Euler 1958). Their observations altered some of Kroeber's postulates, particularly those regarding the amount of farming supposedly done by the Hualapai and their ancestors.

The most recent work in the area took place in 1972, when Charline Smith, of the University of Montana, worked with the Hualapai in an attempt to identify the grass selé and its importance in early Hualapai subsistence (Smith 1973).

Summary and Conclusions

The works discussed in this chapter vary considerably in quality, which renders some of them more valuable than others to an anthropologist working in the area today.

Most of the archaeology in the area has consisted of surveys for which no locational or cultural affiliational data have been published. Descriptions of sites found by these projects were generally preserved in site files, but for the most part these descriptions are of little use in locating sites or identifying their cultural remains.

A number of surveys (including the Cyprus-Bagdad pipeline survey) were necessarily linear in nature, following as they did proposed routes for transmission lines, highways, and pipelines. Some of these surveys were useful to the project, but a number are of little value as virtually nothing is known of the research strategies employed. For instance, the fact that the Gila Pueblo files record a number of sites near sources of water may only indicate that the surveyors followed water courses during their treks, and rarely investigated areas away from those streams.

The majority of the excavation projects have also been limited in scope, being site-specific, with little concern for a regional approach.

The combined site files available indicate that at least 402 sites have been located in the culture area, although the possibility of overlapping from one file to another and the incomplete nature of some of the files indicate that this number is probably inaccurate. However, if one is to relate the data from the Cyprus-Bagdad Project to a larger data base, one is compelled to rely on this sample. Accordingly, this analysis is based on the assumption that these data are in fact representative of the archaeological remains in the culture area.

Fortunately, there is some justification for such an assumption. The Bureau of Land Management survey (one-percent sample) currently underway has already experienced problems with its sampling strategy, according to Pat Giorgi. The original plan of testing a simple random selection of sample units has proven inadequate for lack of sites. Thus, a revised strategy using a stratified random sample based on water availability within the area is being implemented. In sample units randomly selected along water courses and in the vicinity of springs and tanks, the survey is discovering a much denser distribution of sites. This finding lends strong support to an assertion that the majority of the 402 known sites were found near water sources because water was a primary determinant of site location, and that the sample is most likely representative of the overall site distribution in the area. Further support can be drawn from studies by Dobyns (1956), Euler (1958), and Matson (1971), as well as from a survey currently being conducted by Austin (personal communication). Each of these projects, which involved large sample units of land and were not governed by considerations of hydrology, found most sites to be near water sources.

Even the numerous linear surveys can be useful in evaluating Cyprus-Bagdad Project findings. Goodyear (1975) has shown that such surveys generally crosscut several environmental zones, inadequately covering any one zone, and thus denying the archaeologist representative samples of remains within each zone. However, a number of transects can be contrasted, and the pooled data compared with those of more substantial projects. In addition, linear survey projects can be valuable in single site analysis, as each site's function(s) can be inferred via behavioral chain analysis (Phillips 1974; Schiffer 1975c). Site identification can generate inferences concerning subsistence strategies and settlement patterns if the sample is large enough.

Undoubtedly, not all of the 402 sites will provide enough data to be used in such comparisons. However, it would appear at present that a large percentage can be used in this way.

There are also problems with the ethnographic studies. At least two of the studies, those of Gifford (1932) and Drucker (1941), rely solely on information obtained from a single informant. Gifford interviewed his informant for 15 days, then took a one-day drive through Yavapai country (Gifford 1932: 177); the particulars of Drucker's interviews are unknown. It is doubtful whether a representative view of the life of any Indian group can be obtained from a single informant. Gifford's later study (1936) on the Northeastern and Western Yavapai is a little more substantial, as is Kroeber's Walapai Ethnography (1935). Gifford used eight informants in studying the Northeastern Yavapai, and five for the Western bands (Gifford 1936: 250). However, such an approach is less effective than direct observation combined with informant data, a method Kroeber's students used to some extent among the Hualapai.

A second problem involves interpretations by anthropologists. For example, Kroeber's study concluded that agriculture was then and had always been a very minor part of Hualapai life. Dobyns (1956) and Euler (1958) disagreed on the basis of their archaeological and ethnographic studies among the Hualapai 20 years later. They decided that the current lack of emphasis on agriculture among these people resulted from decades of Anglo disruption of their lifeways. Archaeological evidence indicates that agriculture may have provided a substantial portion of their past livelihood. Thus, one must be cautious in accepting ethnologists' interpretations of past behavior.

CHAPTER 4

CULTURE HISTORY

As the findings of the Cyprus-Bagdad Project are to be applied to a broader, regional scope, a review of the history and prehistory of the culture area is in order. This is necessary so that the reader might better comprehend the reasoning which underlies interpretations of cultural affiliation and subsistence postulated in later chapters of this report.

Paleo-Indian

No sites or artifacts indicative of any great antiquity have been discovered in the project area. However, Paleo-Indian use of the Cyprus-Bagdad area can be postulated on the basis of finds to the north and south; these finds were in environments which at present are similar to that of the project area. Gypsum Cave, in southern Nevada, produced human remains in association with extinct fauna, such as ground sloth, horse, dire wolf, and camel. These remains have been dated to about 11,000 years ago (Warren 1967). To the south, Haury (1950) discovered similar evidence in Ventana Cave. Fuller (1975: 12) noted at the north end of Hualapai Valley the presence of a Pleistocene lake bed similar to the one below Gypsum Cave, and remarked that "of all the locales in northwest Arizona, it would seem that the area surrounding Red Lake might be the most productive in any search for Paleo-Indian sites."

Archaic

Whether or not Paleo-Indian groups were present in the region, there is strong evidence indicating that members of the Archaic tradition were. The Archaic tradition, characterized by seasonal transhumance (Davis 1963) and hunting and gathering, represents a distinct environmental adaptation to an arid or semi-arid environment, and probably developed from a generalized hunting, fishing, and gathering pattern in the western United States (Warren 1967: 181). Warren suggests that this tradition was forming as early as 9000 B.C., and was firmly established between 6000 B.C. and 1000 B.C. (1967: 180).

A problem exists regarding the positive identification of Archaic sites. Fuller (1975: 17) points out that the lifeway proposed for the Archaic tradition is very similar to that of subsequent

31

occupants of the region. Such similar adaptations to the environment would likely create similar tool assemblages, thus increasing the chance that sites found could not be easily attributed to this earlier culture. Limitations imposed by the environment on the number of suitable site locales and the resultant continuous reuse of the sites, combined with a lack of detectable stratigraphy at most sites in this region, further increase the difficulty involved in identifying cultural occupation.

San Dieguito

The earliest cultural tradition for which there is conclusive evidence is the San Dieguito. This tradition may have begun slightly before the Desert Culture (as defined by Jennings 1959) to the east, with which it coexisted for many centuries (Warren 1967: 182). Characterized by a flake and core industry, the San Dieguito was a hunting tradition which Warren postulates originated in the northwest and then shifted south. The locales where these sites have been discovered appear to have been more oasis than desert-like at the time of occupation. Evidence from the C. W. Harris Site, Panamint Basin, the Mohave Lake Site, and Gypsum Cave supports this hypothesis (Warren 1967: 179; Davis, Brott, and Weide 1969: 19). Thus, differences between the supposedly coexisting San Dieguito and Desert cultures can possibly be explained as reflecting adaptations to different environments (Warren 1967: 181-82).

The San Dieguito tradition consists of three phases (I, II, and III) (Figure 4). The earliest phase begins about 9000 B.C., and differs in duration from area to area. The sequence developed by Rogers (1966: 140) for the region under discussion (the Southeastern Aspect) begins with a San Dieguito I-II Complex, also known as the Ventana Complex, that lasts from an unknown time until about 8700 B.C. There is no archaeological evidence for the gap between the disappearance of this complex and the beginning of the Amargosa Complex at approximately 5000 B.C.

Rogers located a number of San Dieguito sites within his Southeastern Aspect, including at least four (A-1, A-2, A-12, and A-17) in the project area. (The incompleteness of the available records leads one to speculate whether more such sites may have been found.) Three of these sites dated as early as San Dieguito; all four showed evidence of Amargosa occupations (Rogers 1966: 173, 177).

Amargosa

The San Dieguito was replaced as a lithic tradition by the Amargosa Complex around 5000 B.C. in Rogers' Southeastern Aspect. All four of the sites located by Rogers in the project zone showed evidence

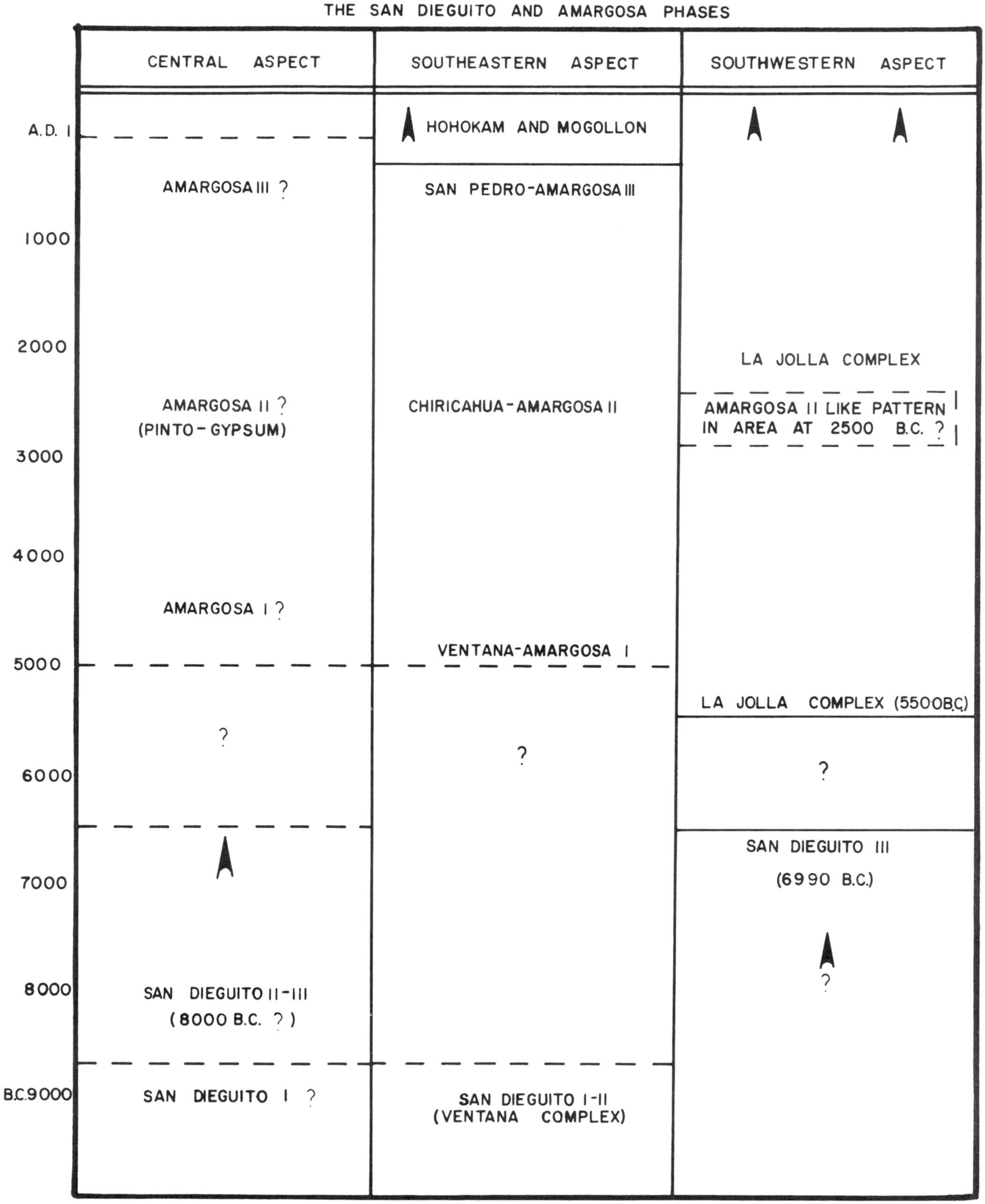

THE SAN DIEGUITO AND AMARGOSA PHASES

	CENTRAL ASPECT	SOUTHEASTERN ASPECT	SOUTHWESTERN ASPECT
A.D. 1		▲ HOHOKAM AND MOGOLLON	▲ ▲
	AMARGOSA III ?	SAN PEDRO-AMARGOSA III	
1000			
2000			LA JOLLA COMPLEX
	AMARGOSA II ? (PINTO-GYPSUM)	CHIRICAHUA-AMARGOSA II	AMARGOSA II LIKE PATTERN IN AREA AT 2500 B.C. ?
3000			
4000			
	AMARGOSA I ?		
5000		VENTANA-AMARGOSA I	
			LA JOLLA COMPLEX (5500 B.C.)
6000	?	?	?
			SAN DIEGUITO III (6990 B.C.)
7000	▲		
			▲ ?
8000	SAN DIEGUITO II-III (8000 B.C. ?)		
B.C. 9000	SAN DIEGUITO I ?	SAN DIEGUITO I-II (VENTANA COMPLEX)	

Figure 4. The San Dieguito and Amargosa phases

of Amargosa presence. This complex is characterized by the occurrence
of ground stone (Rogers 1966: 107-08) and by the presence of pottery in
the later phases. Like the San Dieguito, the Amargosa Complex is
divided into three phases (I, II, and III) with no clear demarcation
between them: Amargosa I begins at about 5000 B.C., Amargosa III ends
about A.D. 1, and Amargosa II lies somewhere in the middle (Figure 4).
The precise duration of each phase is unknown, with the beginning of
each phase marked only by changes in the "quality" and complexity of
the assemblages.

According to Rogers (1939: 27-60), Amargosa I, formerly referred
to as the Pinto-Gypsum Complex, is typified by crude, poorly chipped,
rough stone implements, and seems to have centered in what is now north-
central San Bernardino County, California. Amargosa II originates in
the same area and spreads eastward, with sites located at the centers
of playa surfaces, on playa margins, and on sandy-silt elevations above
water holes (Rogers 1939: 61). It is this phase which is present in
west-central Arizona (Rogers 1966: 173). Amargosa II artifacts exhibit
a general uniformity in raw materials and a decline in the occurrence
of scrapers that continues from the previous phase. The projectile
points (called "dart points" by Rogers) are relatively large and triangular in shape, with side notches parallel to the base (Rogers 1939:
61-64). All Amargosa II sites noted by Rogers were small and had few
artifact clusters.

Amargosa III exhibits a wider variety of projectile points; the
notched varieties appear almost "corner-notched" with the notches
obliquely set. Metates and rough grinding stones appear at this time
along with pottery and implements such as mauls and picks (Rogers 1939:
64-66). Sites are located near springs, water holes, or extant playas
(Rogers 1939: 61). The geographical center of this culture phase lies
to the north in Nevada.

In all of the above phases, it would appear that west-central
Arizona lay on the periphery of the Amargosa Culture. In the immediate
vicinity of the Cyprus-Bagdad Project, Rogers noted at least four sites
which exhibited Amargosa II culture trait complexes. The project itself
located a fifth Amargosa site (AZ M:7:4) of the Amargosa III Phase.

A.D. 1 to European Contact

With the end of the Amargosa around A.D. 1, a second major void
in the archaeological record begins, extending until at least A.D. 500
(Dobyns 1956: 58) and possibly 500 years beyond that (Dobyns and Euler
1956: 14). Rogers, however, contended that,

extending from the western boundary of San Bernardino County
across the desert to the Colorado River and into Mojave
County, Arizona, the Amargosa complex is replaced with a

pattern which needs only the addition of native pottery to
make it Yuman; an element which it eventually acquired
(1945: 173-174).

Rogers describes the material culture as including shallow-basin
metates; unshaped manos; small, round mortars; triangular knives and
projectile points; and bone awls. Houses were circular or oval in
shape and covered with brush, with a circle of rocks outlining the
exterior. Floors were flat or slightly dished. However, with the
exception of the unshaped manos and the addition of native pottery,
these material attributes can also be associated with the later groups
termed Yuman (Drucker 1941). Furthermore, Rogers could not have accurately dated any of these sites, and his "native pottery" remains
unidentified (Dobyns and Euler 1956: 14). Thus, it seems likely that
Rogers actually was referring to Yuman sites which considerably post-
dated the Amargosa.

Hohokam

It is quite possible that the Hohokam culture, centered on the
Gila and Salt rivers to the south and southeast of the culture area,
exerted some influence here, particularly in the eastern portion of the
area. The Hohokam possessed one of the more highly developed prehistoric cultures in the Southwest, beginning perhaps as early as 300
B.C. and lasting until about A.D. 1450 (Haury 1976: 39) (Figure 5).
These people lived primarily through agriculture, relying on extensive
irrigation networks by the late Colonial Period, or about A.D. 800
(Haury 1976: 120). During the Sedentary Period, or by about A.D. 1000,
Hohokam culture traits had reached their maximum distribution. To the
north these traits were identified by McGregor (1941) in the area
around Flagstaff (Winona and Ridge Ruin), while to the west their
influence was felt nearly as far as Prescott (Haury 1976: 6, 8-9).
There is some evidence that the Hohokam had entered the Prescott area
prior to the Sedentary Period. The Henderson Site seems to have been
occupied during the Colonial Period (A.D. 500 to A.D. 900). This site,
east of Prescott in the Agua Fria River Valley, included pit house
structures as well as a canal and a cistern for water storage (Weed and
Ward 1970).

Haury terms these peripheral manifestations of Hohokam influence
"merged Hohokam," reflecting the merging of Hohokam culture traits with
those exhibited by previous occupants of these areas. Thus, although
Hohokam influence may be detected in parts of the Cyprus-Bagdad project
zone, it is probable that no portion of the zone was actually occupied
by Hohokam people. For that matter, only the easternmost portions of
the zone exhibit any Hohokam influence.

Hakataya and Patayan

It is generally agreed that since at least A.D. 1100, the lower Colorado River Valley and the upland areas of northwestern and west-central Arizona were occupied by a people closely related to present-day Yuman groups (McPherson and Pilles 1975: 7). Today the Yumans comprise a group of several Indian tribes living in the same general area. Although substantiating evidence is lacking, Rogers' (1945) idea that the Yumans originated as a seed-gathering culture evolving from the Amargosa has been widely accepted (McPherson and Pilles 1975: 7-8).

The issue of the origins and subsequent sequence of Yuman occupation of western Arizona has been clouded by a myriad of terms which have been arbitrarily applied, redefined, and reapplied by a number of authors. Schroeder (1957) attempted to clarify this confusion some-what, and a brief summary of his discussion follows.

Schroeder points out that the term "Yuman" has literary precedence over its competitors, as indicated by its use in Gladwin and Gladwin (1934: 14 and Figure 1). In 1938, however, Colton objected to the use of the name of a historic Indian language group to identify a prehis-toric culture; therefore, he invented the term "Patayan" to incorporate all prehistoric Yuman groups. Shortly thereafter, Hargrave (1938) used this term to designate a basic culture which included the Prescott, the Cerbat, and the Cohonina. The next year, Colton (1939) revised his own term, dividing it into two branches: the Cerbat, centering around Needles, California; and the Laquish, centering around the Colorado River delta. Rogers (1945: 179) objected to the use of a term most relevant to Arizona archaeology ("Patayan") to refer to what he con-sidered Pacific coastal remains; he further objected to using the term to denote a unified cultural entity, when it in fact included a number of diverse cultural complexes. Rogers readopted the term "Yuman" and advocated the recognition of four branches: Colorado River Valley, California Desert, Western Area, and Eastern Area (Rogers 1945: 180). Baldwin, in apparent confusion, referred to both of Colton's branches as "Patayan", without distinguishing one branch from the other (Baldwin 1950). A symposium at the 1956 Pecos Conference led to the consensus that the term "Hakataya" (which is the word for the Colorado River in Hualapai and Havasupai) would be best suited to denote a region bounded by the Pacific Coast ranges on the west, by the Mogollon Rim on the east, by lower California and the Gila River on the south, and by the Grand Canyon on the north (Schroeder 1957: 177). The term "Patayan" would meanwhile be retained to denote that area occupied prehistorically by the Cerbat, Prescott, and Cohonina (Schroeder 1957: 178).

A meeting at the 1957 Pecos Conference, however, led to the reinstatement of the term "Patayan" to refer to the culture area as a whole. Nonetheless, Schroeder (1960) again used the designation "Hakataya" to refer to a group of traits "that appear to be basic to all cultures of the Yuman root on the lower Colorado River and in western and central Arizona in ceramic times only, as well as in the California desert and northern portions of lower California." According to Euler (1963: 84-85), however, this definition would encompass not only the Amacava, Cohonina, Cerbat, and Prescott, but also the pre-A.D. 1070 Sinagua and the Pioneer Period Hohokam. As summarized by Calvin H. Jennings, the most recent consensus seems to favor the use of "Patayan" to refer to an area south of the Grand Canyon, north of the Bradshaw Mountains, west of the Little Colorado River, and east of the Colorado River below its big bend (Jennings 1971: 49). Although disagreements persist over which prehistoric cultural groups should be included in the Patayan Culture, it is generally agreed that the Cerbat, the Cohonina, and the Prescott are to be included (McPherson and Pilles 1975: 8). These groups are also included iwthin the more inclusive term "Hakataya", as defined by Schroeder (1960).

What anthropologists call these people is of no great consequence. Rather, the significance of this discussion lies in the effort to define the origins and interrelationships of the inhabitants of the culture area. At present, it is perhaps sufficient to note that by A.D. 900 there were a number of populations in the culture area with material cultures sufficiently different to warrant their division into three groups: the Cerbat to the west, the Prescott to the southeast, and the Cohonina to the northeast. At the same time, the material cultures of these groups exhibit enough similarity to warrant their inclusion within the designation "Patayan."

Cerbat

The Cerbat are regarded by Euler and Dobyns as ancestral to the historic Hualapai and Havasupai (Dobyns 1956; Dobyns and Euler 1956; Euler and Dobyns 1956; and Euler 1963). Their view conflicts with that of Schwartz (1956), who believes that the Cohonina were ancestral to the Havasupai. The Cerbat are postulated to have lived west of the Grand Wash Cliffs from about A.D. 700 to 1150. They began moving eastward about A.D. 1150 and replaced the Cohonina throughout the latter group's territorial range by A.D. 1300. Their characteristic pottery was the oxidized Tizon Brown Ware, formed with paddle and anvil (Euler 1963: 83).

The date of origin for this culture is uncertain. Colton (1945: 115), on the basis of associations with datable intrusive wares, presumed that Tizon Brown Wares were being produced in the area as early as A.D. 500. However, subsequent investigations by Dobyns and Euler revealed that the sherds originally examined by Colton were not Tizon Brown Ware (Dobyns and Euler 1956: 14). Schroeder (1952), on the basis of evidence from the Willow Beach Site on the Colorado River, has shown Cerbat Brown (a type of Tizon Brown Ware) to have been produced as early as about A.D. 900 (Euler 1958: 72); to date, this sample is the only one which dates the Cerbat to before A.D. 1000. Euler (1963: 83), however,

suspects that they occupied the area as early as A.D. 700. The Cyprus-
Bagdad Project has produced C-14 dates of A.D. 655 and A.D. 835 in
association with Tizon Brown Ware.

The habitation structures of the Cerbat, a semisedentary people,
were commonly rock shelters or brush wickiups (archaeologically represented by circular rock outlines). In the later periods, U-shaped jacal
structures were occasionally built (Euler 1963: 83). Villages generally
contained about ten domestic units (Euler 1958). Metates were slabs
(generally of sandstone; Dobyns, personal communication) with shallow,
oval, pecked areas on the surface (Euler 1963: 83). Manos were of the
one-handed variety. Projectile points were generally small, triangular-
bladed, with basal and side notches. Other chipped stone implements
included utilized flakes, unifacially retouched knives and scrapers,
and drills. Perishable material culture presumably included coiled
and twined basketry, netting, cordage, sandals of yucca leaves, and
fiber and cotton cloth (Euler 1963).

The lifeways of the Cerbat are still not clearly defined,
although they probably lived much the same way as the historic Pai
groups (McPherson and Pilles 1975: 11). This would indicate a subsistence pattern of nomadic or seminomadic hunting and gathering regulated
by the seasonal availability of wild species.

Prescott

The Prescott Branch is less understood than the Cerbat Branch.
This culture centers on the town of Prescott, with enclaves extending
west toward the Colorado River (Euler 1963: 82-83). Although they
differ considerably from their Yuman neighbors to the west in both
material culture and subsistence modes, the Prescott people have been
included in the Yuman tradition (Gladwin and Gladwin 1934: 14 and
Figure 1).

Gladwin (1957: 125) contends that these people were composed of a
conglomerate of "bands of Reds [sic] coming up from the south and southeast during the eighth century (who) met and merged with some of the
eastern Yuman Foragers, and with the help of a few Basket Makers...
formed the Prescott Branch." Colton (1939) saw fit to include the
Prescott Branch within the Yuman Root. Schroeder cautiously argues
that "archaeologically we have not yet proved that all of the desert
cultures called Yuman by Rogers and Gladwin can be related to the historic Yumans," but he still considers all cultures in the area to be of
Yuman stock (Schroeder 1960: 84). He goes on to hypothesize that the
Prescott Branch became the Yavapai (1960: 96) or were assimilated by
the Cohonina (1960: 99).

Like the Cerbat Branch, the Prescott Branch is dated largely on
the basis of datable intrusive pottery (Euler and Dobyns 1962: 69).

Two phases have been recognized: the Prescott Phase (A.D. 900 to 1100, based on the presence of Black Mesa Black-on-white) and the Chino Phase (A.D. 1025-1200, based on the presence of Flagstaff Black-on-white), which overlaps with the earlier period. Architectural structures of the Prescott Phase include shallow, rectangular pit houses with rounded corners; masonry pueblos; "forts"; and rock outlines. Trough and basin metates, pottery anvils, scrapers, choppers, and projectile points are artifacts typical of this earlier phase. The Chino Phase, though lacking pit houses, essentially retains the earlier architectural forms. Open trough metates, three-quarter grooved axes, and perforated stone disks augment the material culture (Euler and Dobyns 1962: 80). It must be pointed out that this description of Prescott Branch material culture is derived from quite limited excavation samples (Euler and Dobyns 1962; Spicer and Caywood 1936). Euler and Dobyns further note that additional work in the region might significantly alter the currently accepted chronological framework.

The pottery produced by the Prescott people was fired in an uncontrolled atmosphere, was of paddle and anvil construction, and has been called Prescott Gray Ware (Euler 1963: 83). Colton (1958) divided this ware into a number of types, but Euler and Dobyns (1962: 76-77) argue that only one type is involved, "or two types if one distinguishes between the painted and unpainted sherds."

Although they were apparently more sedentary than the Cerbat and practiced agriculture to a larger extent, the Prescott people probably also migrated seasonally in search of wild foods.

Cohonina and Amacava

These two groups may have encroached on the region under discussion. However, they apparently left no traces within the Cyprus-Bagdad project zone. Accordingly, only a cursory description of each will be provided.

Euler (1963: 82) describes the Cohonina as having occupied the area west of Highway 89 (north of Flagstaff), east of the Grand Wash Cliffs, south of the Colorado River, and north of the Mogollon Rim. Jennings (1971: 49) has questioned their inclusion within the Patayan Root. The Cohonina produced San Francisco Mountain Gray Ware, which has been dated from about A.D. 700 to 1150.

Along the Colorado River south of modern Boulder Dam, and west of the project zone, the Amacava occupied seasonal camps detectable today as sherd scatters. Their pottery was oxidized Lower Colorado Buff Ware which dates from about A.D. 700 into historic times. They used slab metates. Schroeder (1960: 96) has hypothesized that the descendants of these people are the modern Mojave.

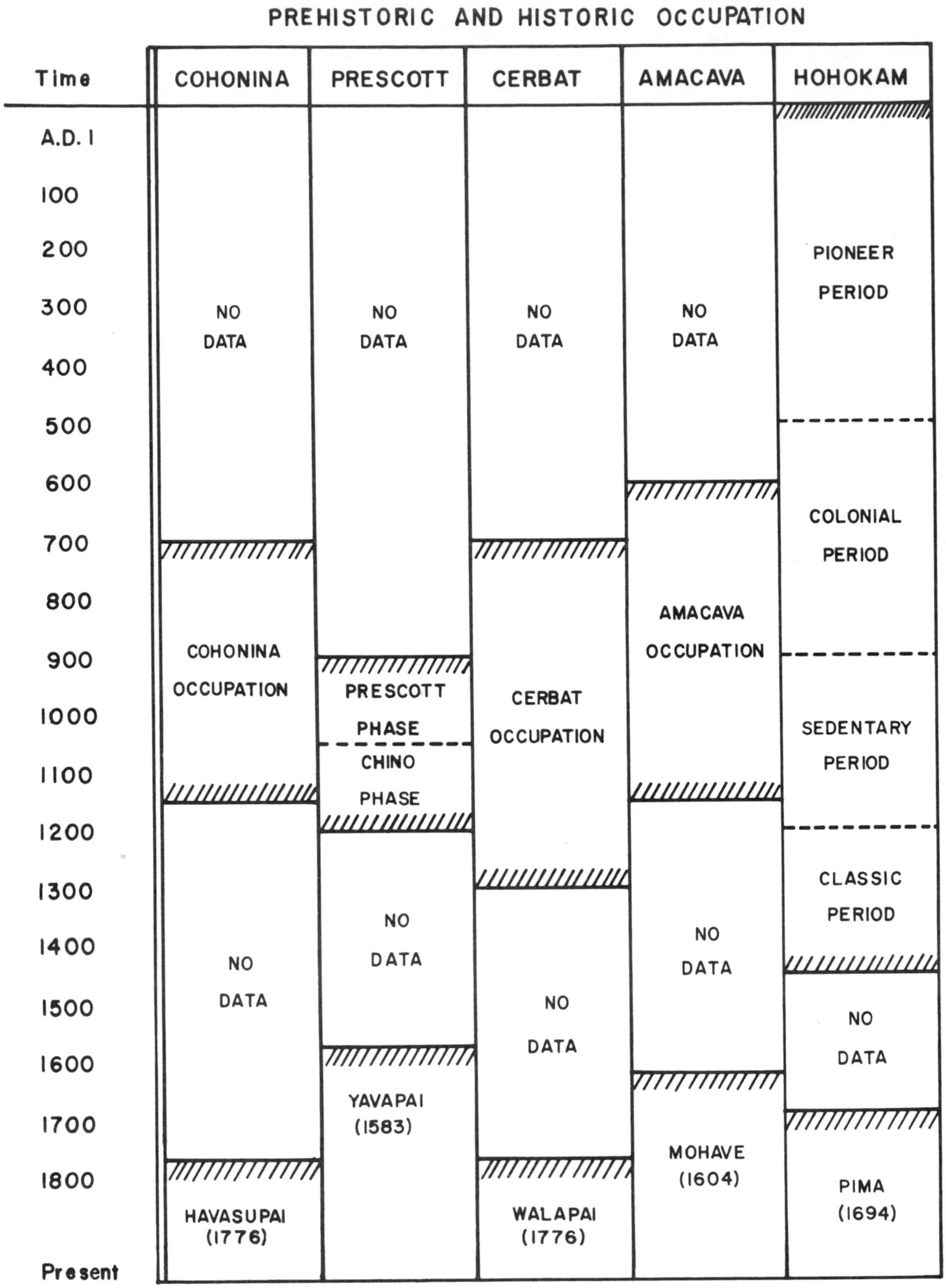

PREHISTORIC AND HISTORIC OCCUPATION

Time	COHONINA	PRESCOTT	CERBAT	AMACAVA	HOHOKAM
A.D. 1					
100					
200					PIONEER PERIOD
300	NO DATA	NO DATA	NO DATA	NO DATA	
400					
500					
600					COLONIAL PERIOD
700					
800				AMACAVA OCCUPATION	
900	COHONINA OCCUPATION	PRESCOTT PHASE	CERBAT OCCUPATION		SEDENTARY PERIOD
1000					
1100		CHINO PHASE			
1200					CLASSIC PERIOD
1300		NO DATA			
1400	NO DATA			NO DATA	
1500			NO DATA		NO DATA
1600					
1700		YAVAPAI (1583)		MOHAVE (1604)	
1800	HAVASUPAI (1776)		WALAPAI (1776)		PIMA (1694)
Present					

Figure 5.   Prehistoric and historic occupation in the Cyprus-Bagdad Project culture area

Protohistoric and Historic Native Cultures

When Europeans first explored western Arizona, they found two culture groups, the Hualapai (or Walapai) and the Yavapai, both speakers of Yuman dialects. Unquestionably, these people were firmly ensconced in the region at the time of the Spanish arrival. However, the length of their prehistoric occupation of the area is still a matter of speculation.

Hualapai

The Cerbat-Hualapai Relationship. Dobyns and Euler, on the basis of archaeological evidence collected through survey (Dobyns 1956) and excavation (Euler 1958), have claimed a continuum between the prehistoric Cerbat and the modern Hualapai. They contend that both groups produced Tizon Brown Ware and that the prehistoric Cerbat occupied almost exactly the same range as the Hualapai. Since no evidence exists that would oppose this contention, it is plausible that the present occupants of the region are descendants of its known prehistoric occupants. However, this postulated continuum has not been adequately demonstrated, and the 300-year void between the end of the archaeological record and the beginning of the historical record warrants a critical assessment of the available evidence.

In support of a proposed continuum, Dobyns (1956: 158) cites the presence of Tizon Brown Ware sherds on historic sites known to have been inhabited by Hualapai Indians. He does not entertain the possibility that these sites might have been occupied more than once. Nonetheless, that the sites may have considerable antiquity remains a distinct possibility, given the unstratified nature of Dobyns' collections and the well-documented practice of reuse of favorable locations by hunting and gathering peoples. The Tizon sherds, which are in the minority at the sites, may very well represent a Cerbat occupation dating to between A.D. 900 and A.D. 1300, even though they are in association with historic European-manufactured goods of a later date.

Euler's (1958) excavations at four sites identified by modern Hualapai as having been most recently occupied by the Hualapai lend limited support to Dobyn's hypothesis. At these sites (Amis Mound [NA 3766 C], Oya Sivli Klavalava [NA 4377], Whala Kitev Giova, and Wha Ha' Vo Cave), the most common pottery was Tizon Brown Ware. Interestingly, Amis Mound has been ethnographically determined to have had a post-1900 occupation, after the postulated end of Tizon Brown Ware manufacture by the Hualapai (Dobyns 1956: 191). However, in none of the sites are the sherds associated with datable hitoric artifacts. Thus, although these sites have been identified by ethnographic informants, the relationship of the ceramic contents to the historic inhabitants remains questionable.

Further evidence in support of the hypothesized connection between the prehistoric Cerbat and the historic Hualapai is derived from the "Wilder pot", obtained from an elderly Hualapai woman and representing, to date, the only known whole Hualapai vessel (Dobyns 1956: 147-150; Dobyns and Euler 1956: 2-4; Euler 1958: 90). This vessel, identified as Aquarius Brown, was claimed by the informant to have been acquired around the turn of the century from her parents-in-law, who told her it was made by a Hualapai (Dobyns 1956: 149). Thus, the information received by Euler and Dobyns concerning this vessel was at best secondhand.

Even if the Wilder pot is Aquarius Brown and can be proven to have been made by a Hualapai, the possibility of independent invention of technique cannot be dismissed. The vessel in question has been identified as an undecorated specimen of Aquarius Brown Ware; however, plainware ceramics, due to their uniformity, are notoriously difficult to classify, even in cases of known cultural affiliation and known prehistoric-historic continuity, such as among the Rio Grande pueblos (R. W. Lange, School of American Research, Santa Fe, personal communication).

The Hualapai in Historic Times. The records of early Spanish explorations indicate that the people today known as Hualapai (and Havasupai) have occupied this region since at least A.D. 1600.

In 1583, Antonio de Espejo may have been the first European to observe the Hualapai, depending on whose interpretation of his itinerary one accepts. According to Bolton (1916: 187), Espejo found a copper mine in Yavapai country. Hammond and Rey (1929: 107) interpret the description of his travels as placing him in the Verde Valley, while Euler (1958: 36) places the mine in Hualapai country. In 1598, Fray Marcos Farfán de los Godos may or may not have retraced Espejo's journey and found the same copper mine (Euler 1958: 37-38). Juan de Oñate followed Farfán as far west as the "juncture of the Santa Maria and the Colorado River" [sic] (Bolton 1916: 269-71). Fray Francisco Atanasio Dominguez, in traveling fron Santa Fe to Monterey, may have skirted the Hualapai territory in 1776 (Bolton 1950: 10).

The first European contact of which there is some certainty occurred in 1776, when Fray Francisco Garcés, of the mission of San Xavier del Bac in southern Arizona, traveled up the Colorado River (Coues 1900: 308). In his travels, Garcés visited the Mojave and various other groups whom Euler (1958: 45-46) defines as Hualapai. Garcés eventually reached Oraibi and then returned to Cataract Canyon, wandering through much of Hualapai country, including Diamond Creek Canyon, Peach Spring Canyon, Hindu Canyon, Milkweed Canyon or possibly Spencer Canyon, and Mata Widita Canyon (Euler 1958: 51-52).

It must be pointed out that most of these earlier Spanish explorers refer to the natives contacted in this region as "Cosnina" or "Co'nina"; Pai peoples are never specifically mentioned. Thus, we are forced to rely upon recent interpretations by modern historians in determining when the first European contact with the Hualapai actually occurred.

The first contact with Americans may have come as early as 1826 when a band of fur trappers led by Jedediah Smith passed through the area on an expedition from the Great Salt Lake to California (Carter 1971: 338). However, the people encountered by Smith called themselves "Ammuchabas" (Morgan 1953: 200), and thus were almost certainly Amacava or Mojave and not Hualapai. Smith, on a second journey through the area in late 1827, heard of and saw signs of another Anglo party in the area. This was probably the party of trappers led by Sylvestre Pratt (Pattie 1930: 150-51), which had only recently been attacked by the Mojave (Morgan 1953: 239). Smith's party, knowing nothing of this skirmish, was attacked by Mojave while crossing the Colorado; the Indians killed ten men and captured two women, all the horses, and most of the supplies. Smith and seven other survivors later had to fight off the Mojave a second time (Morgan 1953: 239-40; Carter 1971: 341).

Also in 1827, a party of settlers passed through Zuni enroute from Santa Fe to San Diego, California; their route may well have taken them through Hualapai country (Euler 1958: 56).

From 1827 to 1830, "the most eccentric mountain man" (Lavender 1954: 26), William Sherley ("Old Bill") Williams, roamed west-central Arizona and may have skirted or traversed the Hualapai country several times in his trapping along the Santa Maria and the stream now known as the Bill Williams Fork (Favour 1936: 71). A group of 40 trappers, including Kit Carson, may have passed through the area in 1829, led by Ewing Young (Lavender 1954: 105-06). In 1834, Bill Williams accompanied a party led by Joseph Walker on a return trip through the region from California (Lavender 1954: 153; Victor 1870: 152-53), but left the group to spend the winter in a Hualapai village in the neighborhood of Bill Williams Mountain (Voelker 1971: 379). This colorful character was known to have visited the area once more in 1837. During his winter with the Hualapai, Williams met a "Padre Gonzales, a wandering Franciscan" staying with the Hualapai (Voelker 1971: 379).

U.S. military contact with the Hualapai began with Captain Lorenzo Sitgreaves, who made peaceful contact with the Truxton Canyon Band of the Hualapai. He was later attacked by the Cerbat Mountain Band (Dobyns and Euler 1960b: 50) and in retaliation plundered a camp identified by Euler as probably Hualapai or Havasupai (Euler 1958: 59-60). In 1853, a party of New Mexicans led by Francois X. Aubry fought off a party of Pai warriors (Dobyns and Euler 1960b: 51).

However, only one year later, Lt. Whipple, while leading a party of railroad explorers across Hualapai territory, encountered only two individuals, who were probably Yavapai (Euler 1968: 61).

Lt. Edward Beale of the U.S. Navy led his camel drive across the region in 1857-1858 and made very little contact with the natives (Leslie 1929). In 1858, Lt. Joseph C. Ives observed Hualapai at Peach Spring, and interestingly surmised that "ours has been the first, and will undoubtedly be the last, party of whites to visit this profitless locality" (Ives 1861: 110).

A group of emigrants later followed Beale's new wagon road between Albuquerque and California. After numerous skirmishes with the Hualapai (perhaps aroused by Mormon propaganda), the party was ambushed by Mojave, who were later soundly defeated by troops marching up the Colorado River Valley. The Hualapai, suitably impressed, embarked upon a period of peaceful relations with the soldiers of Fort Mojave that lasted until 1866 (Dobyns and Euler 1960b: 52-53).

In that year (1866), a Hualapai chief by the name of Wauba Yuma was murdered by a mule skinner, and the western and southern bands rose in vengeance. Thus began the Hualapai War, in which seasoned Civil War veterans were pitted against the Indians. Surprisingly, the Hualapai held out for three years before being subdued in 1869 (Dobyns and Euler 1960b: 54).

Five years later, in 1874, the Hualapai were forcibly removed to the Colorado River Indian Reservation on the lower Colorado River by the Bureau of Indian Affairs. Here they had difficulty in adjusting to the low elevation, riverine environment, new subsistence modes, and strange diseases that killed the infants and the elderly. In 1875, they left the reservation to return to their homeland, receiving no interference from the Army or the Bureau of Indian Affairs (Dobyns and Euler 1960b: 54-55). Upon returning home, the Hualapai were forced to resort to working for Anglo wages to survive, as ranchers now controlled most of the Hualapai ancestral lands. They worked for the ranchers and for mines that were rapidly developing in the area. Their aboriginal life-ways have largely disappeared today (Dobyns and Euler 1960b: 55).

<u>Hualapai Culture and Subsistence</u>. Aboriginally, and in early historic times, the Hualapai were transhumant hunters and gatherers. Villages were built at permanent water sources. During the course of their seasonal rounds, each family used one of three basic living structures: the winter house, the summer brush shelter, and a strong-roofed structure for the stormy fall (Kniffen 1935: 44).

Hualapai population at the time of Kroeber's (1935) study totaled 897 to 1021 individuals, with 3.61 families per band (village),

and 36 to 40 villages (Kniffen 1935: 45). A band was generally
comprised of a lineage, numbering about 25 individuals, and seems to
have been the primary economic unit. Four or more lineages united to
form a larger band structure incorporating close to 100 or more individuals. These groups in turn constituted part of a larger social
structure or congery, of which Dobyns and Euler claim there were three
in aboriginal times (Dobyns and Euler 1960a: 47).

During the spring and summer, families dispersed to gather plant
foods, establishing temporary brush structures. According to Mekeel
(1935: 48-57), agave was "harvested" in April, and various cacti were
consumed in June, July, and August. Mesquite pods were gathered in
late August, and pinyon nuts were collected in September along with
juniper berries. Walnuts were gathered in October and November.
Mulberries, squawberries, wild grapes, wild onions, and grass seeds were
all harvested, with selé being especially preferred, according to Smith
(1973). Tobacco was collected but not cultivated. Mekeel specifically
states that the Hualapai did not use acorns, despite their availability,
but Drucker (1941: 97) contends that sweet acorns were consumed
unleached, raw, and roasted.

There is also some disagreement as to the extent to which these
people practiced agriculture. MacGregor (1935: 57) asserted that it
was practiced by scattered families living next to springs. On the
other hand, Dobyns and Euler (1960a) claim that it was far more important than Kroeber's associates recognized, while Euler (1958) supposed
Hualapai agriculture to have been severely disrupted by prolonged
Anglo contact. The Hualapai are known to have cultivated three to five
colors or varieties of corn, four of beans, pumpkins, and possibly
squash, sunflowers, watermelons and muskmelons, peaches, and possibly
apricots and pears (Mekeel 1935:56; MacGregor 1935: 58; Drucker 1941: 94).

Hunters sought antelope on the plains and deer wherever
encountered. Mountain sheep were hunted in the northern canyon
country, and bear in the Hualapai Mountains. Mountain lion and foxes
were tracked in snow, and coyotes were trapped by deadfalls. Also
included among the larger game were badgers, porcupines, and possibly
wolves. Small game included jackrabbit, while cottontail drives were
organized in winter. Rats and kangaroo rats were trapped, along with
ground squirrels and gophers. Chuckwallas and possibly other lizards
were eaten. Quail, wild turkey, wild pigeons, doves, and other small
birds were shot. Caterpillars were also consumed (McKennan 1935: 61-70;
Drucker 1941: 98-100). Among the large animals, deer, antelope, and
mountain sheep were by far the most important to the Hualapai; jackrabbits and cottontail also furnished a substantial part of their diet
(McKennan 1935: 61, 63).

Dobyns (1957: 188) states that the Burro Creek bottoms provided
the Hualapai with a number of good farming locations; cultivated areas
seem to have been fairly dense here. According to one informant, one

farming site was located on Burro Creek near the mouth of Boulder Creek (Dobyns 1957: 188) in the vicinity of site AZ M:7:2, which also may have been a farming site. Dobyns claims that, in precontact and early historic times, land along Burro Creek was cultivated at numerous points from its headwaters to its mouth. These farms constituted the core settlement area of the eastern canyon region, and were apprently as stable as the farms on the lower Big Sandy (Dobyns 1957: 198). The Hualapai considered this region the southernmost extent of their terri-tory, but they hunted and gathered at least as far south as the Santa Maria River (Dobyns 1957: 205), where they encountered opposition from the Yavapai.

Yavapai

The Yavapai are another group known to have inhabited portions of this region in historic times. Like the Hualapai, they are of Yuman linguistic stock, but they may have arrived in this area somewhat later than the other Yumans (Gifford 1936: 247), possibly as late as A.D. 1400 (Dobyns 1956: 694; Schroeder 1952: 112).

Prehistoric Predecessors of the Yavapai. The Yavapai occupied an area previously inhabited by the Prescott Branch. Based on differ-ences in settlement and habitation patterns, as well as the postulated early disappearance of the ceramic type characterizing the preceding Prescott Culture, Dobyns (personal communication) sees little if any probability of a continuum between these earlier people and the modern Yavapai. However, Gifford (1932 and 1936) continually points out the un-Yuman-like characteristics of the Yavapai Culture. Jeter (personal communication), after considerable field work in the Copper Basin, enter-tains the possibility that the Yavapai of today represent at least a mixture of Yuman and Prescott ancestry.

The Yavapai in Historic Times. Early European contact with the Yavapai is problematic and follows the same proposed sequence as out-lined for the Hualapai, including visits by Espejo, Farfán, and Oñate between 1583 and 1605 (Schroeder 1974: 6). During this time, the South-eastern Yavapai occupied most of the middle Verde Valley from below Fossil Creek to Oak Creek Canyon, including the region around Montezuma National Monument (Schroeder 1952: 111; Gifford 1936: 252). Farfán described these particular Indians as "Cruzados", in reference to their practice of wearing crosses (usually made of wood) around their necks. In 1599, Zaldivar, leading a company of Oñate's men toward the Pacific Ocean (which they did not reach), encountered Indians with crosses used in Roman Catholic fashion (Hammond 1926: 450, 471). After Oñate's trip in 1604, a Fray Velasco passed through the area in 1605 (Schroeder 1952: 114).

In 1662, Peñalosa, then governor of New Mexico, claimed a decisive victory over the Cruzados Coninas (Havasupai), settling them in Hopi villages (Hackett 1926: 264). Schroeder (1952: 114), finding no corroborative evidence for this event in contemporary Spanish records, believes the account to have been fabricated by Peñalosa. If so, there were no known European expeditions into the middle Verde Valley between 1605 and 1860 (Schroeder 1952: 117).

In 1860, with apparently little provocation, a prospector named Jack Swilling led an expedition from the Gila River north into the Prescott area, destroying several rancherías and killing a number of Indians (Schroeder 1974: 11). Three years later, the Yavapai were accused of stealing some horses; the ensuing "punishment" left about 20 Indians dead. When the allegedly stolen horses were later found, the innocent Yavapai retaliated in rage. Late that same year, Major Willis, of Fort Whipple, concluded a tenuous peace (Schroeder 1936: 12); nevertheless, the settlers around Prescott felt compelled to maintain a protective force of 100 men.

Also in 1863, the settlers devised a scheme known as the Pinole Treaty. The Yavapai were invited to a "council" where they were given food. While they were eating, the Anglos opened fire, killing 30 of them. Throughout this year soldiers from Fort McDowell persecuted the Indians, beating, jailing, and killing them for minor crimes or for no reason at all (Schroeder 1974: 13). Open warfare began when soldiers killed a Northeastern Yavapai chief and 27 of his men in the employ of Indian Agent Dunn, who later referred to this episode as outright murder (Schroeder 1974: 14). Many of the Yavapai who remained on the reservations that year faced starvation.

In 1868, a number of Indians were enticed to a council at La Paz, Arizona; in the ensuing ambush, over a dozen were killed (Schroeder 1974: 16). In the following year, settlers induced the Mojave to hold a council, in which the Yavapai were invited to participate; all 35 Yavapai who attended were killed (Schroeder 1974: 17).

By 1873 to 1875, hostilities had more or less ceased, and the vast majority of the Yavapai were placed on military reservations, particularly on the San Carlos Reservation (Schroeder 1974: 19; 1952: 111). Most Yavapai now live on the Camp Verde Reservation, where they were placed in the early 1900s, or in the vicinity of Fort McDowell, Clarkdale, and Prescott (Schroeder 1952: 11; 1974: 20).

Yavapai Culture and Subsistence. The Yavapai are divided into three distinct groups: the Southeastern, Northeastern, and the Western Yavapai (Gifford 1936: 247). Gifford estimated that the population of the combined groups never surpassed 1500 individuals, and attained a density of approximately one person for every 15 square miles.

Among the Southeastern Yavapai, there were two matrilineal clans made up of chiefless, exogamous, nontotemic, matrilineal bands (Gifford 1932: 189); among the Northeastern and Western Yavapai, clans are absent (Gifford 1936: 291-97). These characteristics distinguish the Yavapai from neighboring Yuman tribes, whose clans are patrilineal (Gifford 1936: 291). Although the three groups have never been known to act in concert (Schroeder 1974: 1), the Southeastern and Northeastern groups were close friends, and allies in warfare (Gifford 1932: 183).

Ethnographic data indicate that the Yavapai were more nomadic than the Hualapai and traveled nearly year-round. For shelter all three groups preferred caves and rock shelters (Gifford 1932: 203; 1936: 271), especially in the rainy or winter seasons. They built temporary structures during their migrations, apparently never reusing previous structures. Dwellings generally consisted of domed or beehive huts, thatched among the Southeastern group and made of ocotillo, willow, or mesquite among the Northeastern and Western bands (Gifford 1932: 302; 1936: 271).

Mescal (agave) was the primary wild staple (Gifford 1932: 206-07). Edible year-round, it was either consumed on the spot or collected for later use. During the summer and fall months, the diet was supplemented by (in the order of seasonal availability): saguaro, mesquite (June and July), ironwood seeds (August), palo-verde seeds (August and September), and prickly-pear fruit (September) (Gifford 1936: 258). Doelle (1975: 61) has noted that the Hohokam and Pima commonly used mesquite pods as foods, and may, in times of famine, have consumed the seeds as well. All three Yavapai groups used the pods on a regular basis.

Other plants important to the Yavapai diet included acorns (considered a delicacy), pinyon nuts, and walnuts in the fall. Jojoba beans were parched, ground, and eaten like peanut butter by all three groups. Two varieties of sunflower were eaten in October, as were berries from two species of juniper. Various bulbs and corms were eaten in January, and hackberries were eaten as they ripened during late winter. Squawberries ripened in early May. Wild grapes were also consumed by all three groups. Greasewood leaves were boiled for a medicinal tea by the Southeastern Yavapai. Among the Northeastern and Western Yavapai, children would suck on ocotillo blossoms for the sweet nectar (Gifford 1932: 206-213; 1936: 256-61).

Agriculture was practiced only minimally among the Southeastern Yavapai. Once planted, the crop was not cultivated. This group produced a pink variety of maize, pumpkins, watermelons, and gourds (for use as canteens and rattles) (Gifford 1932: 214). The Northeastern Yavapai seem to have practiced more agriculture than did the Southeastern group, producing several varieties of maize. On the other hand,

the Western Yavapai were much more agriculturally inclined than either
of the other groups, producing several varieties of maize and beans,
pumpkins, watermelons, muskmelons, and gourds. Both the Northeastern
and Western Yavapai were known to have grown a type of tobacco (Gifford
1936: 262-264).

Venison provided the staple meat for all three Yavapai groups;
antelope and mountain sheep were also considered important to their
diet. Jackrabbits and cottontails were shot or clubbed, or pulled from
their burrows with barbed sticks. Among the Southeastern and Western
bands, communal rabbit drives were undertaken, but without the use of
nets. The Southeastern Yavapai might either shoot woodrats or, like
their Northeastern and Western neighbors, trap them with deadfalls.
Among the Northeastern and Western bands, coyotes were consumed when
venison was scarce. These latter groups also ate prairie dogs, ground
squirrels, Arizona tree squirrels, chipmunks, antelope chipmunks, small
stripe-faced chipmunks, porcupines, skunks (striped, spotted, and hog-
nosed), raccoons, ring-tailed cats, and badgers.

People of all three groups trapped quail, while the Northeastern
and Western bands hunted turkey, mourning dove, white-winged dove,
thrasher, hummingbird, mockingbird, Woodhouse jays, Abert's towhee,
orioles, and horned owls.

The desert tortoise was consumed by all three Yavapia groups.
the Northeastern and Western bands also caught and ate chuckwallas. All
three bands consumed at least one species of caterpillar (Gifford 1932:
215-17; 1936: 264-68).

Euler and Dobyns (1956: 8) have been unable to identify any
Yavapai pottery, prehistoric or historic. Gifford's informants claim
that the Southeastern bands produced pottery from a red clay found near
Amanyika, and that red pigment was sometimes added to produce a red
ware (Gifford 1932: 218-19). Informants from the other two groups
provided vague information which suggested that they may have produced
a red ware or a black-and-gray variety. An interesting point in this
regard is their claim to have used ground sherds for temper as well as
fine quartz sand, a procedure differing quite strongly with that of
their Hualapai neighbors (Gifford 1936: 280-81). In any case, informants from all three Yavapai groups related that their pottery was
constructed by the coil method without the use of the paddle and anvil,
a method also quite different from that employed by the Hualapai.

The Yavapai, characteristically very warlike, counted the
Hualapai, Pima, and Maricopa among their traditional enemies. Gifford
describes seven attacks upon or by the Hualapai (Gifford 1936: 326-35).
The Yavapai were known to kill prisoners and burn the bodies. On rare
occasions they ate the flesh of dead prisoners and boasted of this feat
at their next meeting with the victims' kin or friends. (Yavapai

informants claimed that the Hualapai did the same.) In addition, both tribes burned their prisoners alive (Gifford 1936: 304, 328-29). It was probably this warlike behavior which caused the Yavapai to be misidentified as Apache, Apache-Mojave, and Apache-Yuma throughout most of their contact with Anglos (Schroeder 1974: 1).

Historic and Contemporary Anglo Interests

The earliest Anglo interests in the area were the trapping ventures of Bill Williams and his comrades in the 1820s and 1830s. However, not until the region became a territory of the United States were settlements founded. Shortly after the establishment of Arizona Territory in 1864, the year-old gold camp of Lynx Creek was renamed Prescott and made the territorial capital, an honor it held until 1867 when the government was transferred to Tucson. Transferred back to Prescott in 1877, it remained there until Phoenix was made the terri- torial capital in 1889 (Granger 1960: 354-355). Prescott remains today the county seat of Yavapai County. In the same region, Fort Whipple and Camp McPherson were both established in 1864, the former occupied until 1898, the latter abandoned in 1867 with the establish- ment of Camp Date Creek, which became the site of an Indian reserva- tion from 1871 to 1872. Camp Date Creek was eventually abandoned after 1875 (Granger 1960: 341, 363). Camp Verde, farther east in Yavapai County, was founded as a private fort to protect a newly founded agricultural settlement (Granger 1960: 360-61).

Skull Valley was founded in 1869 as a mining community. In that same year, a military scouting party explored and named Burro Creek, whose name indicates that even then, as now, burros were abundant in the area. Granger speculates that disheartened prospectors turned loose their burros, which then multiplied (Granger 1960: 204).

The mining communities of Jerome in Yavapai County and Chloride in Mohave County were both established in 1873 (Granger 1960: 206, 347). The copper mine at Jerome may be the same as that located by Espejo and Farfán in the 16th century.

Signal, established in 1887, was possibly the largest and most widely known mining town of its day, though it is virtually abandoned today. Mining continues at nearby Hillside, founded in 1888 (Granger 1960: 223).

Farther to the north, in Mohave County, the town of Oatman sprang up in 1904 near the site of the Vivian Mine. It was not too far from Kingman, established in 1883 on the Atchison, Topeka, and Santa Fe Railroad route (Granger 1960: 214, 218).

The town of Bagdad, established in 1910, was named for a mining claim located on January 1, 1882 by John Lawler, who also discovered the Hillside deposits. Beginning in 1906, several companies have tried to operate the mine, resulting in a series of rises and declines in the town's population (McPherson and Pilles 1975: 25,27).

Today, mining remains the major financial interest in the area, with some ranching and very limited farming still being done along the Big Sandy and Verde rivers. Large tracts of land are controlled by the Bureau of Land Management, the Forest Service, and several Indian tribes.

CHAPTER 5

METHODOLOGY

Goals

The goals of the Cyprus-Bagdad Project were to "establish (insofar as the data permit) a temporal framework and chronological sequence within the study area with primary emphasis upon human interaction with the effective environment."

Techniques

Field Techniques

Survey. In surveying the proposed 58-km (36-mile) pipeline route, a crew of two spent seven days walking the 50-foot (15.24-m) wide right-of-way. In addition, probable site locations within 30 to 60 meters of the right-of-way and susceptible to indirect impact were also examined. A few surface samples of cultural material were collected to aid in cultural identification.

A total of 88 ha (216 acres) was covered. Six sites were found in the first 29 km (18 miles) from Bagdad, in rough, hilly terrain. No sites were found in the final 29 km of the route, which continued into Wikieup and further north into the low, rough, hilly country along the east side of the Big Sandy River (Hammack 1975: 15-16).

Testing Phase. Following the survey report, a one-week testing program was undertaken, during which a crew of four spent five days in the field. The testing was designed to allow a more accurate estimate of the time required for the data recovery program at each site, and to aid in the formulation of a research design. It also allowed sampling of the cultural materials, as well as a comparison of surface and subsurface remains at individual sites. During this phase of the project, it was discovered that locus AZ M:7:1 had actually resulted from the washing of a small number of sherds into the bed of Boulder Creek from higher ground.

Using site marker(s) placed during survey as datum-points, the crews laid out north-south and east-west base lines and then selected

53

areas which, on the basis of soil color and texture, topography, and artifact density, appeared most likely to reveal subsurface remains.

At AZ M:8:2 (see site map, Chapter 6, Figure 22), four 1 m-by-1 m test pits were excavated to a depth of 5 cm or less, at which point sterile clay was encountered. Bedrock was found at 10 cm. No subsurface features were discovered.

At AZ M:8:3, five 1 m-by-1 m squares were randomly selected and excavated to depths ranging from 5 cm to 15 cm (see site map, Chapter 6, Figure 22). Again, no subsurface cultural remains were discovered and no features were found.

At AZ M:7:3 (see site map, Chapter 6, Figure 19), a stratified random sample of seven 1 m-by-1 m squares was excavated; stratification of the sample was based on the four quadrants of the grid system. Excavators reached sterile soil at 5 cm in one pit, at 10 cm in three others, and at 20 cm in two pits; the deepest pit encountered sterile soil at 35 cm. No features were found, and artifacts were scattered as though by erosion.

AZ M:7:2 (see site map, Chapter 6, Figure 10) was the only site to reveal subsurface cultural remains. This site, on a mesa top, was comprised of two distinct sections; the most heavily used area lay at the tip of the mesa, overlooking Burro Creek, while a thin scatter of lithic materials extended west from this area. In the site's more heavily used portion, two randomly selected 1 m-by-1 m test pits were excavated. One revealed sterile clay at 25 cm, while the other attained a depth of 65 cm, with heavy cultural deposition to this level and below. Exposed in this latter pit was what was thought to be the perimeter of a pit house. A 1 m-by-1 m pit excavated in the lithic scatter to the west disclosed no artifacts, and sterile soil was encountered at 5 cm.

At the final site tested, AZ M:7:4 (see site map, Chapter 6, Figure 6), five test pits were excavated according to a stratified random sample concentrated within the confines of the right-of-way corridor, although the majority of the surface artifacts and suspected deposition lay west of the corridor. This site lies in a natural sink between two mesas and a deep ravine. The pits in the area of least elevation were excavated to a depth of 37 cm to 50 cm and appeared to be in alluvial, sandy soil. The other pits, on slightly higher ground, reached 5 cm, 10 cm, and 15 cm in depth. No cultural deposition was noted which could not be attributed to erosion.

In addition to excavating test pits, the crew examined each site for surface material and to define site boundaries. Although no surface collections were made (other than on the surfaces of the test pit locations), it was often possible to delineate areas of more intensive activity within the sites on the basis of differential artifact density.

Data Recovery Phase.   The data recovery process consisted of three related activities: data collection, mapping and photographing of sites and cultural materials, and a survey of vegetation to collect current environmental data. As the majority of the sites were too large to make total data recovery feasible, each site was sampled. The sampling strategy varied according to site size, disturbance, and other factors (Redman 1975: 151; Asch 1975: 171, 178).

AZ M:7:4 had been severely disturbed by the previous construction of a road, a pipeline, a transmission line, two jeep trails, and a fence line. Since the proposed project corridor was to pass through the least disturbed portion of the site, it had been previously decided to restrict data recovery to the corridor; however, limited collections were undertaken in other portions of the site. A total of 86 contiguous 5 m-by-5 m grid squares collected in the corridor accounted for approximately 50 percent of the corridor space located within the site boundaries. In addition, 24 mostly contiguous 5 m-by-5 m grid squares were collected outside the corridor. In all, 100 squares or 2500 square meters of the site were collected, amounting to approximately 8 percent of its estimated 32,500 square-meter area. In order to estimate the percentage of the total surface material recovered by the collections, a single square was stripped and its contents screened in a one-fourth-inch mesh screen to obtain as much of a 100-percent sample as possible. Finally, four test pits were excavated at randomly selected locations. The results of these tests were similar to those obtained by the testing crew.

Site AZ M:7:2 had apparently been disturbed to a considerably lesser degree. Therefore, sampling at this site was not limited to the corridor, although the majority of work did take place there. In addition, as this site exhibited areas of fairly intensive use, the sample taken was stratified. In Area A, at the east end of the mesa overlooking Burro Creek, the sampling units were comprised of contiguous 2 m-by-2 m grid squares; a total of 148 squares was collected in two blocks. Along the north edge of the mesa, nearest Cornwall Wash, 58 squares were collected in the vicinity of the suspected pit house previously discovered by the testing crew. A shallow but steep, rocky gully separated this set of squares from a block of 90 squares laid out in the same area along the south edge of the mesa. The choice of smaller, contiguous sampling units in Area A proceeded from the evidence of intensive prehistoric activity, and from the hope that more pit houses might be found. On the other hand, Area B of AZ M:7:2, due to its low artifact density and the large area, was collected in alternate 5 m-by-5 m squares.

Area A produced a single habitation structure, which was excavated in ten 2 m-by-2 m squares. These were taken down in 10-cm increments to a point 85 cm below present ground surface; there, an irregular (rather than flat) living surface was encountered. Lack of time later necessitated a shift to a new strategy in which two of the 2 m-by-2 m squares in the southwest corner of the feature were each excavated as a single stratigraphic unit. All material was sifted in a one-fourth-inch mesh screen.

AZ M:7:3, a broad lithic scatter covered with large cores and heavy percussion flakes, was collected in 5 m-by-5 m grid squares. No areas of differential or dense activity were discovered, so the collection sample was not stratified. Collections were not made in areas disturbed by construction, or where gullies crossed the site. Using a marker placed by the survey crew as the datum-point, north-south and east-west base lines were laid out and a total of 98 5 m-by-5 m squares collected in alternating, checkerboard fashion. In this manner, 2450 square meters were collected, approximately 8 percent of the estimated 30,000 square-meter site.

Also at AZ M:7:3, three test trenches, each approximately 5 m long and 0.5 m wide, were excavated through suspected check dams along the western margin of the site. The trenches passed through alignments of volcanic cobbles to a depth of 10 cm to 30 cm. Subsequent pollen analysis revealed that at least one of the cobble alignments was probably a check dam.

Sites AZ M:8:2 and AZ M:8:3 received only limited attention, following the Cyprus-Bagdad Company's decision to reroute the pipeline around them. Because these sites were still suffering disturbance in connection with other aspects of the mine's expansion, permission to undertake limited data collection at these loci was requested.

AZ M:8:2, a small lithic scatter, was collected in its entirety in a series of 25 contiguous 2 m-by-2 m grid squares. No test pits were excavated. AZ M:8:3 lay 80 m north of AZ M:8:2; the two sites may have been related. AZ M:8:2 is located on a small hill, while AZ M:8:3 lies on a broad shoulder of that hill and approximately 18 feet lower in elevation than AZ M:8:2. AZ M:8:3 encompassed approximately 4384 square meters, on two naturally distinct terraces. The upper terrace, which comprises the southernmost portion of the site, is situated on a shallow layer of eroded soil overlying a large, flat outcropping of granite, and is about 3 feet higher than the site's northern section, which is situated on deeper soil. This site is bisected by a bulldozer path, which curves southeast to west over the site and connects two areas of intensive construction activity within the Cyprus-Bagdad Mine itself. A total of 114 2 m-by-2 m grid squares was laid out at AZ M:8:3; half of these, encompassing 228 square meters or 5.2 percent of the total area of the site, were collected in checkerboard fashion. The selection of the grid squares to be collected was affected by the presence of bulldozer damage and, to a lesser extent, by the presence of large outcroppings of granite and dense patches of cactus which could not be removed without extensive disturbance of the surface deposits. No test pits were excavated.

Additional survey by members of the crew along a second pipeline (laid one year before the survey but still related to the mine expansion) located two additional sites along Sycamore Creek northeast of Bagdad, and approximately 8 km from AZ M:8:2 and AZ M:8:3. As the data recovery phase was already in progress when these two sites (AZ M:8:4 and AZ M:8:5) were discovered, no testing was conducted on them. However, they were subjected to intensive data collection following the completion of work at the sites involved in the original contract.

AZ M:8:4, located at Sycamore Well on the high, vertical, rocky south bank of Sycamore Creek, consisted of a light sherd and lithic scatter approximately 1957 meters square. Heavily damaged by a roadbed that had destroyed nearly 20 percent of its surface area, this site was collected by means of a series of 2 m-by-2 m grid squares laid out in two blocks, one on either side of the road. Each block was collected in checkerboard fashion. A total of 34 squares was collected, encompassing 136 square meters or about 6.9 percent of the site area. In addition, five 1 m-by-1 m test pits were excavated, three in the central portion of the site and two near its northeast perimeter in the vicinity of a boulder metate. The test pits revealed the topsoil to be about 5 cm to 10 cm deep, with no cultural deposition. An alignment of rocks in the vicinity of the boulder metate was suspected to be a wall foundation; testing proved this not to be the case.

AZ M:8:5, a sparse sherd and lithic scatter encompassing 652 square meters, is located along the north bank of Sycamore Creek on a gently sloping bench about 0.5 km above the watercourse. The north end of this site had been cut away by a widening of the access road to Sycamore Well and its pump, located about 1 km east at AZ M:8:4. A grid system of 54 2 m-by-2 m squares was laid over the site; 29 of these squares were collected, producing a sample of 17.8 percent of the site area. As with the previous sites, the presence of gullies and other soil disturbance (in addition to the selected checkerboard pattern) determined which squares were collected. Also, four randomly selected 1 m-by-1 m test pits were excavated. These tests indicated that deposition reached 15 cm in depth in some places, and overlay a dense layer of sterile clay. No remains were found below the surface.

Data provided by the collection of material cultural remains and the mapping of each site were augmented by extensive photographic records of the sites and their surroundings, and of the excavations. These records provide a visual record of the topography, hydrology, and vegetation density of each site.

The final aspect of data collection at each site consisted of a vegetation survey, conducted by one individual who traversed the site and its immediate vicinity in order to locate and identify the local plant species. Ideally, these surveys began at the highest point of the hill or mesa on which a particular site was located and proceeded downhill, generally ending in a watercourse. Transects were approximately 100 m wide. Upon reaching a watercourse, the surveyor continued approximately 250 m upstream and downstream, tabulating species found in the floodplain on either bank. This study was intended primarily to ascertain the presence or absence of vegetational resources known to have been important to early historic occupants of this area. Then, by analogy, and with consideration of possible environmental change through time, hypotheses concerning the adaptations of the sites' prehistoric inhabitants were derived. The value of this study is best illustrated by the long transect made between AZ M:7:2, on the west bank of Burro Creek, and AZ M:7:3 on the east bank (see Chapter 6). However, the complete procedure, as outlined above, could be accomplished at only one site, AZ M:7:2.

Analysis

Artifacts were washed, labeled, and catalogued, and then examined by the author and by a number of volunteer analysts.

Chipped Stone. Approximately 15,000 specimens of chipped stone were recovered from the seven sites of the Cyprus-Bagdad Project. Following a procedure suggested by Redman (1975: 149), all items were first cursorily examined, then assigned a general classification and tabulated. More intensive analysis followed. At first, all chipped stone was to be subjected to intensive analysis. After about 20 percent of the items from AZ M:7:2 were analyzed, however, it became obvious that time did not permit analysis of the entire collection. The collection was therefore divided into two parts. The first was a random sample by provenience (but including the 20-percent sample of materials from AZ M:7:2 originally analyzed), stratified by site. This sample included 10 to 80 percent of the chipped stone collected from a given site; factors governing sample size included site size and amount of site disturbance. All artifacts in this sample were thoroughly analyzed and described. The second part of the collection was more cursorily examined; only retouched items were subjected to intensive analysis and description, and other items (such as unretouched flakes) were simply noted using general descriptive terms. Artifacts in each of the two samples, random and unretouched-nonrandom, are listed separately in the tables in later chapters of this report.

Each artifact which underwent further analysis was examined under a 15- to 60-power binocular microscope and described morphologically on the basis of six criteria. These were: 1) raw material, 2) stage of manufacture, 3) fragmentation, 4) cortex, 5) two-dimensional measurements, and 6) thickness. In addition, each item was examined for evidence of alteration and/or utilization; descriptions of utilized portions, marginal retouch, use-wear, and edge-angle were recorded.

Results of these analyses were then encoded on standard IBM Fortran forms (see Appendix A for code, a complete description of each variable, and the reason for its inclusion). The format used is drawn largely from that of Schaafsma (1975, 1976, and 1977). A total of about 3500 items was examined in this way.

Ground Stone. These artifacts were each examined with the aid of a 16-power hand lens, and then described in terms of raw material, general shape, and wear patterns, if any. This information was not computerized. All 125 specimens were analyzed (see Appendix B).

Ceramics. All 2237 potsherds collected during the project were analyzed. On the basis of the type descriptions by Colton (1939, 1958) and consultation with Henry Dobyns, project workers identified pottery primarily on the basis of four criteria: 1) inclusions, 2) texture, 3) coloration (interior as well as exterior and core), and 4) surface treatment (see Appendix B). After examination under a 15- to 60-power binocular microscope, each sherd was identified as either Prescott Gray Ware or one of the varieties of Tizon Brown Ware (Cerbat Brown Ware, Aquarius Brown Ware, Tizon Wiped Ware, or Sandy Brown Ware). Three additional ceramic categories were established: Intermediate (exhibiting elements of both Tizon and Prescott wares), Unidentifiable (too badly eroded or too small for identification), and Other (not corresponding to any of the Prescott or Tizon categories). The few specimens assigned to this last category were later identified as Lino Gray Ware.

In addition to the identification of individual sherds recovered from the seven sites, an experimental attempt was made to produce pottery with similar attributes, using clay from a deposit of bentonite found approximately 6.5 km from AZ M:7:2. Another deposit of this mineral was discovered later in Cornwall Wash, about 1 km from AZ M:7:2 (see Appendix C).

Other Collections. A number of other materials were collected, including pollen samples, soil samples, and bone and shell specimens.

At the two excavated features (the habitation structure at AZ M:7:2 and the check dam at AZ M:7:3), pollen samples were taken. A series of these samples was taken in a stratigraphic column from each of these two sites. Dr. Vera Markgraf and H. L. D'Antoni of Tumamoc Hill Laboratories, Department of Geosciences, University of Arizona performed the analysis, the results of which are discussed in Chapter 6 and Appendix C.

Flotation samples were collected at AZ M:7:2 from the area around the posthole in the habitation structure. These were analyzed by Charles Miksicek of the Tumamoc Hill Laboratories and yielded vegetal remains.

All faunal material recovered by the project was derived from the habitation structure at AZ M:7:2. Most of the bones were burned; however, the structure itself had burned at one time. All the bones were analyzed by Mr. Stanley J. Olsen of the Zooarchaeology Laboratory, Department of Anthropology, University of Arizona.

A very few specimens of charred wood were recovered from the structure at AZ M:7:2. The Laboratory of Tree-Ring Research, University of Arizona, could not date the wood, but was able to identify the species used. These specimens were submitted to the Chronology Laboratory, Department of Geology, University of Georgia, for Carbon-14 dating.

CHAPTER 6

SITE DESCRIPTIONS

In this chapter, each site is described in terms of its environmental setting, physical characteristics, and artifact assemblage. Where possible, cultural affiliations and the age of the site will be discussed.

The most common artifact type at the sites consisted of chipped stone remains. These were classified in terms of descriptive categories, but wear patterns were also considered; as a result, morphologically similar artifacts might be subdivided in terms of supposed function. Few artifacts could be assigned to a specific culture or tradition, although some tentative affiliations will be advanced later in this volume. Most of the criteria used in identifying chipped stone were derived from Crabtree (1972) and Chapman (1973), and were recorded using a computer format similar to that of Schaafsma (1977).

Pottery was more difficult to analyze, due to the small sample recovered and the nature of published descriptions. As a result, the identifications are tentative. An attempt was made to adhere to the criteria described by Dobyns and Euler (1958) in identifying the various types of Tizon Brown Ware, but in the author's opinion the criteria are unreliable. In the course of analysis (which involved only 2241 sherds), it became obvious that a single sherd might fit several of the types described by Dobyns and Euler. Unless one relies on intuition--which is quite commonly used, sometimes justifiably, in Southwestern ceramic analysis (Schiffer and Gumerman 1977)--the various types of Tizon Brown Ware are best seen as variations on a single type, Tizon Brown. Euler and Dobyns (1962) have already reached a similar conclusion about a related ware, Prescott Gray Ware, and Waters (personal communication) has likewise reached this conclusion about Yuman pottery. Nevertheless, the various types of Tizon Brown Ware described by Dobyns and Euler (1958) are distinguished in the pages that follow, as a sample of 2241 sherds is not sufficient to warrant altering type and ware descriptions. However, the author's reservations about these types should be obvious, and further studies of Tizon Brown Ware are clearly needed.

In the following pages, the sites are described in order of excavation.

Site AZ M:7:4

Site AZ M:7:4 (Figures 6 and 7), the northeasternmost site discovered by the Cyprus-Bagdad survey, is located on Bogle Ranch Road approximately 5.5 km east of Highway 93 and at an elevation of about 2950 feet. Irregularly shaped, the site is 200 m long and 190 m wide, and lies in a shallow sink at the foot of a steep-sided basalt mesa. The mesa bounds this sink on the northeast; to the west and south, small hillocks form the remainder of the sink boundaries (see Figure 7). The local geology is of volcanic and sedimentary origin; large basalt boulders and cobbles lie strewn about on a basalt gravel, and are most densely distributed near the basalt mesa. The hillock to the west is steep on its west side (facing away from the site) and slopes downward into an unnamed wash which forms the western boundary and the western half of the northern boundary of the site. Along the site's northern periphery, this wash cuts through sandstone bedrock underlying the volcanic deposits, and ranges from 3 m to 35 m in depth, descending steeply at several points into miniature "canyons" to the west. In the last and deepest of these "canyons," where the wash levels off and flows between the hillocks, a small natural tinaja or bedrock basin was found. No rain had fallen for several months, but a pool of water about 5 m in diameter and 50 cm deep was present (see Figure 8).

Artifact density at the site is heaviest over its western half, and test excavations indicated that the eastern half had been severely eroded. Fine alluvial sand and silty soil extend to a depth of at least 50 cm, the point where excavations ceased due to a lack of cultural remains. Most of the work undertaken in connection with the Cyprus-Bagdad Project was confined to the eastern half of the site, within the direct impact zone. The western half of the site had already been seriously disturbed by previous construction activities.

Environment

The predominant vegetation on the site consists of various forms of cacti, primarily prickly-pear. Growth on the level area of the site is sparse. A few widely scattered creosote-bushes were noted, as well as more numerous blue palo-verde and the aforementioned cacti. Clusters of fleabane daisy grow primarily along the edges of the disturbed areas. Along the edges of the site, which stand above the sink, the vegetation becomes denser and more varied, with several varieties of cacti still predominating. These include barrel cactus, buck-thorn cholla, pencil cholla, Christmas cactus, beavertail, hedgehog, and fishhook. Along the highest elevations are a few saguaro.

Yucca and agave are common on the rocky slopes of the mesa to the northeast of the site, along with a wide assortment of grasses:

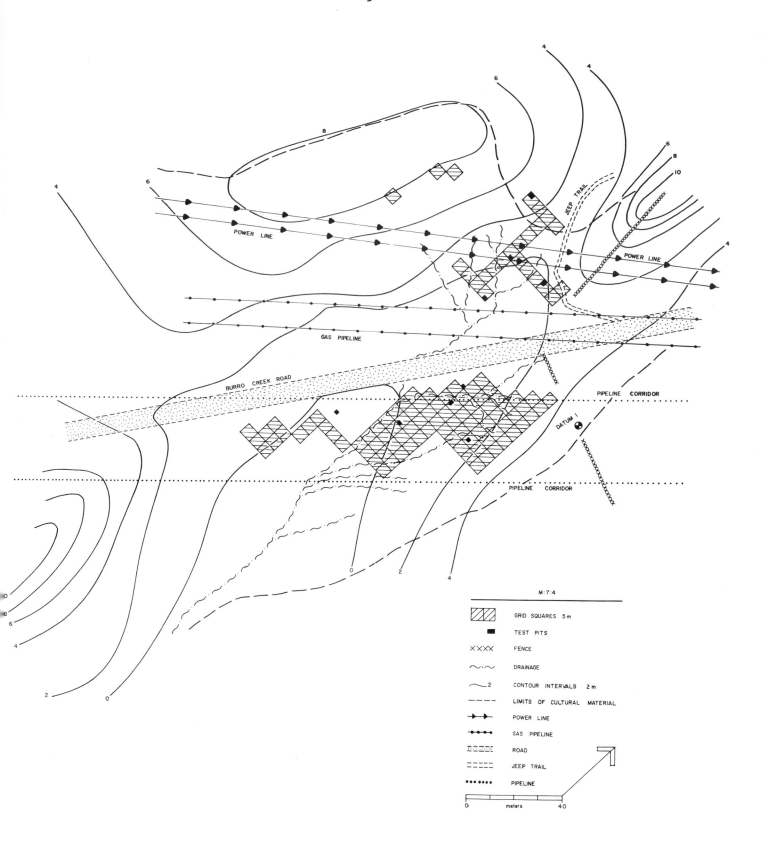

Figure 6. Map of AZ M:7:4, showing areas tested

64

Figure 7.   AZ M:7:4

Figure 8.   Bedrock basin near AZ M:7:4

squirrel-tail, wild barley, sixweeks needle grama, sixweeks grama, stink-grass, pingüe, and trailing-four-o'clock.

Ocotillo are plentiful along the slopes and heights of the mesa and hills surrounding the site, as are the blue palo-verde and all varieties of thorn.

In the canyon and riverbed to the north and west of the site, the plant community includes mesquite, catclaw, catclaw mimosa, white-thorn acacia, bitter condalia, oak, and salt-bush. Along the slope of the hill above the wash (facing west and away from the site) are found wild lettuce and wild mustard.

Juniper, though sparse, occurs along the edge of the mesa over-looking the site, at the edge of the canyon to the north of the site, and in the wash.

Although the flora on the site proper are rather sparse, AZ M:7:4 and its immediate environs (the area within 250 m of the site) actually exhibit the largest variety of species at any of the sites.

Chipped Stone Artifacts

A total of 8773 pieces of chipped stone were recovered from the surface of AZ M:7:4. Of these, a random sample of 1190 artifacts (13.6 percent) was subjected to a careful analysis which included inspection with a binocular microscope. In addition, all other re-touched artifacts from the total collection (267 artifacts, 3.0 percent) were subjected to the same analysis. The remaining 7316 pieces (83.4 percent), consisting of utilized and unutilized flakes, were cursorily examined to identify their morphological features. Flake types for this remainder and their relative frequencies are presented in Table 2.

Table 2. Flake Types from AZ M:7:4

Flake Type	Frequency	Percent
Hard-hammer flakes	2008	27.4
Soft-hammer flakes	3486	47.6
Shatter	1237	16.9
Thinning flakes	585	8.0
Totals	7316	100.0

The analysis to which the random sample and the retouched artifacts were subjected was aimed at tentatively identifying the functions of these artifacts. A number of characteristics were observed and recorded, including raw material, stage of manufacture, retouch, use-wear, edge angle, and presence of cortex. Using this information, tentative functional identifications were made for each artifact (see Appendix A for a more detailed description of the methodology used in the lithic analysis). The frequency distribution of artifact types found at AZ M:7:4 is given in Table 3.

Most of the artifacts from AZ M:7:4 were fashioned from one of several varieties of rhyolite, a source of which occurs nearby in an outcropping high in the side of the steep mesa northeast of the site.

Table 3 shows that unutilized flakes constitute the most numerous category found at AZ M:7:4, comprising 60.4 percent of the chipped stone assemblage. Based on use-wear patterns, the most common tool type recovered was the knife, which in its various forms made up 17.7 percent of the assemblage. Various types of scrapers (including spokeshaves) comprised 8.1 percent of the assemblage, while 2.4 percent were knife-scrapers (see Figure 9). Altogether, knives and scrapers represented 29.1 percent of the assemblage of chipped stone implements from AZ M:7:4. Projectile points, bifacial knives, and other bifacial items (including preforms) comprised only 2.4 percent of the total assemblage; nonetheless, this group of bifacial items (see Figure 9) is the largest found at any of the three sites with sample sizes greater than 100. The majority of the points can be dated on stylistic grounds to the Amargosa III Period.

Ground Stone Artifacts

Several ground stone artifacts were found at AZ M:7:4; they comprise slightly less than 0.3 percent of the total artifact collection. With the exception of three quartz hammerstones, all of these artifacts were of basalt.

Due to the exposed nature of the site, nearly all of the ground stone was fragmentary. Although most of this damage presumably was caused by weathering, the heavy construction activity at the site may have contributed to the destruction. In addition, the high percentage (80 percent) of broken artifacts may reflect the prior removal of whole artifacts by vandals.

As shown by Table 4, mano fragments constituted the most common type of ground stone artifact recovered. A single, large, round mano (Type I) was recovered intact from a fresh grading of the Bogle Ranch Road about seven months after the excavations had been completed. Otherwise, the fragments were all of Type II (small, oval to rectangular with rounded corners, one-hand specimens).

Table 3. Frequency distribution of tentative lithic artifact
classifications for AZ M:7:4

Category Label	Code*	Frequency (random)	Percent (random)	Frequency (nonrandom)
Primary core	1	39	3.3	23
Secondary core	2	4	.3	4
Core nucleus (expended)	3	17	1.4	48
Core/hammerstone	10	1	.1	0
Core/scraper	20	4	.3	8
Core/chopper	30	3	.3	1
Chopper	31	2	.2	0
Core/knife	40	1	.1	1
Unutilized flake	100	719	60.4	1
Retouch flake	101	10	.8	0
Hammerstone	110	1	.1	0
End scraper	121	15	1.3	20
Side-end scraper	122	12	1.0	16
Single-side scraper	123	50	4.2	25
Double-side scraper	124	12	1.0	6
Convergent-side scraper	125	1	.1	0
Transverse scraper	126	3	.3	1
Scraper, indeterminate fragment	127	6	.5	6
Spokeshave	128	6	.5	17
Knife/scraper	131	28	2.4	13

Table 3. (continued)

Category Label	Code*	Frequency (random)	Percent (random)	Frequency (nonrandom)
Knife/gouge	132	2	.2	0
Scraper/gouge	133	1	.1	0
Scraper/graver	134	0	0.0	0
Scraper/spokeshave	135	0	0.0	5
Flake knife	141	206	17.3	23
Knife projection	142	3	.3	0
Knife/scraper/gouge	143	1	.1	0
Knife/spokeshave	144	0	0.0	1
Gouge	150	4	.3	1
Graver	151	4	.3	1
Drill, Type II-B	156	1	.1	0
Drill, Type IV	158	1	.1	2
Drill, indeterminate fragment	159	1	.1	0
Projectile point, Type I-A-2	202	0	0.0	0
Projectile point, Type I-A-3	203	0	0.0	1
Projectile point, Type I-A-4	204	0	0.0	0
Projectile point, Type I-A-5	205	0	0.0	0
Projectile point, Type I-A-6	206	0	0.0	0

Table 3. (continued)

Category Label	Code*	Frequency (random)	Percent (random)	Frequency (nonrandom)
Projectile point, Type I-B-1	211	0	0.0	0
Projectile point, Type I-B-4	214	1	.1	0
Projectile point, Type II-A-1	221	1	.1	0
Projectile point, Type II-A-2	222	2	.2	0
Projectile point, Type II-B-2	232	1	.1	0
Projectile point, Type II-C-1	241	0	0.0	0
Projectile point, Type II-C-2	242	0	0.0	0
Projectile point, Type III-B	261	1	.1	0
Projectile point, Type III-C	262	1	.1	0
Projectile point fragment	271	9	.8	3
Serrated projectile point fragment	272	0	0.0	0
Projectile point, other varieties	281	0	0.0	0
Projectile point preform	282	0	0.0	0
Biface	289	11	.9	21
Bifacial knife	290	2	.2	9

Table 3.   (continued)

	Code*	Frequency (random)	Percent (random)	Frequency (nonrandom)
Bifacial resharpening flake	291	0	0.0	0
Flaked axe	301	0	0.0	0
Unknown	303	3	.3	10
Totals		1190	100.0	267

For definitions of artifact types, refer to Appendix A.

*"Code" refers to the computerized identification number assigned to the individual type during analysis.   See Appendix A.

Figure 9. Projectile points, knives, and scrapers from AZ M:7:4

Table 4. Ground stone artifacts from AZ M:7:4

Type	Frequency	Percent
Manos	(13)	(52.0)
Type I	1	4.0
Type II	0	0.0
Type III	0	0.0
Fragments	12	48.0
Grinding Stones	1	4.0
Metates	(1)	(4.0)
Type I	0	0.0
Type II	0	0.0
Fragments	1	4.0
Mortars	0	0.0
Hammerstones	(3)	(12.0)
Complete	3	12.0
Fragments	0	0.0
Slabs	(7)	(28.0)
Complete	0	0.0
Fragmentary	7	28.0
Totals	25	100.0

(For type descriptions, see Appendix B.)

Ground stone artifacts were mainly found in the more disturbed western portion of the site. The small number of items, their usually fragmented condition, and the high probability of previous artifact removal render the figures in Table 4 of limited statistical value.

Ceramics

The number of potsherds found was even less than that of ground stone items (see Table 5). The sherds were also heavily weathered, and have been reduced to sizes of 2 to 4 cm in diameter at most.

Table 5. Frequencies of ceramic types from AZ M:7:4

Type	Frequency	Percent
Prescott Gray Ware	7	36.8
Tizon Brown Ware	(9)	(47.4)
Cerbat Brown	1	5.3
Aquarius Brown	8	42.1
Aquarius Black-on-brown	0	0.0
Sandy Brown	0	0.0
Tizon Wiped	0	0.0
Transitional*	0	0.0
Unidentifiable**	0	0.0
Exotic***	3	15.8
Totals	19	100.0
Rim sherds	(0)	(0.0)

*Transitional: Those sherds resembling both Prescott Gray Ware and Tizon Brown Ware, to the point of being indistinguishable.

**Unidentifiable: Those sherds too small or too badly disfigured to positively identify.

***Exotic: Those sherds of types foreign to the region: trade wares.

Tizon Brown Wares predominated slightly over Prescott Gray Ware, as one might expect considering the location of the site. The high incidence of Prescott and Tizon sherds may reflect repeated occupations by different populations, a theory supported by the lithic analysis.

Bifacial tools were found dating to Amargosa III, which is at least 1000 years before the introduction of pottery. No rim sherds or whole vessels were found at AZ M:7:4.

As in the case of the ground stone artifacts, sherds were densest in the heavily disturbed western portion of the site. The sample may have been skewed as a result of the prior removal of larger, better preserved sherds by vandals.

Site AZ M:7:2

AZ M:7:2 (Figures 10 and 14), located 11 km east of AZ M:7:4, lies on the east bank of Burro Creek at the edge of a steep sedimentary mesa known locally as Burro Leg Mesa. At an elevation of 2250 feet, AZ M:7:2 is situated approximately 100 feet above the floodplain of Burro Creek and is bounded on the north by Cornwall Wash, a major tributary of Burro Creek. This point is approximately 3 km southwest of the juncture of Burro Creek and Boulder Creek and about 1 km southwest of the Burro Creek Ranch headquarters.

The site covers most of the top of the mesa; however, the densest concentrations of artifacts lie at its eastern (lowest) end, directly above Burro Creek (see Figure 10). Both the nature of the deposits and artifact distribution indicate that these concentrations are due to cultural factors rather than erosion.

Area A, at the western end of the mesa (which corresponds to the areas designated A and B in the survey report), produced a considerable amount of ground stone and pottery. This area was characterized by a high density of surface artifacts (2.4 per square meter) extending 35 to 40 m to the west (uphill) before dropping to a density of about 0.3 artifacts per square meter in Area C. No obvious physical demarcation separates the two areas.

Area C extends north-south across the eastern end of the mesa. As one travels west (uphill), the artifacts end abruptly along the southern half of the mesa; artifact density decreases more gradually along its northern half. The western perimeter of Area C lies 85 to 90 m west of the eastern rim of the mesa and is about 14 m higher than the rim. From this point, the mesa begins to rise more steeply to an elevation 60 meters higher than that of Area A (or 90 meters above Burro Creek). Area C produced no pottery and only a single metate fragment, which was discovered near the boundary with Area A.

Although the damage at this site hardly compares with the destruction of cultural resources at AZ M:7:4, some disturbance has resulted from two bulldozer cuts which nearly bisect the mesa. The more destructive of these was cut into the mesa from the north and is nearly 40 m long and 12 m wide; varves on either side give the path a

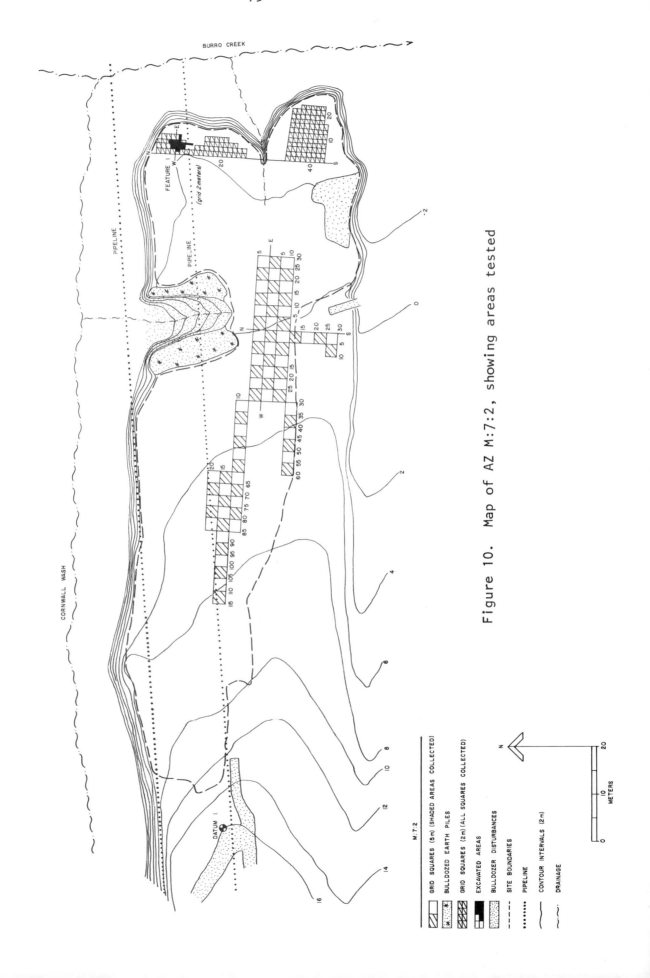

Figure 10. Map of AZ M:7:2, showing areas tested

total width of 35 m. This steep-sided cut creates a pathway to the
floor of Cornwall Wash. A second, less extensive cut lies directly
opposite the first. Only 12 to 13 m long and 4 m wide, this cut,
which never exceeds 0.5 m in depth, plunges off the southern edge
of the mesa into the natural fold and eroded cleft below.

Another bulldozer cut has been made at a point just west of (and
above) the western boundary of Area C. It is difficult to determine
whether the site actually ended at this point, or whether part of it
had been covered or removed by bulldozers.

Environment

The plant species observed at AZ M:7:2 show less diversity, but
greater density, than those at AZ M:7:4. Site AZ M:7:3 is located
across Burro Creek and less than 2 km west of AZ M:7:2. A transect
through the major vegetational communities between the two sites was
made by Christopher S. Causey (Figure 11). This transect shows the
demarcations of the vegetation zones, which are to a large extent
determined by the topography of the area. One should note that only
the dominant species of each zone are listed.

On the site proper, saguaro, buck-thorn cholla, hedgehog cacti,
beavertail cacti, barrel cacti, pencil cholla, and Christmas cacti
abound. Near the edges of the mesa, particularly along its eastern
and northern perimeters, are numerous yellow palo-verde and blue palo-
verde. Juniper and Utah juniper are less abundant. A number of agave
are also present throughout the site area.

The sides of the mesa exhibit an abundance of shrubs, grasses,
and weeds. Creosote-bushes are perhaps the most abundant. Nuttal
milk-vetch, ground-fig spurge, New Mexico thistle, sunflower, shepherds-
purse, sacred datura, loco-weed, clammy-weed, skeleton-weed, squirrel-
tail, and green fox-tail also grow along the mesa sides. Wild lettuce
and rubber rabbit-brush were also observed.

The riparian community in the floodplain of Burro Creek and
Cornwall Wash includes mesquite, acacia, and catclaw mimosa. The hills
surrounding the site are generally covered with juniper, Utah juniper,
and palo-verde.

AZ M:7:2 was visited for short periods by field crews in October
1975, April 1976, and May 1976; continuously from mid-June to the
beginning of August 1976; and again in February 1977. At the time of
each visit, Burro Creek was flowing. The heaviest flow observed by the
archaeologists occurred in April 1976; informants, however, knew of
heavy flooding which had occurred in January 1975. Rainfall patterns
for this area lead one to expect Burro Creek to flow with greatest

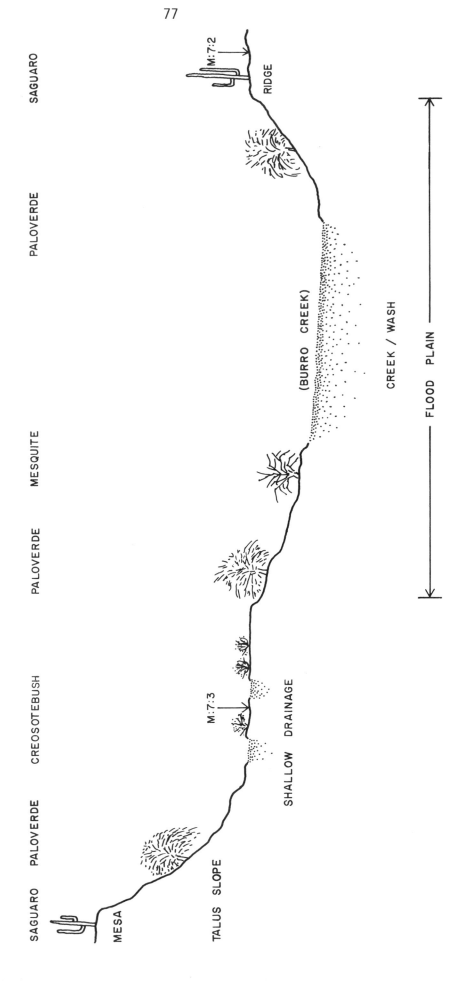

Figure 11. Cross section of vegetational transect between AZ M:7:2 and AZ M:7:3

volume in August and September, and again in midwinter. The fact
that it was flowing in midsummer 1976 (the dryest part of an unusually
dry year) indicates that the flow is permanent.

Architectural Features

The single structure encountered during the project was discovered in the area of highest artifact density at AZ M:7:2. This
structure was subterranean, had no standing walls or features, and
had been heavily disturbed by rodent activity, which, combined with
the lack of excavation time and of comparative data, prevents any
precise determination of this structure's form or purpose. On the
basis of data from the testing phase of the project, the structure had
been presumed to be a common pit house. Allocations of time for its
excavation were based on this presumption; unfortunately, the allotted
time proved insufficient to excavate the structure completely, despite
changes in excavation procedures. A volunteer crew attempted to finish
the excavation after the field phase of the project had ended; unfortunately, construction had by then exceeded the specified right-of-way
boundaries, resulting in the structure's destruction.

The structure (see Figures 12, 13, and 15) was about 4.5 m wide
(east-west), over 10 m long (the location of the south wall was never
satisfactorily established), and apparently ovoid in shape. It extended
90 cm below the modern surface and was originally 55 cm deep. The
floor sloped upward to form vertical walls. On the transverse midline
of the feature, and 4.5 m from the southern wall, a single posthole
was found. It was 20 cm in diameter and tapered to a rounded bottom
48 cm below the floor. Flotation analysis showed that the post had
been of cottonwood, available today near the junction of Burro and
Boulder creeks, 3 km from the site. No postholes or rock alignments
were found along the perimeter of the structure, nor was any firepit
discovered.

The entire floor of the structure had been burned and was
covered with a thin (1-2 cm) layer of ash. The floor itself had
turned reddish-orange, contrasting with the light brown soil around it.
The floor, however, was so sandy that even light sweeping with paint
brushes stripped it away. As a result, archaeomagnetic sampling was
not attempted.

A dense layer of ashy soil was found about 25 cm above the
floor of the structure; within this layer were two pieces of palo-verde
which later yielded dates of A.D. 655 $\pm$ 60 and A.D. 835 $\pm$ 60. A number
of burned rocks and metates were also associated with this lens
(Figure 16).

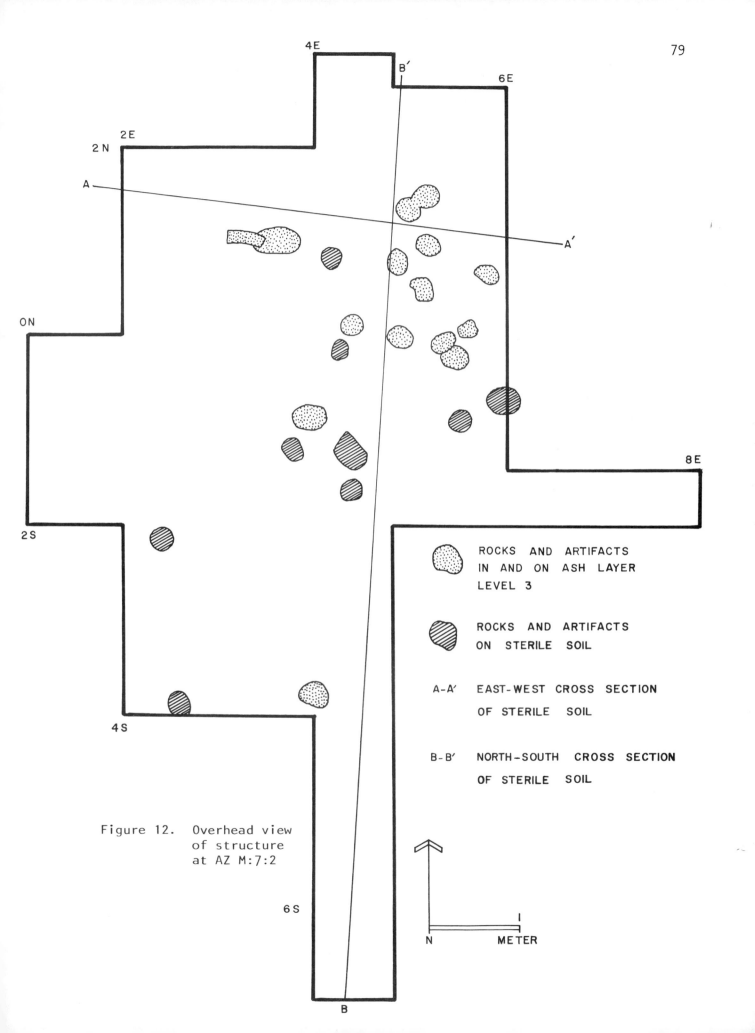

Figure 12. Overhead view
of structure
at AZ M:7:2

ROCKS   AND   ARTIFACTS
IN   AND ON ASH LAYER
LEVEL 3

ROCKS   AND   ARTIFACTS
ON   STERILE SOIL

A-A'   EAST-WEST CROSS SECTION
OF STERILE SOIL

B-B'   NORTH-SOUTH CROSS SECTION
OF STERILE SOIL

N   METER

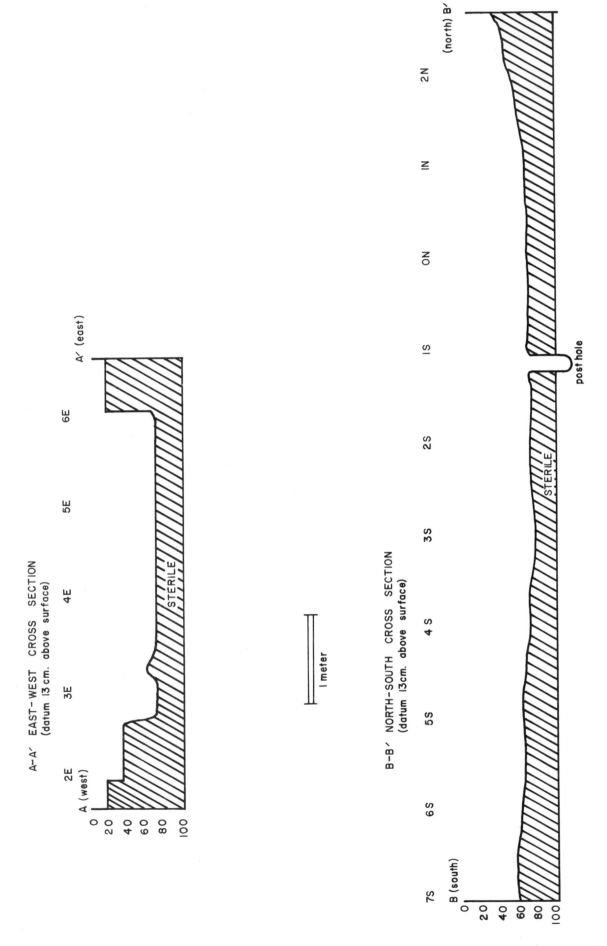

A-A' EAST-WEST CROSS SECTION
(datum 13cm. above surface)

B-B' NORTH-SOUTH CROSS SECTION
(datum 13cm. above surface)

1 meter

STERILE

post hole

STERILE

Figure 13. Cross section of structure at AZ M:7:2

Figure 14.   AZ M:7:2

Figure 15.   Structure at AZ M:7:2

Due to the time restrictions previously discussed, about 4 square meters in the southwest corner of the structure were rapidly excavated as a single stratigraphic unit. In this area a cremation was identified, though not in situ. It is uncertain whether the cremation is associated with the layer of ashy soil or with the structure's floor.

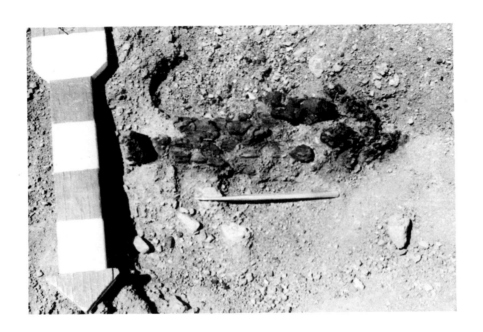

Figure 16. Radiocarbon sample in situ at AZ M:7:2

Chipped Stone Artifacts

Items of chipped stone recovered from AZ M:7:2 totalled 3847, including those from the subsurface levels of Feature 1. Of these, 2538 specimens (66.4 percent) consisting of utilized and unutilized flakes showing no signs of retouch were categorized into the classifications shown in Table 6. The remaining 1309 specimens (33.6 percent) were intensively analyzed with the aid of a binocular microscope. These included a random sample of 1225 artifacts (31.4 percent) and an additional 84 retouched artifacts (2.2 percent). These artifacts were all classified according to their inferred functions. Table 7 gives the results of the classification.

Table 6. Flake types from AZ M:7:2

Flake Type	Frequency	Percent
Hard-hammer flakes	720	28.4
Soft-hammer flakes	1432	56.4
Shatter	196	7.7
Thinning flakes	190	7.5
Totals	2538	100.0

The 1309 artifacts analyzed more intensively were manufactured mainly of chert or chalcedony, in contrast to the predominance of rhyolite at AZ M:7:4. The cherts and chalcedonies are, with few exceptions, of a higher chipping quality than the rhyolites and have been found to be as readily available locally as are the rhyolites at AZ M:7:4. AZ M:7:3, across Burro Creek from AZ M:7:2, seems to have been a quarry or procurement area for a gray to white granular chert. This chert can range from fine white chalcedony (which is very rare) to a granular gray quartzitic variety found in single cobbles. Such material is plentiful among the artifacts at AZ M:7:2. However, the main source of chipping materials for this site seems to have been an outcropping to the west of the site, less than 0.5 km upstream in the side of Cornwall Wash. The chert-chalcedony from this source is of a tabular, high-quality variety ranging in color from gray-brown to pink to light gray, with a brown limestone cortex.

Table 7 shows that at AZ M:7:2, like AZ M:7:4, the most commonly found artifacts were unutilized flakes, which make up 64.8 percent of the assemblage. Based on use-wear, knives are even more common at AZ M:7:2 than they were at AZ M:7:4 (though they exhibit less variety), comprising 21.7 percent of the total assemblage. The various scrapers (including spokeshaves) constitute only 5.6 percent, while those tools combining elements of both knives and scrapers comprise 1.6 percent. Thus, knives and scrapers total 28.9 percent of the entire assemblage, a figure very close to the corresponding percentage (30.9) from AZ M:7:4. Bifacial items recovered at this site comprise only 1.4 percent of the chipped stone assemblage, and include small, acute-triangular, serrated points generally less than 2.5 cm long. As yet, no projectile point type has been established as characteristic of the Cerbat or the Hualapai. It may well be that these points, which resemble somewhat those manufactured by the Hohokam, represent such a type. They do not resemble points typical of the Prescott Branch (see Figure 17).

Ground Stone Artifacts

Fifty-two pieces of ground stone were recovered at AZ M:7:2, or 1.0 percent of all artifacts recovered. Although this is nearly four times the corresponding percentage (and twice the number) of ground stone artifacts recovered at AZ M:7:4, this figure still represents a small absolute number of items.

With the exception of a fragment found in Area C, ground stone was restricted to Area A. No whole metates or mortars were recovered. Two of the seven hammerstones were made of rhyolite, one was of quartz, and one of schist. All the remaining ground stone artifacts (92 percent) were made of basalt. The variety of basalt used exhibits small holes or "pockmarks" over the entire cortex, but is solid inside the stone.

Evidence of surface disturbance was found in the fact that six fragments from the same metate were collected from four different grid squares up to 12 m apart. The broken surfaces had weathered, and most of the fragments were at least half buried. In view of the large selection of metates lining the fence of Burro Creek Ranch house 1 km away (and the rancher's own admission that the number of metates at the site had once been greater), it seems likely that the proportionately large number of fragmented ground stone artifacts at this site reflects the wholesale removal of complete specimens in the recent past.

As Table 8 shows, metate fragments were the most common form of ground stone at AZ M:7:2, both on the surface and in the subsurface deposits of Feature 1. As at AZ M:7:4, only basin-type metates were recovered. The surface of one fragment is convex enough to lend credence to Dobyns' theory that such metates were used to pound rather than grind upon. However, they were found in association with one-hand manos exhibiting distinct grinding wear upon their flat faces and no discernible pounding wear on the ends. Incidentally, no mano could be found to fit any metate basin exactly (that is, with mano length equaling basin width, and the curvature of the mano surface matching the curvature of the basin).

Table 7. Frequency distribution of tentative lithic artifact classifications for AZ M:7:2

Category Label	Code*	Frequency (random)	Percent (random)	Frequency (nonrandom)
Primary core	1	14	1.1	5
Secondary core	2	12	1.0	1
Core nucleus (expended)	3	5	.4	19
Core/hammerstone	10	1	.1	0
Core/scraper	20	2	.2	2
Core/chopper	30	0	0.0	0
Chopper	31	0	0.0	0
Core/knife	40	0	0.0	0
Unutilized flake	100	793	64.8	0
Retouch flake	101	15	1.2	0
Hammerstone	110	0	0.0	0
End scraper	121	20	1.2	9
Side-end scraper	122	2	.2	3
Single-side scraper	123	33	2.7	8
Double-side scraper	124	2	.2	2
Convergent-side scraper	125	1	.1	0
Transverse scraper	126	2	.2	0
Scraper, indeterminate fragment	127	4	.3	1
Spokeshave	128	3	.2	3
Knife/scraper	131	20	1.6	2

Table 7. (continued)

Category Label	Code*	Frequency (random)	Percent (random)	Frequency (nonrandom)
Knife/gouge	132	1	.1	0
Scraper/gouge	133	0	0.0	0
Scraper/graver	134	1	.1	0
Scraper/spokeshave	135	0	0.0	0
Flake knife	141	265	21.7	1
Knife projection	142	0	0.0	0
Knife/scraper/gouge	143	0	0.0	0
Knife/spokeshave	144	0	0.0	0
Gouge	150	2	.2	0
Graver	151	0	0.0	0
Drill, Type II-B	156	0	0.0	0
Drill, Type IV	158	3	.2	0
Drill, indeterminate fragment	159	0	0.0	0
Drill/scraper	160	1	.1	0
Projectile point, Type I-A-2	202	0	0.0	2
Projectile point, Type I-A-3	203	0	0.0	1
Projectile point, Type I-A-4	204	3	.2	4
Projectile Point, Type I-A-5	205	0	0.0	0

Table 7.   (continued)

Category Label	Code*	Frequency (random)	Percent (random)	Frequency (nonrandom)
Projectile point, Type I-A-6	206	0	0.0	2
Projectile point, Type I-B-1	211	0	0.0	1
Projectile point, Type I-B-4	214	0	0.0	1
Projectile point, Type II-A-1	221	0	0.0	0
Projectile point, Type II-A-2	222	0	0.0	0
Projectile point, Type II-B-2	232	0	0.0	0
Projectile point, Type II-C-1	241	1	.1	0
Projectile point, Type II-C-2	242	1	.1	0
Projectile point, Type III-B	261	0	0.0	1
Projectile point fragment	271	3	.2	3
Serrated projectile point fragment	272	2	.2	4
Projectile point, other varieties	281	0	0.0	0
Projectile point preform	282	0	0.0	0
Biface	289	4	.3	3
Bifacial knife	290	3	.2	2

Table 7. (continued)

Category Label	Code*	Frequency (random)	Percent (random)	Frequency (nonrandom)
Bifacial resharpening flake	291	0	0.0	0
Flaked axe	301	1	.1	0
Unknown	303	5	.4	3
Totals		1225	100.0	84

For definitions of artifact types, refer to Appendix A.

*"Code" refers to the computerized identification number assigned to the individual type during analysis. See Appendix A.

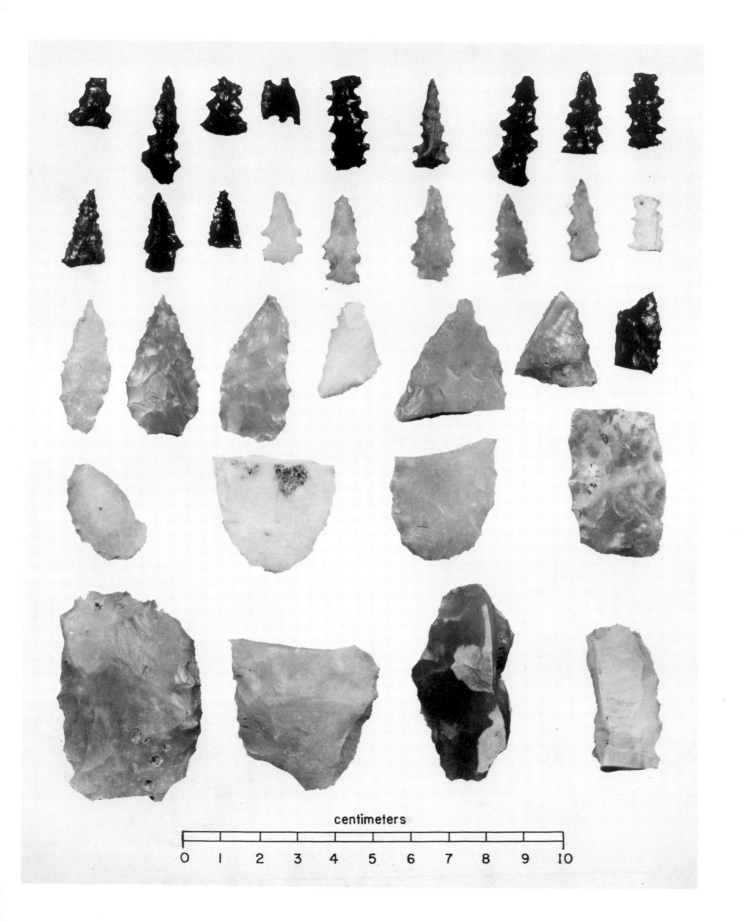

Figure 17.   Projectile points, knives, and scrapers from AZ M:7:2

Table 8. Ground stone artifacts from AZ M:7:2

Type	Frequency	Percent
Manos	(15)	(28.9)
Type I	1	1.9
Type II	7	13.5
Fragments	7	13.5
Grinding Stones	4	7.7
Metates	(14)	(26.9)
Type I	0	0.0
Type II	0	0.0
Fragments	14	26.9
Mortars	0	0.0
Hammerstones	(7)	(13.4)
Complete	5	9.6
Fragments	2	3.8
Slabs	(12)	(23.1)
Complete	0	0.0
Fragments	12	23.1
Totals	52	100.0

(For type descriptions, see Appendix B.)

Ceramics

AZ M:7:2 produced the largest assortment of pottery recovered by the Cyprus-Bagdad Project. As indicated by Table 9, most of the sherds (87.7 percent) represent varieties of Tizon Brown Ware. All of the sherds were recovered from Area A, most of them from the subsurface levels of Feature 1. Nearly 64 percent of the ceramics was recovered from the habitation structure; even here, however, there

was a mixture of wares. The overall low incidence of Prescott Gray
Ware sherds suggests the possibility that they represent trade wares.

Table 9. Frequencies of ceramic types from AZ M:7:2

Type	Frequency	Percent
Prescott Gray Ware	86	7.9
Tizon Brown Ware	(951)	(87.7)
Cerbat Brown	373	34.4
Aquarius Brown	517	47.7
Aquarius Black-on-brown	1	0.1
Sandy Brown	25	2.3
Tizon Wiped	35	3.2
Transitional	28	2.6
Unidentifiable	20	1.8
Exotic	0	0.0
Totals	1085	100.0
Rim sherds	(14)	(1.3)

Several rim sherds were discovered, and they reveal some
interesting patterns, as shown in Figure 18. The Tizon Brown Wares
generally exhibit a flattened rim, as though the rim had been wiped
or scraped with a hard, straight edge while still soft. This flattening may be perpendicular to the long axis of the sherd or may tilt
to the inside or outside vessel wall. The flattening is often accom-
panied by an adjacent buildup or ridge of excess clay, which appears
to have once been the apex of the rim, displaced in the forming of the
facet. At AZ M:7:2, the Cerbat Brown rim sherds lack this flattening;
however, it is frequently associated with this ware at the other sites,
just as it is on the Aquarius Brown rim sherds at AZ M:7:2. The small
number of rim sherds recovered rendered this criterion of little value

in identifying ceramic types, but it may be of some classificatory value if complete Tizon vessels are recovered in the future.

As at AZ M:7:4, the sherds recovered were small, excepting some from subsurface proveniences. In addition, not even partial reconstructions of vessels were possible. Consequently, the shapes and functions of pottery at AZ M:7:2 (as at AZ M:7:4) remain unknown.

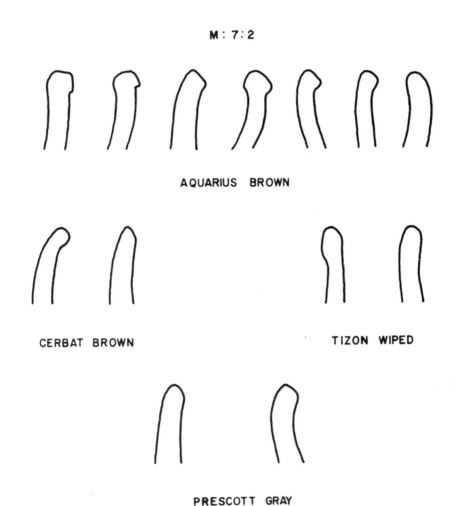

Figure 18. Ceramic rim forms and type correlations at AZ M:7:2

Site AZ M:7:3

Site AZ M:7:3 (see Figures 19 and 20) is located on the east
bank of Burro Creek, across the creek from AZ M:7:2, and just over
1 km east of that site. The site lies on the third bench above Burro
Creek at the western base of Centipede Mesa, at a point approximately
3 km south of the juncture of Burro Creek and Boulder Creek. Its
elevation (2250 feet) corresponds to that of AZ M:7:2. Figure 11
illustrates the relationships among AZ M:7:3, AZ M:7:2, and Burro
Creek.

AZ M:7:3 is an extensive lithic scatter, 190 m (east-west) by
at least 240 m (north-south). Lithic artifacts continue to appear,
though with less frequency, more than a kilometer to the south and well
out of the impact zone of this project. The site is located on a broad
terrace between the talus slope of Centipede Mesa to the east and a low
volcanic ridge to the west, which drops 20 feet to the second bench
above Burro Creek. The terrace is liberally strewn with basalt cobbles
over much of its surface, and is filled with alluvial sandy soil
35 cm deep in places and overlying bedrock. Subsurface deposits are
sterile.

Surface artifact density is greatest where the talus slope of
Centipede Mesa begins to level off onto the terrace, and decreases
with distance from the slope. Along the western edge of the site, the
basalt flow abruptly ends, leaving a band of barren sandy soil between
the cobble pavement and the basalt ridge that forms the site's western
boundary. At several points along the pavement's edge are apparently
man-made alignments of cobbles. Pollen tests indicate that at least
one of these alighments was a check dam, and that the adjacent sandy,
barren area once served as an agricultural field.

Environment

The single most common plant on the site is creosote-bush, which
covers the basin wherein the site lies. Cacti, though less abundant
than at other sites, occur on the surface of the site proper, and
primarily consist of prickly-pear and beavertail. Buckthorn cholla
occur near the site's edge. Pencil cacti also appear beneath many of
the creosote-bushes. A few saguaro are present around the site, but
are generally restricted to the rocky slopes and top of Centipede Mesa.
Both species of palo-verde predominate on the talus slope of Centipede
Mesa, and also on the ridge and slope west of the site, where a thick
band of vegetation (including creosote-bush, acacia, mimosa, and
sunflower) grows. The only grass noted at this site was squirrel-tail,
which was seen mainly on the rocky slopes of the mesa and on the rocky
slope descending toward the second bench above Burro Creek.

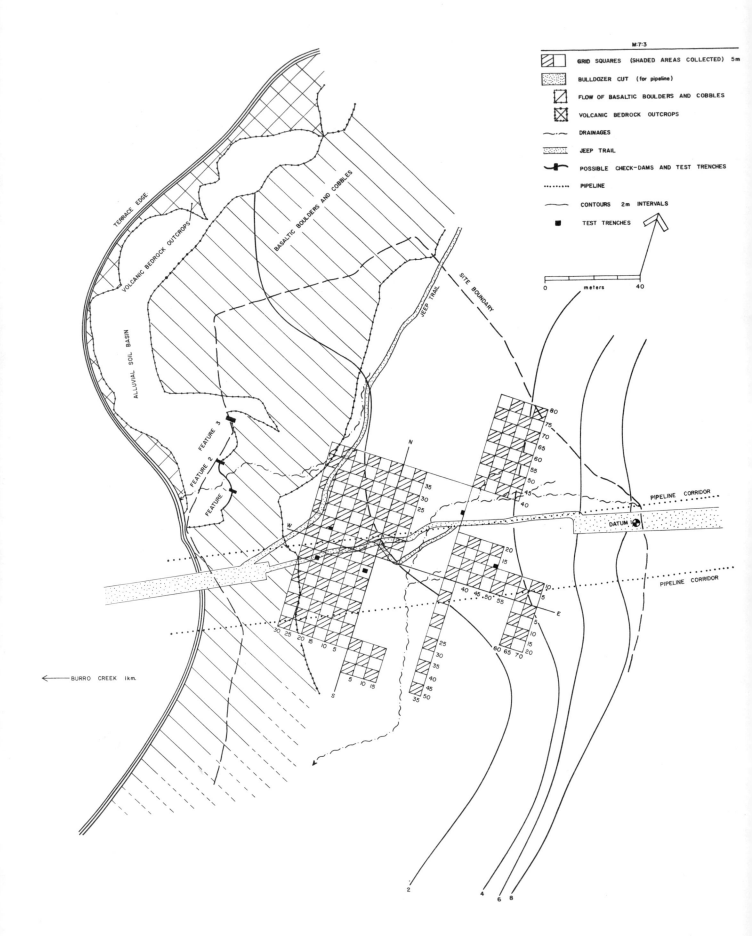

Figure 19. Map of AZ M:7:3, showing areas tested

Agricultural Features

AZ M:7:3 was the only site with agricultural features. As noted above, a series of three alignments of basalt cobbles was discovered at the western edge of the cobble pavement at the site; these alignments did not appear to be natural. Excavation showed that one of the alignments had been formed by piling up three layers of cobbles. Pollen samples taken from this alignment (designated Feature 1) indicate that maize was grown in association with it.

Feature 1 (see Figures 19 and 21) was 15 m long and curved inward toward its uphill (eastern) side; the center of the alignment was approximately 5 m deep in curvature. Feature 1 connects with a second alignment (Feature 2) at the former's northern end, with Feature 2 curving outward to the downhill (western) side. The two features combine to form an "S"-shaped curve. Pollen samples collected from Feature 2 or Feature 3 (a third alignment, approximately 20 m north of Feature 2, and part of the same discontinuous alignment marking the western perimeter of the cobble pavement) were not analyzed; thus, it cannot with any certainty be asserted that these latter two features were also check dams.

At first it was thought that the dam had been constructed to retain water on its eastern (uphill) side. However, water would then have been retained only in the area of the cobble pavement, which is hardly susceptible to cultivation. Then it was noted that the volcanic ridge bordering the terrace on the west formed a natural dam on that side, as the outcroppings of basalt are somewhat elevated above the level of the soil. Thus, by constructing a dam to the east of the outcroppings, water could have been trapped simply by restricting the dissipation of precipitation, runoff, or even water carried up from Burro Creek for irrigation. Several small gullies indicate that runoff could still have entered the enclosed area, where it would have been trapped. It is unknown whether the enclosed area was naturally devoid of cobbles, or whether the pavement at one time had extended up to the basalt ridge and had been cleared for agricultural purposes. Although little was growing in this enclosed area at the time of the excavations, it is possible that annual vegetation might grow there. In addition, the dense stand of vegetation along the western margin of the area shows that, with little human interference, this area supports more vegetation than does any other portion of the site.

The test trenches excavated on this site indicate that the soil around these features is looser and more silty than that found in control trenches.

Figure 20.   AZ M:7:3

Figure 21.   Check dam (Feature 1) at AZ M:7:3

Chipped Stone Artifacts

A total of 1615 pieces of chipped stone was recovered from the site from 88 5 m-by-5 m grid squares. The surface artifact density averaged 0.7 items per square meter, but was somewhat higher in that portion of the site lying at the base of the talus slope of Centipede Mesa.

Of the total, 1335 unretouched flakes (82.8 percent) were examined to determine their morphology and stage of manufacture. Table 10 lists the frequencies in which various types of flakes occurred.

Table 10. Flake types from AZ M:7:3

Flake Type	Frequency	Percent
Hard-hammer flakes	569	42.6
Soft-hammer flakes	516	38.7
Shatter	199	14.9
Thinning flakes	51	3.8
Totals	1335	100.0

The outstanding feature of this frequency distribution is that, unlike any of the other sites, AZ M:7:3 exhibits more hard-hammer flakes than soft-hammer flakes. In addition, shatter occurs in a higher proportion than at all other sites except AZ M:7:4.

From AZ M:7:3, 280 artifacts, including 247 artifacts in a random sample (15.3 percent) and 33 retouched tools (2.0 percent), were subjected to a more careful analysis to identify their functions. Table 11 shows the frequencies of the various tool types from AZ M:7:3. Unutilized flakes are again the most common item, comprising 60.7 percent of the total lithic assemblage. For those items exhibiting use-wear, cutting seems to have been the activity performed most often, with knives making up 15.8 percent of the assemblage. Scrapers and knife-scrapers constituted respectively 4.4 percent and 2.0 percent of the collection. Thus, tools designed for cutting and/or scraping totalled 22.3 percent of the recovered chipped stone assemblage, a percentage considerably lower than those from AZ M:7:2 and AZ M:7:4. On the other hand, the percentage of cores recovered from AZ M:7:3 is

Table 11. Frequency distribution of tentative lithic artifact
classifications for AZ M:7:3

Category Label	Code*	Frequency (random)	Percent (random)	Frequency (nonrandom)
Primary core	1	31	12.6	11
Secondary core	2	1	.4	1
Core nucleus	3	2	.8	8
Core/hammerstone	10	3	1.2	2
Core/scraper	20	0	0.0	1
Core/chopper	30	1	.4	0
Unutilized flake	100	150	60.7	0
Retouch flake	101	2	.8	0
Hammerstone	110	1	.4	0
End scraper	121	1	.4	1
Side-end scraper	122	1	.4	0
Single-side scraper	123	6	2.4	0
Double-side scraper	124	1	.4	0
Transverse scraper	126	1	.4	0
Scraper, indeterminate fragment	127	0	0.0	1
Spokeshave	128	1	.4	0
Knife/scraper	131	5	2.0	1
Scraper/spokeshave	135	0	0.0	1
Flake knife	141	39	15.8	0
Unknown	303	1	.4	0
Quartz crystal	304	0	0.0	6
Totals		247	100.0	33

larger than those from the other two sites: cores found at AZ M:7:3 comprise 15.4 percent of the chipped stone complex, while those from AZ M:7:4 make up only 5.7 percent, and those from AZ M:7:2 only 2.8 percent of their respective lithic assemblages.

The majority of the lithic items found at AZ M:7:3 were made of a gray to white granular chert which often resembled quartzite. This material was derived from the large cobbles and boulders strewn profusely over the talus slope of Centipede Mesa, above the site. An individual cobble, it was noticed, might exhibit a complete range of gray to white-colored materials and contain both granular and crystalline structures. This material originated as an ancient redeposited gravel, and is not associated with any specific outcropping in the area (see Appendix C).

Ground Stone Artifacts

A single hammerstone and two small, round, pecked pebbles were recovered from AZ M:7:3 (Table 12). The hammerstone is made of the same material as were most of the chipped stone artifacts; the two small pebbles are of basalt. The latter artifacts, discovered some 20 m apart, are each approximately 2.5 cm in diameter, and have been pecked over their entire surfaces, apparently in an effort to shape them. They are too small and granular to have served as hammerstones, and too rough to have been utilized for polishing ceramic vessels. Their function is not known.

Table 12. Ground stone artifacts from AZ M:7:3

Type	Frequency	Percent
Manos	0	0.0
Grinding Stones	0	0.0
Metates	0	0.0
Mortars	0	0.0
Hammerstones	(1)	(33.3)
Complete	1	33.3
Fragments	0	0.0
Slabs	0	0.0
Pecked Pebbles	2	66.7
Totals	3	100.0

Ceramics

No sherds were found at AZ M:7:3, despite a special search for such items.

Site AZ M:8:2

AZ M:8:2 and AZ M:8:3 (see Figure 22) are located on the property of the Cyprus-Bagdad Copper Company mine, and are so close to one another that their environmental settings are identical. Analysis of the artifacts from these sites indicates that they may, in fact, have been related.

AZ M:8:2 is a small lithic scatter on a hill (see Figure 23) opposite the mine's new mill. This hill forms a terrace above and east of the eastern end of Centipede Mesa about 8 km due east and 1 km south of AZ M:7:3. Higher terraces rise to the east, and a series of small hills lie to the south. AZ M:8:2 measures only 10 m by 10 m and lies at the foot of a low outcropping of granite which forms a line of boulders bordering the site to the east. The geology of this region differs from that of the three sites previously discussed; while the geologic formations are still comprised of igneous layers overlying sedimentary ones, the uppermost layers are plutonic rather than volcanic in nature. The topsoil is quite shallow, with bedrock lying less than 5 cm below the surface. The soil is sandy and less gravelly than at those sites situated in volcanic zones. Elevation is about 3800 feet.

Environment

The vegetation at AZ M:8:2 and AZ M:8:3 is dominated by juniper and ocotillo. Agave are numerous, occurring either singly or in clusters of ten or more plants. Prickly-pear cacti also abound, as do beavertail cacti. Buck-thorn cholla are somewhat less abundant. Species not encountered at the previously described sites include oak and mountain-mahogany, which occur in dense clusters on and around both AZ M:8:2 and AZ M:8:3. Acacia and Apache-plume were also found, though in lesser abundance than were the plants previously mentioned. Artemisia, mallow, squirrel-tail grass, and grama grass were quite common among the rocks.

No evidence of architectural or agricultural features was discovered at either site. In addition, it is impossible to determine whether water was available near this location in prehistoric times, owing to recent and severe disturbance to the topography in the vicinity. Copper Creek, which enters Boulder Creek just west of the open pit mine, may have had its headwaters in this area, as evidenced by the presence

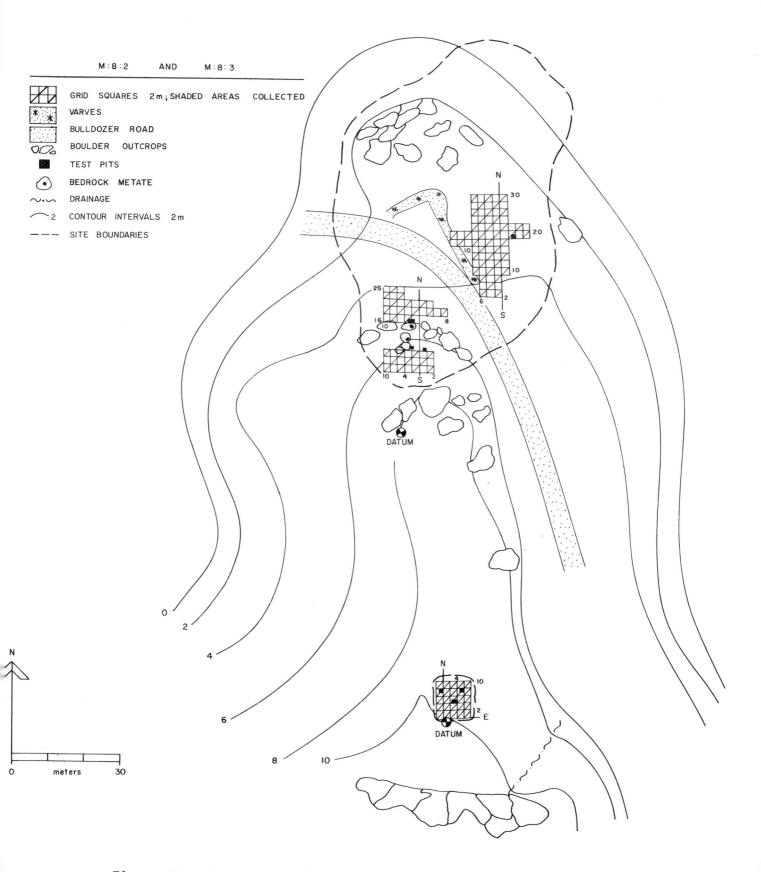

Figure 22. Map of AZ M:8:2 and AZ M:8:3, showing areas tested

Figure 23.   AZ M:8:2

Figure 24.   AZ M:8:3

of wells and water tanks east of and above the new mill. The probability that water was close by, and still may be close to the surface, is indicated by the presence of various vegetal species (such as oak) which are generally associated with riparian communities.

Though these two sites share a similar environment and biotic resources, their respective artifact assemblages differ substantially and will be discussed separately.

Chipped Stone Artifacts

AZ M:8:2, a lithic scatter, produced 92 pieces of chipped stone. A total of 69 pieces (75.0 percent) was analyzed under the binocular microscope; this group includes a random sample of 66 artifacts (71.7 percent) and three retouched artifacts (3.3 percent). The results of this analysis are presented in Table 14. The remaining 23 flakes (25.0 percent) were identified as to their morphological features and stage of manufacture (see Table 13).

Table 13. Flake types from AZ M:8:2

Flake Type	Frequency	Percent
Hard-hammer flakes	0	0.0
Soft-hammer flakes	13	56.5
Shatter	1	4.3
Thinning flakes	9	39.1
Totals	23	100.0

Although the small sample size makes any conclusions tentative, the absence of hard-hammer flakes and high incidence of thinning flakes suggest that refined lithic manufacture was occurring at this locus. The materials used were primarily a fairly high-quality chert and chalcedony. These same materials were common at AZ M:8:3, where a broader range of lithic manufacturing activities was represented. The occupants of AZ M:8:3 may possibly have utilized AZ M:8:2 to manufacture finished implements, although the lack of secure dates for either of the sites precludes any definite establishment of such a relationship. It is apparent, however, that raw materials available to the occupants of AZ M:8:2 were also available to those of AZ M:8:3.

Analysis of the wear patterns exhibited by artifacts of the two assemblages suggests a different intersite relationship. As shown by Tables 14 and 16, AZ M:8:2 exhibits a far lower percentage of unutilized flakes than does AZ M:8:3, indicating that chipping was a more prominent activity at AZ M:8:3. The virtual lack of cores or core nuclei from AZ M:8:2 likewise indicates that chipping was not a major function here. On the other hand, the amount of cutting activity that was apparently occurring at AZ M:8:2 far exceeds that of any other site on this project; knives account for three times as much of the chipped stone assemblage from AZ M:8:2 as they do at AZ M:8:3.

Therefore, it is suggested that chipping at AZ M:8:2 was secondary in importance to some other activity. That this other activity may have been hunting is indicated by the high incidence of knives (34.8 percent) and the comparatively low proportion (3.0 percent) of scrapers, which suggest that not even hide preparation was carried out at AZ M:8:2. The complete absence of ceramic and ground stone artifacts at AZ M:8:2 lends further support to the hypothesis that this site enjoyed only temporary occupation, perhaps by a mobile band of hunters.

Table 14. Frequency distribution of tentative lithic artifact classifications for AZ M:8:2

Category Label	Code	Frequency (random)	Percent (random)	Frequency (nonrandom)
Core/hammerstone	10	1	1.5	0
Unutilized flake	100	37	56.1	0
Single-side scraper	123	1	1.5	0
Scraper, indeterminate fragment	127	1	1.5	0
Knife/scraper	131	1	1.5	0
Flake knife	141	23	34.8	0
Biface	289	1	1.5	0
Bifacial knife	290	1	1.5	2
Unknown	303	0	0.0	1
Totals		66	100.0	3

Ground Stone Artifacts

Site AZ M:8:2 was devoid of ground stone artifacts, with the sole exception of a quartz hammerstone discovered at a point between this site and AZ M:8:3. (Notably, the survey crew had found a hammerstone lying much closer to AZ M:8:2; this item may have been the same as that just described. If so, it provides further evidence of disturbance occurring in this area between the times of the survey and data recovery phases of the project.)

Ceramics

No sherds were found. As the original survey also failed to note any pottery, its lack is not due to recent disturbance.

Site AZ M:8:3

AZ M:8:3 lies approximately 80 m north of AZ M:8:2 (see Figures 22 and 24). Slightly lower than AZ M:8:2 in elevation (just under 3800 feet), the site lies on two terraces separated by a granite outcrop. The portion of the site north of the outcrop is about 1.5 m lower than the southern portion, which is closer to AZ M:8:2. AZ M:8:3 measures 98 m (north-south) by 60 m (east-west), and is irregular in shape.

The site has been bisected by a bulldozer cut 5 to 7 m wide, which serves as a road. The cut enters the site from the southeast, makes an almost 45-degree turn near the center of the site, and then exits to the west. Just north of where the road curves, a considerable amount of additional bulldozer damage is apparent.

The topsoil reaches a maximum depth of 20 cm, which is deeper than the soil at AZ M:8:2. Surface artifact density is heaviest near the center of the site, north of the road and outside the bulldozer damage. Artifacts continue to occur, though with less frequency, to the north and down the gradual slope leading to Centipede Mesa. Three bedrock metates, all exhibiting light to moderate wear, were found in the granite outcroppings separating the northern from the southern portion of the site.

Environment

The environment of this site is identical to that of AZ M:8:2, discussed previously.

Chipped Stone Artifacts

AZ M:8:3, a larger site than AZ M:8:2, also produced a broader range of artifacts and a larger number of chipped stone items. A total of 441 chipped stone artifacts was collected from AZ M:8:3. Of these, 113 specimens (24.7 percent) were analyzed under the binocular microscope, including 98 artifacts in a random sample (22.0 percent) and 15 retouched tools (2.7 percent). The remaining 328 flakes (76.1 percent) were analyzed to determine their morphological features and stage of manufacture (see Tables 15 and 16).

Table 15. Flake types from AZ M:8:3

Flake type	Frequency	Percent
Hard-hammer flakes	34	10.4
Soft-hammer flakes	245	74.7
Shatter	37	11.3
Thinning flakes	12	3.7
Totals	328	100.0

AZ M:8:3 exhibits a much broader range of lithic manufacturing activities than does AZ M:8:2. Evidence of chipping activity particularly abounds. This site shows a higher proportion of unutilized flakes (80.6 percent) than does any other project site, although the number of cores in the collection is small (1.0 percent). While the relative frequency of knives (13.3 percent) approximates the corresponding figures from other sites, scraping tools are absent from the random sample. (There is one scraper in the nonrandom sample.) Because of the small size of the random sample, the absence of scrapers may not be significant.

Ground Stone Artifacts

The collection of ground stone artifacts from AZ M:8:3 is the second largest (after AZ M:7:2) made by the project. These items comprised 2.5 percent of the total artifact assemblage. In addition to the bedrock metates situated in the granitic outcrop which divides the site, a number of metate and mano fragments were found. In nearly every case, these objects had been disturbed; they were found, for example, in the bulldozer cut or piled neatly about the bedrock metates.

Table 16. Frequency distribution of tentative lithic artifact
classifications for AZ M:8:3

Category Label	Code	Frequency (random)	Percent (random)	Frequency (nonrandom)
Secondary core	2	1	1.0	0
Core nucleus	3	0	0.0	3
Unutilized flake	100	79	80.6	1
Retouch flake	101	1	1.0	0
Double-side scraper	124	0	0.0	1
Flake knife	141	13	13.3	1
Graver	151	1	1.0	0
Projectile point, Type 1-A-4	204	0	0.0	2
Projectile point, Type 1-B-4	214	1	1.0	0
Projectile point fragment	271	0	0.0	1
Biface	289	0	0.0	1
Bifacial knife	290	0	0.0	1
Unknown	303	1	1.0	1
Quartz crystal	304	1	1.0	3
Totals		98	100.0	15

As Table 17 illustrates, with the exception of a single hammerstone (recovered at the northern perimeter of the site), all ground
stone implements were fragmentary.

It should also be noted that all such recoveries were made from
the site's surface. Judging from the disturbance of ground stone, and
from the fact that the site had been vandalized by construction workers,
it is likely that more ground stone artifacts were once present on the
site.

Table 17. Ground stone artifacts from AZ M:8:3

Types	Frequency	Percent
Manos	(4)	(11.4)
Type I	0	0.0
Type II	0	0.0
Fragments	4	11.4
Grinding Stones	0	0.0
Metates	(10)	(28.6)
Type I	0	0.0
Type II	0	0.0
Fragments	10	28.6
Mortars	0	0.0
Slabs	(20)	(57.1)
Complete	0	0.0
Fragments	20	57.1
Hammerstones	1	2.9
Totals	35	100.0

The ground stone assemblages of AZ M:8:2 and AZ M:8:3 differ even more than do their respective chipped stone complexes. The project survey crew had previously reported these same differences. Because the survey had been conducted before the period of greatest disturbance to the sites, it is assumed here that the disturbance has contributed only slightly to the differences in site assemblages found by the excavation crew.

Ceramics

At AZ M:8:3, potsherds comprised 66.5 percent of the artifact collection. This predominance of ceramics over lithics is unique among the sites excavated during this project. As shown by Table 18,

Tizon Brown Ware made up more than two-thirds of the ceramic assemblage. Sherds averaged less than 3 cm in diameter, which reflects recent collecting by construction workers. The survey crew had noted larger sherds on the site, while construction workers told of large painted sherds collected from the site since the time of the survey. However, not a single painted sherd was found by the excavation crew.

Table 18. Frequencies of ceramic types from AZ M:8:3

Type	Frequency	Percent
Prescott Gray Ware	248	26.6
Tizon Brown Ware	(631)	(67.8)
Cerbat Brown	260	27.9
Aquarius Brown	327	35.1
Aquarius Black-on-brown	0	0.0
Sandy Brown	22*	2.4
Tizon Wiped	22	2.4
Transitional	21	2.3
Unidentifiable	31	3.3
Exotic	0	0.0
Totals	931	100.0
Rim sherds	(21)	(2.3)

*Five of the Sandy Brown sherds, though recovered between AZ M:8:2 and AZ M:8:3, were much closer to the latter site, and thus have been included in these tabulations.

A number of rim sherds were discovered. As shown in Figure 25, their forms vary widely from type to type and even within a given type. Comparison of these forms with those present at AZ M:7:2 (see Figure 18) shows that certain patterns are present in both collections. For

M:8:3

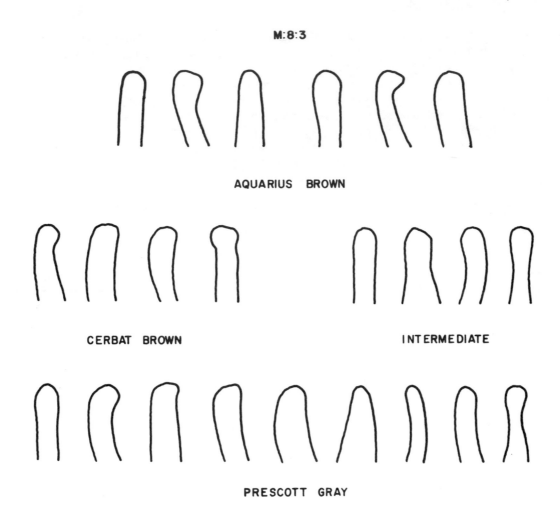

AQUARIUS BROWN

CERBAT BROWN

INTERMEDIATE

PRESCOTT GRAY

Figure 25. Ceramic rim forms and type correlations at AZ M:8:3

instance, the Tizon wares show a flattened facet somewhere along the rim, as opposed to the generally rounded appearance of the rims on Prescott ware; this was also the case at AZ M:8:3.

Site AZ M:8:4

AZ M:8:4 and AZ M:8:5 are two small sites located along Sycamore Wash about 5.6 km northeast of Bagdad. They had been disturbed by construction of a transmission line and parallel pipeline about one year prior to the project's work in the area. Although it is generally not the policy of the Arizona State Museum to perform "post-facto" survey and excavation, the area was examined in view of its potential contributions toward fulfilling the research design. A two-day survey of the 3.2 kilometers of pipeline and transmission line located the two sites.

Discovered at Sycamore Well at an elevation of 4000 feet, AZ M:8:4 consists of a small lithic and sherd scatter measuring 50 m (east-west) by 45 m (north-south) (Figures 26 and 29). The site is located on a gradual slope comprising the first terrace on the south side of Sycamore Creek, which has cut a 10-m to 12-m vertical bank into the terrace. The north bank of the creek is lower and more gradually inclined. The site has been disturbed by a road cut that enters from the northwest, traverses three-fourths of the site, and then turns sharply back to the southwest at about a 45-degree angle. The area damaged by the road and its varves ranges from 5 to 10 m wide and is about 85 m long within the boundaries of the site. To the west of the site, more extensive damage had been done by the installation of the water pipeline; this construction, however, apparently did not disturb any cultural remains. A large (20 m by 15 m) area had also been cleared by bulldozer around Sycamore Well on the southwest peri-meter of the site.

Environment

AZ M:8:4 is at a higher elevation than the sites previously discussed; as a result, the vegetation is denser and includes several species not found at those sites. Shrubs and small trees predominate; mountain-mahogany, juniper, mesquite, palo-verde, acacia, and oak all abound on the site and on the steep slopes of the mesa above it. Larger trees such as cottonwood, sycamore, and willow grow densely in the bed of Sycamore Creek at the base of the terrace.

Cacti are more limited; prickly-pear, beavertail, and hedgehog are the only species. Yucca and agave are common, as are various grasses, including squirrel-tail, Mediterranean, grama, sixweeks grama, and wild barley. Thistle, blueweed, tansy-mustard, desert-mallow, trailing-four-o'clock, and portulaca also were observed. Although the excavations at both AZ M:8:4 and AZ M:3:5 took place at the beginning of the rainy season, water flowed in Sycamore Creek only for a few hours after a heavy rain. Nonetheless, the amount of vegetation along the creek far exceeded that seen in Burro Creek, Boulder Creek, or Copper Creek, all of which are to the west and at lower elevations. Apparently, subsurface water is available at no great depth.

Chipped Stone Artifacts

Only 37 chipped stone artifacts were recovered from AZ M:8:4. Twenty-nine artifacts (78.4 percent) were analyzed with the binocular

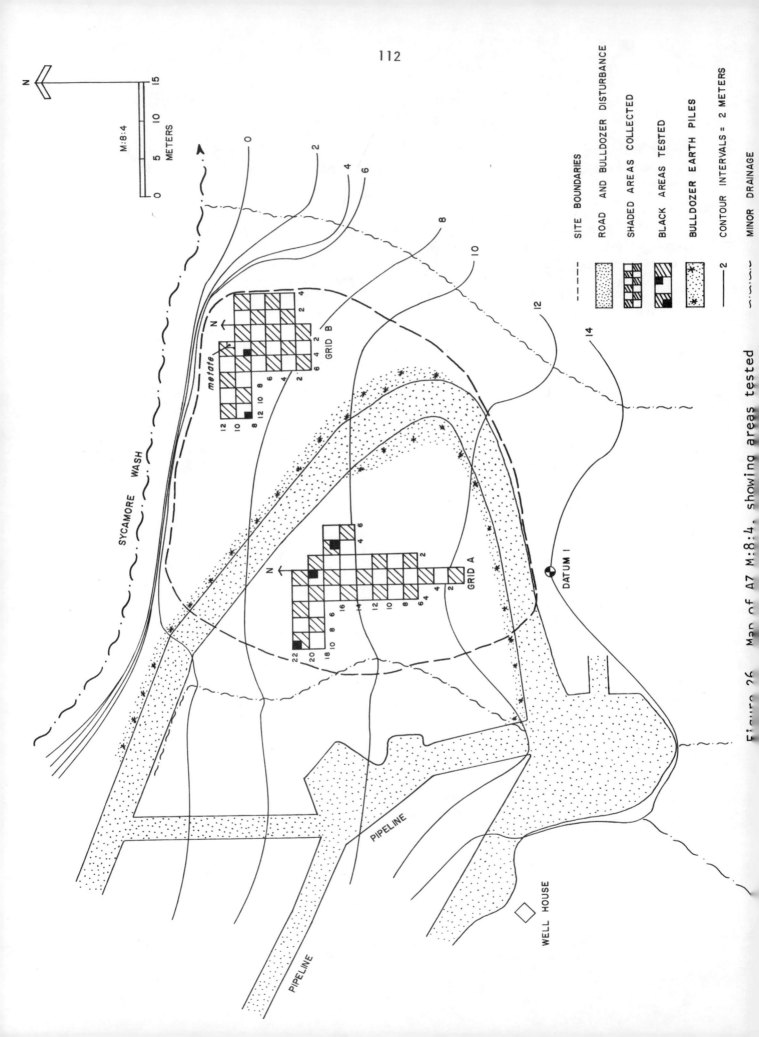

Figure 26. Map of A7 M:8:4, showing areas tested

microscope, including a random sample of 25 artifacts (67.6 percent) and 4 retouched tools (10.8 percent). The remaining eight specimens (21.6 percent) were classified according to their morphological features and stage of manufacture (see Table 19).

Table 19. Flake types from AZ M:8:4

Flake type	Frequency	Percent
Hard-hammer flakes	1	12.5
Soft-hammer flakes	6	75.0
Shatter	0	0.0
Thinning flakes	1	12.5
Totals	8	100.0

The 29 artifacts which were more intensively analyzed were classified on the basis of wear patterns into 12 categories (see Table 20). Unutilized flakes occurred most commonly, comprising 60.9 percent of the assemblage. Together, knives and scrapers make up 24.0 percent of the assemblage. Interestingly, scrapers (including spokeshaves) are more prevalent than knives, although this may be due to the small size of the lithic sample.

Slightly over 41 percent of the items were chipped from quartzite, and less than 38 percent from chert. This preponderance of quartzite implements is shared by AZ M:8:5 and sets these two sites apart from all others investigated in the course of the project.

Table 20. Frequency distribution of tentative lithic artifact classifications for AZ M:8:4

Category Label	Code	Frequency (random)	Percent (random)	Frequency (nonrandom)
Core/hammerstone	10	1	4.0	0
Unutilized flake	100	15	60.0	0
End scraper	121	1	4.0	0
Single-side scraper	123	1	4.0	0
Scraper, indeterminate fragment	127	1	4.0	0
Spokeshave	128	0	0.0	1
Scraper/graver	134	1	4.0	0
Flake knife	141	2	8.0	1
Knife/spokeshave	144	1	4.0	0
Gouge	150	1	4.0	0
Biface	289	0	0.0	1
Bifacial knife	290	1	4.0	1
Totals		25	100.0	4

Ground Stone Artifacts

The assemblage of ground stone from AZ M:8:4 was also rather small. A total of five items (all fashioned from basalt and found on the surface) was recovered, including four fragments of grinding implements and a single hammerstone. In addition, at the northeastern extremity of the site a large "boulder metate" was discovered (see Figure 30). Other, possibly whole specimens may have been removed from the site in the recent past.

Table 21. Ground stone artifacts from AZ M:8:4

Types	Frequency	Percent
Manos	(2)	(40.0)
Type I	0	0.0
Type II	0	0.0
Fragments	2	40.0
Grinding Stones	0	0.0
Metates	0	0.0
Mortars	0	0.0
Slabs	(2)	(40.0)
Complete	0	0.0
Fragments	2	40.0
Hammerstones	1	20.0
Totals	5	100.0

Ceramics

AZ M:8:4 produced 30 sherds, comprising 41.7 percent of the
site's recovered artifact assemblage. Type frequencies are listed in
Table 22.

All sherds were surface finds and averaged no more than 3 cm
in diameter. The small size of this sample precludes anything more
than tentative observations; nonetheless, it is interesting to note
the continued dominance of Tizon Brown Wares this far to the east.
Rim forms are shown in Figure 27.

Table 22. Frequencies of ceramic types from AZ M:8:4

Type	Frequency	Percent
Prescott Gray Ware*	6	20.0
Tizon Brown Ware	(20)	(66.7)
Cerbat Brown	2	6.7
Aquarius Brown	17	56.7
Aquarius Black-on-brown	0	0.0
Sandy Brown	1	3.3
Tizon Wiped	0	0.0
Transitional	2	6.7
Unidentifiable**	2	6.7
Exotic	0	0.0
Totals	30	100.0
Rim sherds	(3)	(10.0)

*Includes 1 Prescott Black-on-gray.

**Both are corrugated, probably of exotic origin.

M:8:4

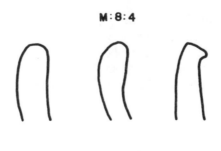

AQUARIUS BROWN

Figure 27. Ceramic rim forms and type correlations at AZ M:8:4

Site AZ M:8:5

Located along Sycamore Creek, AZ M:8:5 is less than 1 km west of AZ M:8:4 at an elevation of about 3950 feet. This site is directly adjacent to the stream bed rather than on the terrace above it.

During the construction of the water pipeline and power lines from Sycamore Well to Bagdad, a previously existing road was widened and straightened for use as an access road. As a result, the northern end of the site was destroyed, and the site was made accessible to pot hunters.

AZ M:8:5 is a small sherd and lithic scatter measuring 35 m (north-south) by 20 m (east-west) (see Figures 28 and 31). No architectural or agricultural features were discovered. Aside from the road cut to the north and the presence of recent trash, the site seems to have suffered little disturbance.

Environment

The vegetation observed at AZ M:8:5 resembles that at AZ M:8:4, although the large cottonwoods and sycamores growing in the stream bed below AZ M:8:4 are absent at AZ M:8:5. Mountain-mahogany, juniper, palo-verde, mesquite, oak, and acacia abound on the site proper and on the slopes north and south of the site.

Prickly-pear, beavertail, and hedgehog cacti are less abundant than at AZ M:8:4. Absent from the site itself, but observed on nearby slopes, are yucca and agave. Grasses present include squirrel-tail, Mediterranean, wild barley, grama, and sixweek grama. Thistle, blue-weed, tansy-mustard, desert-mallow, trailing-four-o'clock, and portulaca were all noted.

Chipped Stone Artifacts

Of the 30 specimens collected, a random sample of 28 artifacts (93.3 percent) and one additional retouched tool (3.3 percent) was analyzed under the binocular microscope; a single soft-hammer flake (3.3 percent) was not included in this analysis.

Each of the 29 artifacts analyzed was classified into one of ten categories according to its inferred function (see Table 23). As at other sites, unutilized flakes were most common, comprising 46.4 percent of the total lithic assemblage. Together, cutting tools and scraping tools also make up 46.4 percent of the collection; each of these categories alone makes up 21.4 percent of the collection.

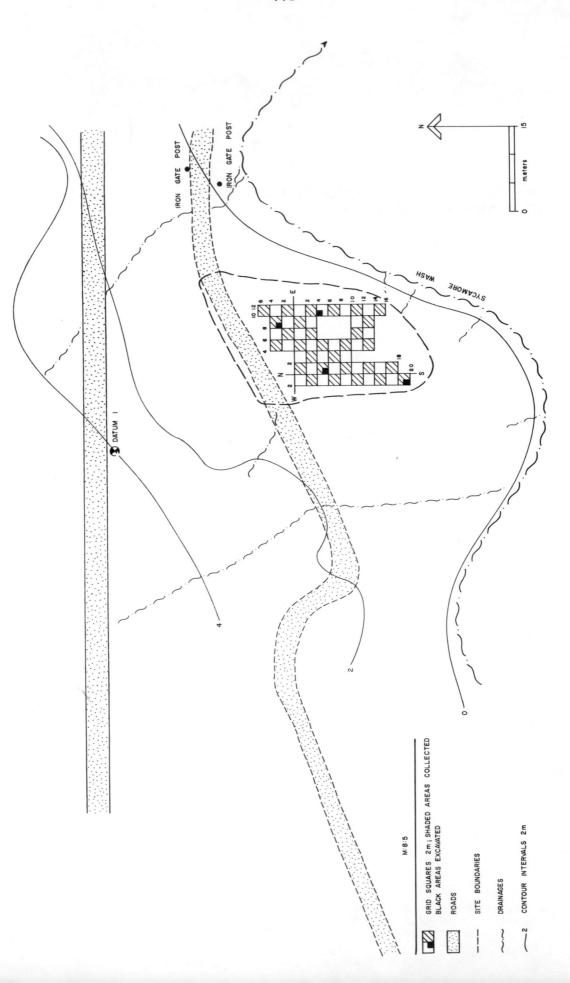

Figure 28. Map of AZ M:8:5, showing areas tested

Figure 29.   AZ M:8:4

Figure 30.   Boulder metate at AZ M:8:4

Figure 31.   AZ M:8:5

As in the case of AZ M:8:4, the majority of the chipped stone tools (64.3 percent) were made of quartzite. Chalcedony, from which 14.3 percent of the tools were manufactured, was the second most commonly used material; this situation contrasts strongly with that at AZ M:8:4, where almost 40 percent of the chipped stone items were made of chert.

The sources of the various raw materials were not pinpointed. These materials are quite different from any of those found at the more westerly sites, including AZ M:7:2 and AZ M:8:3.

Table 23. Frequency distribution of tentative lithic artifact classifications for AZ M:8:5

Category Label	Code	Frequency (random)	Percent (random)	Frequency (nonrandom)
Core nucleus	3	1	3.6	0
Unutilized flake	100	13	46.4	0
Single-side scraper	123	1	3.6	0
Double-side scraper	124	1	3.6	0
Scraper, indeterminate fragment	127	2	7.1	0
Spokeshave	128	2	7.1	0
Knife/scraper	131	1	3.6	0
Flake knife	141	6	21.4	0
Projectile point fragment	271	1	3.6	0
Bifacial knife	290	0	0.0	1
Totals		28	100.0	1

Ground Stone Artifacts

Only three ground stone items were found at AZ M:8:5; these comprised 1.5 percent of the artifacts recovered from the site. A basalt mano fragment and a basalt slab fragment were found on the site, while approximately 100 m north and east of the site, a large cylindrical piece of granitic schist was discovered. Although both ends of the cylinder had been broken off, each of the "new" ends, though of irregular shape, exhibited extensive battering, as though the object had been used as a pestle. The sides had been pecked and ground to a smooth finish. The object is approximately 18 cm long with an elliptical cross section 4.5 to 5.5 cm in diameter.

Table 24. Ground stone artifacts from AZ M:8:5

Types	Frequency	Percent
Manos	(1)	(33.3)
Type I	0	0.0
Type II	0	0.0
Fragments	1	33.3
Grinding Stones	0	0.0
Metates	0	0.0
Mortars	0	0.0
Slabs	(1)	(33.3)
Complete	0	0.0
Fragments	1	33.3
Hammerstones	0	0.0
Granite Cylinder	1	33.3
Totals	3	100.0

Ceramics

Table 25 illustrates the typological distributions of the 172 ceramic specimens recovered from AZ M:8:5. No rim sherds were found. Even this far east, Tizon Brown Ware remained the predominant ceramic type and made up 76.2 percent of the assemblage. Thus, there is no good evidence to indicate that Prescott Gray Ware increases in frequency to the east of the project area; in fact, AZ M:7:4, the westernmost site investigated by the project, produced the highest percentages of this type. However, two factors should be weighed in evaluating these conclusions: the removal of sherds from sites by amateur collectors, and the continuing difficulty in identifying ceramic types.

Table 25. Frequencies of ceramic types from AZ M:8:5

Types	Frequency	Percent
Prescott Gray Ware	30	17.4
Tizon Brown Ware	(131)	(76.2)
Cerbat Brown	68	39.5
Aquarius Brown	56	32.6
Aquarius Black-on-brown	0	0.0
Sandy Brown	3	1.8
Tizon Wiped	4	2.3
Transitional	9	5.2
Unidentifiable	2	1.2
Exotic	0	0.0
Totals	172	100.0
Rim sherds	(0)	(0.0)

CHAPTER 7

FUNCTIONAL VARIABILITY AMONG SITES

The sites discovered by the Cyprus-Bagdad Project differ substantially from one another at nearly all levels of comparison, and as a result any identification of site function must make clear the relationship between functional labels and remains at individual sites. In this report, the approach known as behavioral chain analysis (Schiffer 1972) serves as an inspiration for relating arti- fact variability to prehistoric activity and site function.

Binford (1964: 265) has asserted that archaeological remains are "a 'fossil' record of the actual operation of an extinct society." Schiffer (1972: 156), however, takes exception to this view, pointing out that cultural remains are subjected to a number of cultural and natural "formation processes" which make the archaeological record a distorted picture, at best, of prehistoric behavior (see also Jelinek 1976). However, once these "formation processes" (refuse disposal patterns, loss of perishable items, etc.) are considered, the behav- ioral patterns leading to a given archaeological record can be reconstructed. Once this has been done, it is possible to test hypotheses (such as those in Chapter 2) about culture and human behavior.

The approach used here is based on "behavioral chain" models developed by Schiffer (1976) and Collins (1975). Other models using the same general approach have been established by Phillips (in McDonald and others 1974), Spain (1975), and Linford (n.d.b). The approach used assumes that the total range of events in the use-life of a tool includes five stages: procurement, manufacture, use, maintenance, and discard. At least two of these stages, use and discard, will have occurred at the site at which the tool was found; one assumes that an item would not have been brought to a site simply to dispose of it. The remaining stages must be inferred from associated remains; for example, manufacture of retouched or modified flake tools can be deduced from the presence of small "thinning" flakes. The project, however, was less concerned with identifying specific activities that took place at the sites than with relating those activities to site function. The fact that projectile points were discarded at a site is of interest only because it implies that the site was used as a base for hunting.

Unfortunately, some items are not very useful in behavioral chain analysis. Pottery and ground stone do not lend themselves to

123

study on the basis of stages of artifact use-life. Use presumably occurred at sites where such items were discarded, but procurement, manufacture, and maintenance usually cannot be detected archaeologically. Chipped stone, on the other hand, is easily discussed in terms of these stages, largely because procurement, manufacture, and discard create obvious waste products. In addition, different uses produce characteristic wear patterns on chipped stone tools (Tringham and others 1974; Chapman 1973; Crabtree 1972) or can be related to measurements of edge angle on the tools (Wilmsen 1968, 1970). Drawing from such studies and from functional definitions themselves, it is possible to derive a series of characteristics of various functional types of sites.

Expected Characteristics of Functional Site Types

Procurement and Initial Reduction of Chippable Stone

Sites whose major function was the procurement and initial reduction of chippable stone should have the following characteristics:

1. Naturally occurring chippable stone should be present.

2. Chipped stone should predominate within the artifact assemblage.

3. A large proportion of worked parent materials, or cores in various stages of reduction, should be found.

4. A high incidence of cortical flakes (the waste from core preparation and initial reduction) should be present.

5. A large percentage of shatter (unintentional waste from stone-chipping) should be found.

6. A low incidence of chipped stone tools (artifacts with use-wear, marginal retouch, or unifacial or bifacial modification) should be present. This is based on the assumption that such tools will be found at sites where they were last used, rather than at those sites at which they were made.

7. A low incidence of breakage of such tools as are found should be observed. This presumes that breakage occurs as a result of tool use.

8. Hammerstones (for stoneworking) should be present.

Preparation of Chipped Stone Tools

Sites whose major function was the preparation of chipped stone tools should display the following attributes:

1. Chipped stone should predominate within the artifact assemblage.

2. A sizable number of cores, particularly core nuclei, should be present.

3. Cortical flakes should be present in lesser numbers than at procurement and initial reduction sites (reflecting an emphasis on flake production rather than core preparation in the handling of cores).

4. Soft-hammer flakes (associated with tool preparation) should be more common than hard-hammer flakes (associated with initial reduction of chippable stone), and both should make up larger proportions of the chipped stone assemblage than at other kinds of sites.

5. There should be a low incidence of tools, and such tools as are found should be unbroken.

6. A large amount of shatter (representing unintentional manufacturing waste) and of thinning flakes (representing intentional modification of flakes into tools) should be present.

7. Hammerstones (for stoneworking) should be present.

Extended Habitation

Sites used for habitation should have several characteristics:

1. A large and diversified artifact complex, with no over-whelming predominance of any artifact type, should be found.

2. A relatively high incidence of artifacts with use-wear, marginal retouch, or modification should be in evidence. This reflects the assumption that tools are discarded at the loci where they were last used.

3. There should be a low incidence of cortical flakes, as initial core reduction should, for the most part, have taken place at sites other than those at which finished tools were used and discarded.

4. A high frequency of fragmentary artifacts should be noted. This reflects the breakage of tools as part of their use.

5. Ground stone tools should be present in large numbers, having been used for food preparation.

6. Pottery should be found in quantity (assuming a ceramic period occupation), reflecting its use in food storage and preparation.

7. Features, especially shelters of some sort, should be present.

Plant Food Gathering and Preparation

Sites from which plant foods were collected and prepared should have the following attributes:

1. The chipped stone assemblage should be limited and should show a lack of modification or retouch, reflecting its minor role in plant food preparation.

2. Ground stone should be abundant, as it is the most obvious tool for plant food preparation.

3. Pottery should also be abundant (assuming a ceramic period occupation); in this case, however, its main use may be for storage rather than for cooking.

4. Features should be related to food storage or preparation.

Hunting

Sites from which hunting took place (as opposed to the actual kill sites, not considered here) should have, on a relative scale, more projectile points than other sites. Admittedly, this is a weak test, but in the absence of well-preserved bone remains, the relative frequency of points will have to serve as a criterion.

Farming

Sites at which farming was undertaken are difficult to identify. However, if soil- or water-control features were used, these may be detected. Additional evidence for farming may come from the finding of plant remains or pollen, but again this depends on preservation at the site.

A given site, of course, may subsume several of these functions. In that case, the remains of the site should reflect a balance of the characteristics just outlined.

Evaluation of the Sites

During the field work phases of the project, several hypotheses of site function were advanced; these are examined in the following pages. For each site, the proposed function is stated as a hypothesis; the site's artifact assemblage is then compared with those of other sites, using the functional characteristics just outlined as test implications.

Two aspects of this analysis deserve explanation. First, when a given site is contrasted with others, it is contrasted only with those other sites which the test implications predict would differ from that site in a particular case. For example, AZ M:7:2 is hypothesized to have been an extended habitation site, and as such should have a relatively high proportion of pottery in its artifact assemblage. However, AZ M:8:3 and AZ M:8:4, as plant food-processing sites, should also have fairly high proportions of pottery. Thus, while the proportion of pottery at AZ M:7:2 is contrasted with that at other sites as part of the analysis, AZ M:8:3 and AZ M:8:4 are excluded from the comparison, as the proportion of pottery at the latter sites would not be predictably lower than at AZ M:7:2. In similar ways, one site or another has been excluded from site comparisons when, according to the test implications, their presence would mask any functional differences which existed.

The second aspect of the analysis deserving mention is the samples used in analysis involving chipped stone. For certain items, such as frequencies of thinning flakes, the relevant information was recorded for the entire collection. For others, such as breakage in tools, the needed information was available only for the more limited "random sample" of intensively studied chipped stone. In each analysis, the largest sample possible was used.

Keeping in mind these facts and the functional implications outlined previously, it is possible to test hypotheses of individual site function.

Functions of Individual Project Sites

AZ M:7:2

Hypothesis: AZ M:7:2 was a long-term, semipermanent habitation site.

This hypothesis is generally supported (Table 27). AZ M:7:2 has the second-largest and the second most diversified chipped stone assemblage of any site, after AZ M:7:4 (Table 26). (Note the close correlation between diversity and sample size; these two features covary, and they may be aspects of a single, more inclusive variable.) The proportion of tools to manufacturing waste, however, does not set this site apart from the others. Similarly, the proportions of modified tools (partial or complete unifaces and bifaces) are not significantly different from those at other sites, although the test implications would lead one to expect some difference.

Cortical flakes are relatively uncommon, as would be expected for a site not used primarily for the procurement of chippable stone. However, the amount of breakage in tools is similar to that at other sites. Ground stone and pottery are, as anticipated, fairly common. Finally, the existence of a large habitation structure at the site, as well as the size of the artifact assemblage, strongly supports the hypothesis.

Alternate functions. The presence of some cores and cortical flakes shows that some core reduction and flaking took place at AZ M:7:2. In the same way, the presence of ground stone suggests that plant food-processing took place at the site, and the presence of a number of projectile points suggests that some hunting was carried out from this base. However, the proportions of such artifacts are low enough to indicate that these activities were not site specializations, but rather were part of a general subsistence round associated with extended habitation.

AZ M:7:3

Hypothesis: AZ M:7:3 served primarily as a site for the procurement and initial reduction of chippable stone.

This hypothesis is strongly supported (Table 28). All but three of the 250 artifacts collected are chipped stone, and raw materials occur at the site. About four percent of the chipped stone takes the form of cores or parent material; this is the highest proportion of such items for any of the sites studied. Cortical flakes and shatter are also relatively abundant. Tools are slightly less common than at other sites, but the difference may in this case be due to sampling error. Despite the test implications, the amount of breakage in tools was no different than at other sites. However, retouch was, as predicted, less common at this presumed procurement site. One hammer-stone was found; the only other ground stone at the site consisted of two pecked pebbles.

Alternate functions. Specialized tool manufacture seems ruled out by the relatively low proportion of soft-hammer flakes and thinning

Table 26. Range of artifact types by site

Site	Total Number of Types Represented	Rank by Number of Types Represented	Number of Types Represented by 5 or More Items	Rank by Number of Types with 5 or More Items	Sample Size
AZ M:7:2	31	2	10	2	1225
AZ M:7:3	17	3	5	3	247
AZ M:7:4	40	1	14	1	8773
AZ M:8:2	8	6	2	4	66
AZ M:8:3	8	6	2	4	98
AZ M:8:4	10	4	1	7	25
AZ M:8:5	9	5	2	4	28

NOTE: Based on the random sample of chipped stone artifacts.

Table 27. Comparison of artifact assemblage from AZ M:7:2 with those from other sites

Category	AZ M:7:2	Other Sites	Chi-square (with Yates Correction)
A. Tools vs. Manufacturing Waste[1]			$x^2 = 0.1$, 1 d.f., $p > .10$
Tools[2]	381	528	
Waste[3]	839	1122	
Tools:Waste	.45:1	.47:1	
B. Modified Tools[4]			$x^2 = 1.47$, 1 d.f., $p > .10$
Unifaces and Bifaces	47	107	
Other Chipped Stone	3800	10,876	
Modified:Other	.01:1	.01:1	
C. Marginal Retouch[4]			$x^2 = .02$, 1 d.f., $p > .10$
Unretouched	3733	10,664	
Retouched	114	319	
Retouched:Unretouched	.03:1	.03:1	
D. Cortical Flakes[1,5]			$x^2 = 17.31$, 1 d.f., $p < .001$
Dorsal Surface Completely Cortical	28	100	
Other	1025	1491	
Cortical:Other	.03:1	.07:1	
E. Breakage in Tools[1,2]			$x^2 = 1.99$, 1 d.f., $p > .10$
Whole or Nearly Whole	243	365	
Fragmentary	210	376	
Whole:Fragmentary	1.16:1	.97:1	
F. Ground Stone vs. Chipped Stone[4,6]			$x^2 = 44.57$, 1 d.f., $p < .001$
Ground Stone[7]	45	27	
Chipped Stone	3847	10,510	
Ground:Chipped	.01:1	.003:1	

Table 27. (continued)

Category	AZ M:7:2	Other Sites	Chi-square (with Yates Correction)
G. Pottery vs. Chipped Stone[4,6]			$x^2 = 1837.62$, 1 d.f., $p < .001$
Pottery	1085	191	
Chipped Stone	3847	10,510	
Pottery:Chipped Stone	.42:1	.02:1	

NOTES:

[1]Random sample of chipped stone used.

[2]Types excluded are numbers 1-3, 101, 303, and 304 in Field 23.

[3]Same as types excluded in Note 2.

[4]All chipped stone collected used.

[5]Excluding items patinated after flaking.

[6]Excluding AZ M:8:3 and AZ M:8:4.

[7]Excluding hammerstones.

Table 28. Comparison of lithic assemblage from AZ M:7:3 with those
from other sites

Category	AZ M:7:3	Other Sites	Chi-square (with Yates Correction)
A. Cores and Utilized Parent Material[1,2]			$x^2 = 20.94$, 1 d.f., $p < .001$
Cores and Parent Material	65	83	
Other Chipped Stone	1550	4267	
Cores and Parent Material: Other	.04:1	.02:1	
B. Cortical Flakes[3,4,5]			$x^2 = 6.60$, 1 d.f., $p < .05$
Dorsal Surface Completely Cortical	15	34	
Other	225	1201	
Cortical:Other	.07:1	.03:1	
C. Shatter[1,2]			$x^2 = 41.86$, 1 d.f., $p < .001$
Shatter	264	444	
Other Chipped Stone	1351	3906	
Shatter:Other	.20:1	.11:1	
D. Tools vs. Manufacturing Waste[2,3]			$x^2 = 3.77$, 1 d.f., $.10>p>.05$
Tools[6]	60	422	
Waste[7]	186	949	
Tools:Waste	.32:1	.44:1	
E. Breakage in Tools[2,3]			$x^2 = .03$, 1 d.f., $p > .10$
Whole or Nearly Whole	35	266	
Fragmentary	34	239	
Whole:Fragmentary	1.03:1	1.11:1	

Table 28.   (continued)

Category	AZ M:7:3	Other Sites	Chi-square (with Yates Correction)
F. Marginal Retouch[1,8]			x^2 = 23.91, 1 d.f., p < .001
Unretouched	1603	3733	
Retouched	12	114	
Retouched:Unretouched	.01:1	.03:1	

NOTES:

[1]All chipped stone collected used.

[2]AZ M:7:4 and AZ M:3:2 excluded.

[3]Random sample of chipped stone used.

[4]AZ M:7:4 excluded.

[5]Excluding items patinated after flaking.

[6]Types excluded are numbers 1-3, 101, 303, and 304.

[7]Same as types excluded in Note 6.

[8]AZ M:7:2 only site included in "Other Sites."

flakes (Table 29). Extended habitation is unlikely due to the fairly low number of artifacts, the lack of unifacial or bifacial tools, the low proportion of tools in general, and the lack of features. The lack of grinding tools rules out plant food-processing as a site function; the same would seem to hold for hunting, given the lack of projectile points.

Farming cannot be ruled out, however. AZ M:7:3 is the only site to show evidence of this activity (see Chapter 6). But with this reservation in mind, it would seem that the site's hypothesized function can be accepted on the strength of the successful test implications, and because of the lack of likely alternative functions.

Table 29. Comparison of lithic assemblages from AZ M:7:3, AZ M:7:4, and AZ M:8:2

Category	AZ M:7:3	AZ M:7:4	AZ M:8:2	Chi-square
A. Soft-Hammer and Hard-Hammer Flakes[1]				$x^2 = 81.15$, 2 d.f., $p < .001$
Hard-Hammer	638	2450	13	
Soft-Hammer	567	3803	30	
Hard:Soft-Hammer	1.12:1	.64:1	.43:1	
B. Thinning Flakes[1,2]				$x^2 = 148.22$, 2 d.f., $p < .001$
Thinning Flakes	74	675	36	
Other Chipped Stone	1541	8098	56	
Thinning Flakes:Total Chipped Stone	.05:1	.08:1	.64:1	

NOTES:

[1]All chipped stone collected used.

[2]Yates Correction used in chi-square test.

AZ M:7:4

Hypothesis: AZ M:7:4 was a site for the procurement and reduction of chippable stone, and also for the manufacture of chipped stone tools.

The support for this hypothesis is equivocal (Table 30). AZ M:7:4 is characterized by an extremely high proportion of chipped stone to total artifacts (8751 out of 8792 items), and chippable stone does occur at the site. However, the proportion of cores and parent material is not as high as might be expected--no higher, for that matter, than at other sites. Curiously, the proportion of cortical flakes is relatively large, as would be expected; why this frequency, but not the frequency of cores and parent material, would be as predicted is not known.

The proportion of shatter is high, as expected. The proportions of tools and tool breakage, however, do not seem to differ from those at other sites. Retouch is no less common than at other sites, despite the test implications. Three hammerstones, which might have been used for stone-chipping, were found at the site.

The proportions of soft-hammer and hard-hammer flakes deserve more involved consideration. If hard-hammer flakes are characteristic of initial reduction of stone and if soft-hammer flakes are typical of tool manufacture, then AZ M:7:4 (which shares both these functions) should have "intermediate" proportions of such flakes. The problem, of course, is to determine what those "intermediate" proportions are. In this case, it is possible to use AZ M:7:3 as an example of a site where initial reduction was predominant, and AZ M:8:2 as a site where toolmaking was the primary activity. If the hypothesized functions of all three sites are correct, we would expect AZ M:7:4 to have the highest proportion of hard-hammer flakes, and AZ M:8:2 the lowest; AZ M:7:4 would fall somewhere in between. This is precisely the case, and the differences are significant (Table 29). The ratio of hard-hammer to soft-hammer flakes at AZ M:7:3 is 1.12 to 1; at AZ M:7:4, it is .64 to 1; and at AZ M:8:2, .43 to 1.

The same treatment can be accorded proportions of thinning flakes, the distribution of which should parallel that of soft-hammer flakes. Again, there are significant differences which fit the expected trend (Table 29). At AZ M:7:3, thinning flakes comprise only five percent of the chipped stone; at AZ M:7:4 they make up eight percent of the chipped stone; and at AZ M:8:2 they comprise 64 percent of the chipped stone. The distributions of hard- and soft-hammer flakes and of thinning flakes, therefore, fit the test implications perfectly.

Alternative functions. No features were found, and pottery was rare. However, the chipped stone assemblage exhibits the widest range of types of any site (Table 26), and the site was extensive. The density of the assemblage seems to be a function of sample size; the largest assemblage of any of the seven sites investigated by the project was collected at AZ M:7:4. Ground stone and projectile points were present in some quantity (Tables 3, 30), which suggests that

Table 30. Comparison of lithic assemblage from AZ M:7:4 with those from other sites

Category	AZ M:7:4	Other Sites	Chi-square (with Yates Correction)
A. Cores and Utilized Parent Material[1,2]			x^2 = .03, 1 d.f., p > .10
Cores and Parent Material	162	83	
Other Chipped Stone	8611	4267	
Cores and Parent Material: Other	.02:1	.02:1	
B. Cortical Flakes[3,4,5]			x^2 = 20.62, 1 d.f., p < .001
Dorsal Surface Completely Cortical	79	34	
Other	1090	1201	
Cortical:Other	.07:1	.03:1	
C. Shatter[1,2]			x^2 = 137.19, 1 d.f., p < .001
Shatter	1586	444	
Other Chipped Stone	7187	3906	
Shatter:Other	.22:1	.11:1	
D. Tools vs. Manufacturing Waste[2,3]			x^2 = 2.08, 1 d.f., p > .10
Tools[6]	398	422	
Waste[7]	789	949	
Tools:Waste	.50:1	.44:1	
E. Tool Breakage[2,3]			x^2 = .92, 1 d.f., p > .10
Whole or Nearly Whole	292	266	
Fragmentary	297	239	
Whole:Fragmentary	.98:1	1.11:1	

Table 30.   (continued)

Category	AZ M:7:4	Other Sites	Chi-square (with Yates Correction)
F. Marginal Retouch[1,8]			x^2 = .31, 1 d.f.,
Unretouched	8495	3733	p > .10
Retouched	278	114	
Retouched:Unretouched	.03:1	.03:1	

NOTES:

[1]All chipped stone collected used.

[2]AZ M:7:3 and AZ M:8:2 excluded.

[3]Random sample of chipped stone used.

[4]AZ M:7:3 excluded.

[5]Excluding items patinated after flaking.

[6]Types excluded are numbers 1-3, 101, 303, and 304.

[7]Same as types excluded in Note 6.

[8]AZ M:7:2 only site included in "Other Sites."

plant food preparation and hunting-related activities were taking place at the site. Thus, while no single alternate function can be suggested for AZ M:7:4, it apparently served functions beyond the preparation of chippable stone and its working into tools. While stoneworking was clearly the major activity at the site, it seems clear that the hypothesis must be modified and that AZ M:7:4 in some ways resembles an extended-occupation site or "base camp."

AZ M:8:2

Hypothesis: AZ M:8:2 was a specialized site for the preparation of chipped stone tools.

This hypothesis is strongly supported (Table 31). Chipped stone comprises the whole of the artifact assemblage. However, no cores were found. At a site as small as this one (92 artifacts), several explanations can be advanced for the lack of cores. Sampling error is the most obvious explanation for this lack. Alternately, such few cores as had existed may have been reduced to shatter; they may have been removed in prehistoric times for further use at another site; or they may have been removed by natural action or vandalism. Finally, chippable stone may have been brought into the site in the form of flakes. Thus, while the lack of cores weakens the hypothesis (following the test implications), it cannot be rejected for this reason.

There are few cortical flakes present, but not demonstrably fewer, proportionally speaking, than at AZ M:7:3 and AZ M:7:4 (the stone procurement and reduction sites). The proportions of hard-hammer and soft-hammer flakes, already discussed in the section on AZ M:7:4, are as predicted: soft-hammer flakes predominate.

Chipped stone tools are relatively common at AZ M:8:2, although the reverse would be expected from the test implications. The frequencies of retouch are too low to be tested statistically, but retouched tools seem more common that at other sites. Differences in the amounts of shatter and of breakage in tools do not seem to be significant.

Although no hammerstones were found at the site, the presence of shatter and thinning flakes shows that stoneworking did take place there. Thinning flakes in particular account for 36 of the 92 artifacts found, a predominance consistent with the site's proposed function.

Alternate functions. Procurement and initial reduction of chippable stone was an unlikely site function, given the lack of raw materials and cores. (However, some cortical and partly cortical

Table 31. Comparison of lithic assemblage from AZ M:8:2 with those from other sites

Category	AZ M:8:2	Other Sites	Chi-square (with Yates Correction)
A. Cortical Flakes[1,2,3]			Inapplicable
Dorsal Surface Completely Cortical	3	94	
Other	58	1330	
Cortical:Other	.05:1	.07:1	
B. Tools vs. Manufacturing Waste[1,4]			x^2 = 4.47, 1 d.f., p < .05
Tools[5]	29	422	
Waste[6]	37	949	
Tools:Waste	.78:1	.44:1	
C. Marginal Retouch[7,8]			Inapplicable
Unretouched	86	3733	
Retouched	6	114	
Retouched:Unretouched	.07:1	.03:1	
D. Breakage of Tools[1,2]			x^2 = .08, 1 d.f., p > .10
Whole or Nearly Whole	15	266	
Fragmentary	16	239	
Whole:Fragmentary	.94:1	1.11:1	
E. Thinning Flakes[7]			x^2 = 130.31, 1 d.f., p < .001
Thinning Flakes	36	1068	
Other Chipped Stone	56	13,670	
Thinning Flakes:Other	.64:1	.08:1	
F. Shatter[4,7]			x^2 = .97, 1 d.f., p > .10
Shatter	6	444	
Other Chipped Stone	86	3906	
Shatter:Other	.07:1	.11:1	

Notes on following page

Table 31.   (continued)

NOTES:

    [1]Random sample of chipped stone used.

    [2]Sites used in comparison are AZ M:7:3 and AZ M:7:4.

    [3]Excluding items patinated after flaking.

    [4]Excluding AZ M:7:3 and AZ M:7:4.

    [5]Excluding type numbers 1-3, 101, 303, and 304.

    [6]Same as types excluded in Note 5.

    [7]All chipped stone collected used.

    [8]AZ M:7:2 only site included.

flakes were found, so some initial reduction--and subsequent core removal--may have taken place.) Plant food-processing and hunting are ruled out by the lack of pottery, ground stone, and projectile points. Extended occupation is clearly ruled out when one considers the lack of features and the dearth of artifacts. In all, the hypothesis that AZ M:8:2 was a site of tool-manufacturing is supported.

AZ M:8:3

Hypothesis: AZ M:8:3 was a specialized site for the processing of
               plant foods.

This hypothesis is supported (Table 32). The site has the second-lowest ratio, among those studied, of chipped stone to total artifacts. Furthermore, although the small sample size is probably a factor, the chipped stone assemblage shows little diversity (Table 26); thus, 81 percent of the random sample of chipped stone consisted of unutilized flakes, while another 13 percent was comprised of flake knives (Table 16). Modified tools and retouched items are rare, but no rarer than at other sites.

The strongest evidence in support of the hypothesis comes from the ground stone collection, which was the second-largest from any site. AZ M:8:3 also has the second-largest ratio of ground to chipped stone (.08 to 1) of any site (after AZ M:8:4, where there is a problem with sample size). Pottery shows a similar distribution; again, the sherd collection is the second-largest recovered, and the site has a high ratio of sherds to chipped stone (2.14 to 1). The only features at the site were three bedrock metates, which lends further support to the proposed site function.

Alternate functions. The lack of raw material and cores and the rarity of cortical flakes rule out procurement and initial reduction of chipped stone as activities at the site. The few thinning flakes present suggest limited tool-working or refreshing, but such activity was minor at most; retouch, for example, is found on only 12 of 424 pieces of chipped stone. Extended habitation seems unlikely given the lack of suitable features and the simplicity of the chipped stone assemblage (Table 26). Hunting was possibly an activity at AZ M:8:3 given the finding of three projectile points, but at most would have been a minor aspect of the site's occupation. In sum, there are no likely alternative functions which can be argued for, and the site seems to have been predominantly oriented towards plant food collection and preparation.

Table 32.   Comparison of artifact assemblage from AZ M:8:3 with those from other sites

Category	AZ M:8:3	Other Sites	Chi-square (with Yates Correction)
A. Modified Tools[1,2]			Inapplicable
Unifaces and Bifaces	6	144	
Other Chipped Stone	424	14,357	
Modified Tools:Other	.01:1	.01:1	
B. Marginal Retouch[3,4]			$X^2 = .01$, 1 d.f., $p > .10$
Unretouched	424	3733	
Retouched	12	114	
Retouched:Unretouched	.03:1	.03:1	
C. Ground Stone vs. Chipped Stone[1,2]			Inapplicable
Ground Stone[5]	35	76	
Chipped Stone	436	14,357	
Ground:Chipped	.08:1	.01:1	
D. Pottery vs. Chipped Stone[1,6]			$X^2 = 6314.44$, 1 d.f., $p < .001$
Potsherds	931	191	
Chipped Stone	436	10,510	
Potsherds:Chipped Stone	2.14:1	.02:1	

NOTES:

[1]Random sample of chipped stone used.

[2]Excluding AZ M:8:4.

[3]All chipped stone collected used.

[4]Including only AZ M:7:2.

[5]Excluding hammerstones.

[6]Excluding AZ M:7:2 and AZ M:8:4.

AZ M:8:4

Hypothesis: AZ M:8:4 was a specialized site for the processing of plant foods.

The hypothesis is supported only weakly (Table 33). The assemblage of chipped stone is small and lacks diversity, as would be expected (Table 26). However, only four pieces of ground stone (excluding a hammerstone) were found. Pottery is relatively abundant, as would be expected from the test implications. The only feature at the site, a boulder metate, lends some additional support to the hypothesized site function. It may be noted that the site is located in an area where a number of wild plant foods are available (see Appendix C); this circumstance, while not proving the hypothesis, is at least consistent with it.

Alternate functions. Procurement and initial reduction of chipped stone are unlikely activities because of the lack of raw materials at the site and the rarity of cores and cortical flakes. Chipped stone toolmaking is a doubtful site specialization given the lack of thinning flakes and of chipped stone in general. Extended occupation is precluded as a site function by the lack of features (excepting a boulder metate) and the limited chipped stone assemblage (Table 26). Finally, hunting can be ruled out as a site specialization because no projectile points were found. The identification of AZ M:8:4 as a plant food-processing site, therefore, is only weakly supported by the direct evidence, but is bolstered by the lack of acceptable alternatives.

AZ M:8:5

Hypothesis: AZ M:8:5 was a short-term campsite used by a group in transit from one point to another, and having no significant relationship to local biotic resources.

Evidence for such a site function is essentially negative in that other site functions must be ruled out, and for the most part, alternate functions can be suggested. While the chipped stone assemblage is the smallest of any site, three stone grinding tools were found, and pottery is relatively common. The sherds are largely from a single concentration, which might represent only one or two vessels; however, the type analysis suggests that a minimum of seven varieties of pottery are present at the site. This hardly seems consistent with a hypothesized single, transient use of the site.

Alternate functions. Procurement and initial reduction of stone are ruled out by the lack of local natural deposits of chippable stone. However, the presence of a core, shatter, and unutilized

Table 33. Comparison of artifact assemblage from AZ M:8:4 with those
from other sites

Category	AZ M:8:4	Other Sites	Chi-square (with Yates Correction)
A. Ground Stone vs. Chipped Stone[1,2]			Inapplicable
Ground Stone	4	76	
Chipped Stone	37	14,357	
Ground:Chipped	.11:1	.01:1	
B. Pottery vs. Chipped Stone[1,4]			x^2 = 4106.23, 1 d.f., p < .001
Potsherds	172	191	
Chipped Stone	37	10,510	
Potsherds:Chipped Stone	4.64:1	.02:1	
C. Marginal Retouch[1,2]			Inapplicable
Unretouched	31	3730	
Retouched	6	114	
Retouched:Unretouched	.19:1	.03:1	
D. Modified Tools[1,2]			Inapplicable
Unifaces and Bifaces	3	144	
Other Chipped Stone	34	14,357	
Modified Tools:Other	.09:1	.01:1	

NOTES:

[1]All chipped stone collected used.

[2]Excluding AZ M:8:3.

[3]Excluding hammerstones.

[4]Excluding AZ M:7:2 and AZ M:8:3.

flakes suggests that toolmaking (as opposed to tool use) was a minor activity at the site. The possibility of extended occupation is ruled out by the small number of items found and by the lack of features; however, plant food-processing is suggested by the ground stone and pottery present. The possibility that hunting was a subsidiary activity at AZ M:8:5 is hinted at by the recovery of a single projectile point. Ultimately, no alternate specialization can be argued for AZ M:8:5, but the site seems to some degree related to local biotic resources. This fact, combined with the amount of debris found, militates against the original hypothesis. AZ M:8:5 was most likely a short-term camp without functional specialization, but related to the gathering of local resources.

Discussion of the Analysis

Hypotheses of site function advanced during field work held up under testing in some cases and were modified in others. AZ M:7:2 was an extended habitation site (or "base camp"), and AZ M:7:3 a procurement and initial reduction site for chipped stone. At AZ M:7:4, the importance of stone procurement and initial reduction was confirmed, but the assemblage suggests that the site also functioned in some ways as a base camp. AZ M:8:2 was confirmed as a specialized, toolmaking site, and AZ M:8:3 is fairly clearly a plant food-processing site.

The final two sites are more of a problem. AZ M:8:4 was only weakly upheld as a plant food-processing site. AZ M:8:5 was, as originally hypothesized, a short-term campsite, but seems to have had some relationship to local biotic resources. It does not seem, as was originally thought, to have been a way station for some group traveling through the area. It is perhaps not surprising that these last two sites failed to produce sharply distinctive assemblages, functionally speaking, when one considers that they were occupied for relatively short periods.

In no case were all the test implications for a particular hypothesis supported. While negative results weaken the hypothesis in question, it is also possible to examine the validity of the test implications themselves. One attribute with a distribution often contrary to expectations was the frequency of marginal retouch. If this attribute reflects the refreshening of tool edges after some use, then it should be more common at sites where chipped stone tools were used extensively than at sites where such tools were only prepared, or used just slightly. However, this was not the case. An alternate hypothesis would be that marginal "retouch" is often part of the initial preparation of a chipped stone tool. Thus, retouch would be common at toolmaking sites as well as at tool-use sites.

A second attribute which consistently failed to show the anticipated distribution was breakage in tools. If tools were broken due to use, then the proportion of broken tools should be highest at sites where they were most heavily used. This, again, was not the case. Apparently, breakage during manufacture (or after discard?) may be as important as breakage during use, in terms of the frequencies of breakage noted by the archaeologist.

A third characteristic which did not conform to expectations was the relative proportions of tools and manufacturing waste (cores, unutilized flakes, thinning flakes, and shatter). The problem may lie in part with the heavy reliance, in this report, on use-wear as a defining attribute of tools. There is, of course, the problem of natural edge damage on tools, which would occur after discard and which would mask (or duplicate) use-wear patterns on the tool edge. More basic, however, is the uncertain relationship between specific tool uses and specific wear patterns. The study of wear patterns on chipped stone is a fairly new field of study in archaeology, and its problems are far from resolved. Consider, for example, the following statement from an ethnoarchaeological study of use of Australian native tools:

> Flake-knives will always be a problem for the archaeologist, since they are rarely retouched intentionally or used enough to acquire extensive edge-damage or use-wear to be identi- fiable as tools or distinguishable from certain waste flakes (Gould 1978: 824).

At the Cyprus-Bagdad sites, "unutilized flakes" were consistently the largest single artifact type. Perhaps the reason these items are so common is that many of them were, in fact, tools. Perhaps if such tools could also be taken into account, and if use-wear could be dis- tinguished more easily from natural edge damage, the discrepancy between observed and expected frequencies of tools and manufacturing waste would not be as great.

Finally, one aspect of chipped stone not considered in this study may deserve further attention. Scraping tools (defined here on the basis of use-wear) are often associated with hunting activity, especially hide preparation, although in this analysis only projectile points were used as evidence of hunting. It is noteworthy that scraping tools were slightly but significantly more common at the two sites with projectile point assemblages of any consequence (Table 34). Although hunting-related activities would probably account for only part of the scraping-tool variability noted, and although a number of factors could make the association a spurious one, this relationship between points and scraping tools deserves consideration in future studies in this area.

Table 34. Distribution of scraping tools relative to projectile
points

	Scraping Tools	Other Chipped Stone	Scraping Tools: Other
Sites with relatively large numbers of points (AZ M:7:2 and AZ M:7:4)	221	2193	.10:1
Sites with few or no points	27	437	.06:1

Chi-square (with Yates Correction): $X^2 = 5.08$, 1 d.f., $p < .05$

NOTE: The random sample of chipped stone was used; scraping tools were
defined to be types 20, 121-217, 131, 133-135, 143, 160. Yates
Correction used in determining the chi-square value.

In summary, the analysis of site function was not completely
successful, if one considers success to be a complete affirmation of
proposed hypotheses. However, site functions were clarified through
hypothesis testing. The analysis also permitted a review of certain
assumptions commonly made by archaeologists about the ways in which
tools are made, used, or left as archaeological remains. In the long
run, this improved appreciation of possible behavioral-material cor-
relates may prove more valuable than the identification of specific
site functions.

CHAPTER 8

REGIONAL IMPLICATIONS

The following hypotheses are part of the research design
discussed in Chapter 2. It was hoped that the data from the analysis
could be applied to regional problems, despite the limited sample of
cultural material investigated by the Cyprus-Bagdad Project. These
data cannot provide a complete picture of prehistoric conditions, nor
can they supply conclusive proof of the following hypotheses. Yet,
if a number of small projects such as this were to apply their data
to these or similar hypotheses, patterns in the archaeological record
might become evident.

Hypothesis I: The availability of water was the primary determinant
                 for the location of settlement sites (base camps),
                 and was instrumental in the location of all other
                 types of sites.

Test Implications   (The hypothesis will be supported if):

T1:   All sites with habitation structures are located near permanent
      or semipermanent water sources.

        This implication is supported. AZ M:7:2, the only site found
to have a habitation structure, was located on a mesa top immediately
above Burro Creek. This creek has been shown to be (at least in modern
times) as permanent a water supply as is available in the region (see
Chapter 6).

T2a: Those sites with or without habitation structures, but with
      evidence of numerous and varied activities, are located near
      permanent or semipermanent water sources.

        This implication is also supported. As pointed out in T1,
AZ M:7:2, the habitation site, was located adjacent to Burro Creek.
AZ M:7:4, which had the largest and most varied chipped stone assem-
blage found, was located near a large bedrock tank. AZ M:7:3, with
the third largest and most diverse assemblage, was located next to
Burro Creek. Thus, the locations of three sites support the implication.

T2b: Sites not located near such water sources were loci of specialized, limited activity.

This implication cannot be evaluated properly with the data at hand. AZ M:8:4 and AZ M:8:5 were found near Sycamore Creek, a sizable but dry waterway, as the implication would suggest. AZ M:8:2 and AZ M:8:3, however, were located in a zone of severe disturbance inside the Cyprus-Bagdad open-pit mine, and so it is not possible to tell if water was once available nearby.

T3a: The strongest evidence for prolonged or repeated occupation is derived from sites located near such water sources.

T3a is also supported. AZ M:7:2, with its habitation structure, evidences the only apparent continuous occupation and, as has been pointed out above, is next to Burro Creek. AZ M:7:4, the stone procurement and toolmaking site which produced the most definite evidence of repeated occupations, is located above an unnamed wash and natural pool which contained water even during the driest part of 1976, an unusually dry year. AZ M:7:3, the lithic raw material procurement locus which produced a lithic complex diversified and densely distributed enough to suggest repeated use, was located on the bank of Burro Creek.

T3b: Sites immediately adjacent to permanent or semipermanent water sources exhibit the most complete chronological sequence from the earliest cultural occupations to the latest.

The evidence in this case is limited. AZ M:7:4 does show an early occupation, based on the presence of Archaic-type (Amargosa) points datable to as early as 2000 B.C. In addition, the presence of Prescott Gray Ware on the site apparently indicates occupation between A.D. 700 and A.D. 1400 (Jeter 1977), while the presence of Tizon Brown Ware suggests continued occupation to as late as A.D. 1800 (Dobyns 1956: 158). The fact that this site was located at a source of lithic material (rhyolite) and had a relatively permanent water source nearby (in the form of the natural pool) must have made this a rather desirable location. The generally inferior quality of the chipping material suggests that such considerations were perhaps secondary to those of water availability in deciding site location.

Hypothesis II: Given that the availability of water was the primary determinant of settlement location, all sites were also functionally related to other biotic and abiotic resource locations.

Test Implications (The hypothesis will be considered supported if):

T1: Along permanent or semipermanent water courses (which cross a variety of biotic zones), sites are located primarily within zones with a potential for intensive biotic resource exploitation (as determined by ethnographic data).

The data tend to support this implication. For example, AZ M:7:2 is located quite close to a large stand of mesquite situated in the bed of Burro Creek. AZ M:8:3 is situated in a zone currently dominated by juniper, agave, and numerous cacti. Oak and agave are the dominant species in the environment surrounding AZ M:8:4 and AZ M:8:5.

T2a: For those sites near impermanent sources of water, there is a direct correlation between the season of plant resource avail- ability and the seasonal availability of water.

Table 35 shows that this test implication is supported for the sites investigated by the project, with the possible exceptions of AZ M:8:2 and AZ M:8:3. It should be pointed out, however, that the table takes into account periods of maximum rainfall as well as of observed or probable surface flow. Because desert plants tend to fruit during or just after periods of heaviest rainfall, the correla- tion between seasonal plant resources and seasonal rainfall may be a trivial one. The test implication might be more useful if in the future it considered only actual runoff or catchment of surface water.

T2b: The artifact assemblage (tool kit) at each food-processing site reflects activities directly related to the procurement and use of available biotic resources.

At present, it is not possible to test this implication. While several sites have grinding stones, for example, there is no way to show that such tools were used with those specific resources available at each site. Pollen analysis may be useful in demonstrating on-site presence of given food resources, but otherwise the inability to cor- relate tool types with specific resources is a limitation of current archaeological methods.

T3: Sites not related to biotic resources will be directly related to an abiotic resource.

The final test implication is also supported. Three sites, AZ M:7:3, AZ M:7:4, and AZ M:8:2, have all been shown to exhibit arti- fact assemblages reflecting functions unrelated to the procurement of foodstuffs. At the same time, it has been demonstrated that two of these sites (AZ M:7:3 and AZ M:7:4) served as loci for the procurement of lithic raw materials. Furthermore, the assemblages from the latter two sites indicate that the functions of these sites included the extraction of these raw materials and the manufacture of chipped stone tools.

The third site, AZ M:8:2, was also a chipping station. No known source of raw material is located nearby, but it is by far the smallest site of the three.

Table 35. Vegetal resources and water availability for project sites.

MONTH	AZ M:7:4 Vegetal Foods Available	AZ M:7:4 Water Available	AZ M:7:2 Vegetal Foods Available	AZ M:7:2 Water Available	AZ M:7:3 Vegetal Foods Available	AZ M:7:3 Water Available	AZ M:8:2, AZ M:8:3 Vegetal Foods Available	AZ M:8:2, AZ M:8:3 Water Available	AZ M:8:4, AZ M:8:5 Vegetal Foods Available	AZ M:8:4, AZ M:8:5 Water Available
January		P		O		O		P		I
February		P		O		O		P		I
March		P		P		P		P		I
April		O		O		O		P		
May		O		O		O		P		
June	V	O	V	O	V	O	V	P	V	
July	V	O	V	O	V	O	V	P	V	I
August	V	O	V	O	V	O		P	V	I
September	V	O		P		P	V	P	V	
October	V	P		O		O	V	P	V	
November		P		P		P		P	V	
December		P		P		P		P	V	I

Code

Vegetal Resources = V

Water Availability:

0 = Observed

P = Probable (based on observations of other months and Sellers and Hill 1972)

I = Intermittent

Hypothesis III: Agriculture was an important method of subsistence
                 for the prehistoric inhabitants of this area.

Test Implications (The hypothesis is considered supported if):

T1:   Agricultural features (such as terraces, check dams, or irriga-
       tion ditches) are discovered, indicating that a sizable amount
       of time was invested in preparation of plots for horticulture.

       The data support this implication, but only very weakly. At
AZ M:7:3, a single structure has been identified as a check dam used
in conjunction with the cultivation of maize. It is situated on the
third terrace above Burro Creek, which is more than 1 km distant.
The actual cultivation area lies on the "downhill" side of the dam
(on the other side of the pool is a natural outcropping of basalt
which would have kept the water from continuing down the slope). Thus,
the "dam" was most likely a device intended to control runoff coming
down the slope of Centipede Mesa to the east (several erosion vectors
converged at the dam) and to concentrate it at the naturally occurring
basin.

T2:   Agricultural fields were situated in areas amenable to
       natural watering (through runoff or channel overflow), but in
       areas protected from violent floods which would have washed
       the seeds or young plants away.

       This implication is partially supported. The plot at AZ M:7:3
is safe from floods and swiftly running water, and is also situated
so as to benefit from the runoff coming down Centipede Mesa.

T3a: Sites nearest the identifiable agricultural fields were occupied
       during the growing season in order to facilitate cultivation.

       Although hypotheses and observations have been introduced con-
cerning the periods of water and wild plant food availability, no
tangible evidence relating to season(s) of site occupation has been
uncovered.

T3b: Crops were processed at nearby sites, rather than at the loca-
       tion of their growth and maturity.

       The data support this implication. AZ M:7:3, where the check
dam was located, showed no evidence of habitation or occupation. No
pottery or ground stone was recovered, nor was any structure found.
Thus, evidence suggests that this site was only visited on a day-by-
day basis.

       Furthermore, evidence found at AZ M:7:2, directly across Burro
Creek, suggests that that site was a locus of rather permanent habitation. At this site was also found evidence of maize consumption.

Thus, it seems possible that the maize cultivators at AZ M:7:3 actually lived across Burro Creek at AZ M:7:2.

T3c: Agricultural and food-processing tools (hoes and picks, manos and metates) are found at nearby habitation sites.

This implication remains unsupported, in that no evidence of hoes or picks was recovered; however, these implements may have been made of wood (Dobyns 1956) and would thus have disappeared from the archaeological record. Manos and metates were recovered at AZ M:7:2, but it cannot be determined whether they were used for processing cultivated foods.

CHAPTER 9

CONCLUSIONS

The goals of the Cyprus-Bagdad Project called for a research
design which could be applied to data from a limited number of sites,
but which would employ those data within a broad-scale, regional study.
Thus, while specific data from each site are presented, the scope of
the project was not limited to just these seven sites. It is felt
that, through the determination of the function of each site, a
better understanding of the relationship between the region's inhabitants and their relatively inhospitable environment can be attained.

In Chapter Six, each site was described in considerable detail.
The following chapter interprets the differences in the artifact
assemblages in terms of inferred activities of the occupants of each
site. In this manner, it has been demonstrated that each site represents a different aspect of human interaction with the environment.

As only one site contained (admittedly tenuous) information on
dates of occupation, this report has not attempted to assert that
these sites all represent occupations by the same people. Instead,
it has been assumed that lifeways changed little in this region in
prehistoric (and even protohistoric) times. Thus, these seven sites
can be viewed as divulging information concerning the human occupation
of this region over a number of centuries.

Site Functions

In order to address the set of regional hypotheses presented in
Chapter Two, it was necessary to determine the function of each site.
This was accomplished by examining several critical variables: site
location (in relation to biotic and abiotic resources), site configura-
tion (size, density, and composition), and artifact assemblages. When
these factors were considered, the following site functions were
established:

   AZ M:7:2: Extended occupation; probably a base camp.

   AZ M:7:3: Procurement and initial reduction of chippable stone;
              also, limited farming.

AZ M:7:4: Procurement and initial reduction of chippable stone, combined with other activities suggesting extended occupation or use of the site.

AZ M:8:2: Specialized production of chipped stone tools.

AZ M:8:3: Procurement and processing of wild plant foods.

AZ M:8:4: Procurement and processing of wild plant foods.

AZ M:8:5: Temporary campsite and wild food-processing site.

Several findings of the project deserve special mention. The structure discovered at AZ M:7:2 is difficult to identify, as it does not resemble other prehistoric structures found in the Southwest, nor do its remains correspond to those from known protohistoric and historic dwellings. The foundation of the structure was excavated 25 cm to 30 cm into the original surface; the structure itself was rounded-rectangular in plan and 4.5 meters wide (east to west) by over 10 meters long (the southern boundary was never satisfactorily defined). A single posthole (20 cm in diameter) was found in its approximate center. No other postholes or evidence of wall structures could be found either inside the pit or around its perimeter.

The evidence of agriculture at AZ M:7:3 consisted of an alignment of stones at the western edge of the site, which was apparently intended to divert water (runoff) into a large, irregular basin between the alignment and an outcropping of basalt. Excavations showed the stones to have been stacked three high, and pollen samples produced a single grain of maize pollen. While this may seem only slight evidence of the growing of maize, technicians at the Tumamoc Hill Laboratories of the University of Arizona Department of Geosciences consider it to be conclusive. As no habitation structure was located on this site, the growers and consumers of the maize may have been residing across Burro Creek at AZ M:7:2, where excavations recovered a maize kernel fragment. This postulation is supported by strong similarities in the raw materials used by the inhabitants of both sites; AZ M:7:3 was a major source of chippable stone for the inhabitants of AZ M:7:2.

The selection and subsequent occupation of AZ M:7:4 seems likely to have been affected by the presence of a natural pool in a deep ravine northwest of the site. The site itself produced evidence of repeated occupations over a long period, with Archaic-type (Amargosa) points and ceramics found in association. The artifact distribution at AZ M:7:4 was the densest of all sites investigated, due to the presence nearby of a large supply of rhyolite, the raw material from which about 80 percent of the chipped stone artifacts were made. Yet,

unlike the other raw material procurement site, AZ M:7:3, this site
produced evidence of a broad range of daily activities. As evidence
of these other activities was more limited than that for chipped
stone production, and as no structures were discovered at the site, it
can be suggested that the occupations were transitory. The presence
of the lithic materials along with the natural pool undoubtedly made
this site a desirable and possibly regular stopping point in the
seasonal rounds of the inhabitants of the region.

AZ M:8:2 was an isolated chipping station and was oriented
towards tool manufacture rather than core reduction. The large proportion of thinning flakes collected suggests that unifacial or
bifacial tools were completed at the site. AZ M:8:3 and AZ M:8:4
were sites at which plant foods were collected, prepared, and possibly
stored. The last site, AZ M:8:5, seems to have been a temporary campsite, but some food collection was probably carried out there.

Site description and functional identification completed the
first and perhaps most crucial stage of analysis for the Cyprus-Bagdad
Project. This small block of data was then applied to a series of
hypotheses whose continued testing may eventually produce a much fuller
picture of the lifeways of prehistoric peoples in the Sonoran and
Mojave deserts. More tests involving different data are required to
validate these findings. However, if they hold true, they might have
a far-reaching effect on future archaeology in this region. Additional
support for the first hypothesis would suggest that if future land-
altering activities were to avoid water courses and natural retaining
ponds, fewer sites would be encountered, thus reducing losses in time,
money, and cultural resources. Awareness of the relationship between
water availability and site location might be useful in planning future
archaeological survey strategies. In terms of time expended, researchers
might profitably spend less time investigating open areas away from
water sources.

Further investigation of the second hypothesis--on use of biotic
resources--might eventually produce a much clearer and more concise
picture of the interaction between local prehistoric peoples and the
environment. Additional support for the last hypothesis--on agricul-
ture--might help to settle the disagreement between Kroeber (1935), who
believed farming to have been of minor concern to the Hualapai, and
Dobyns and Euler, who feel that cultivated food sources were an important part of the subsistence base of this group.

Future Research

The Cyprus-Bagdad Project encountered and addressed a number of
problems. As a direct result of these problems, two symposia were
convened in May and November of 1977 to discuss them with other

researchers concerned with work in west-central Arizona. At the
first meeting, a list of research problems was drawn up, along with
a list of difficulties inherent in working in the region, difficulties
which must be dealt with before the research problems can be resolved.
Papers dealing with topics on these lists were presented at the second
meeting, and may be published as an issue of The Kiva.

However, these papers did not cover all topics on these lists,
nor was any topic exhausted. These lists, in that they reflect the
results of cooperation among more than 20 archaeologists interested in
west-central Arizona, go far beyond the interests of any one author.
Many of the topics are interrelated; some are specifically directed
to this region, while others could be applied anywhere. They are
reproduced here for the benefit of future researchers in the hope that
they will prove useful in the development of future research designs.

Research Problems:

1. Subsistence: Gathering strategies
                 Hunting strategies
                 Agriculture

2. Settlement patterns and "culture boundaries"

3. Trade

4. Resource locations: Obsidian
                        Potter's clay

5. Site function(s)

6. Intrasite activities

7. Population interactions

8. Floral and faunal change

9. Hohokam influence

10. Alternatives to ceramics: As chronological markers
                               In defining cultural (population)
                                  affiliation

11. Prehistoric-historic population continuums

Inherent Difficulties:

1. Defining chronologies: Cultural
                           Site-specific

2. Defining cultural affiliation

3. Knowledge of vegetation: Types: Desertscrub
                                    Chaparral
                                    Grassland
                                    Pinyon-juniper
                                    Ponderosa

                          Meanings of changes

4. Ceramic identification

5. Lithic identification

6. Identifying culture-trait complexes: Habitation structures
                                         Ceramics
                                         Ground stone
                                         Chipped stone

7. Interpretation of early published data

8. Lack of geologic data: USGS maps
                           Geological interpretations

The most important factor in the continuation of research in
this region lies in the broadening of horizons. The Cyprus-Bagdad
Project dealt with only seven sites within a linear corridor. The
data provided by this minute sample are not particularly enlightening
when viewed in isolation. However, within a regional perspective,
the sites gain additional import. Some of the assertions presented
in relation to these data may stand; others will certainly be disproven.
They all need to be tested, a task to be accomplished only through the
use of this and previous studies in conjunction with future projects.
This is particularly true in the case of contract projects, which are
generally limited in scope. The use of findings from a number of
projects offers the opportunity to synthesize within a regional perspective what might otherwise remain an assortment of small, unrelated
studies.

APPENDIX A

LITHIC TERMINOLOGY

Chipped Stone Artifacts

The largest assemblage of artifacts recovered during the course
of the Cyprus-Bagdad Project was comprised of chipped stone. All
chipped stone artifacts exhibit a common set of attributes (thus
enabling their identification as such), as well as additional attributes
(such as shape, retouch patterns, and wear patterns) which are directly
related to their intended functions. The terms used to describe these
attributes have been discussed at great length by Chapman (1973),
Crabtree (1972), and Wilmsen (1970), to whom the reader is referred for
more detailed explanations. A glossary of the terms used by the project
is included in this appendix.

Analysis of chipped stone materials from the seven sites tested
produced a classification which, based on clusters of attributes,
included 56 varieties of artifacts. For the purposes of this report,
each of the artifact types was assigned a tentative functional label.

The analysis procedure was drawn largely from that developed by
Schaafsma (1977), although a number of elements have here been added
to or deleted from his format. Besides the various provenience data,
a total of ten attributes were utilized in the analysis, most of which
are derived from Schaafsma's work. Each of these is defined and
described in detail below in the discussion of the computer card design.

Each of the artifacts included in this analysis was examined
under a 14- to 60-power, zoom, binocular microscope, under high-intensity
light. Identification of the various attributes was facilitated through
consultation of Chapman (1973), Tringham and others (1974), and
Crabtree (1972).

The analysis was performed by the author and a crew of volunteers,
working in teams of two; the work was periodically checked by the author.
Observations were performed by one team member and recorded on standard
IBM data sheets by the other. At the end of the analysis, the data
were transferred to punch cards and placed on computer tape for further
use and storage. Selected results of the analysis are included in
Chapters 6 and 7.

Descriptions of Attributes

Included below is the computer-card format used for this project (Table 36), along with an explanation or definition of each of the ten attributes used in identifying the functions of individual artifacts (Table 37). On the basis of its determined function, each artifact was then assigned a tentative name (Field 23, Codes 1 through 304). These names are here considered tentative due to the variability of terminology from one analyst to the next; what may be a "knife/scraper" in one person's view might just as easily be called a "cutting and scraping implement" by someone else. Anyone reusing this data can omit Field 23, and apply his own definitions should he so desire.

Field 1: Analysis Type

Code 1: Entire Sample Analyzed. This classification means that all artifacts, including debitage as well as unretouched artifacts, from the given provenience (or artifact bag) were intensively analyzed.

Code 2: Selected Artifacts Analyzed. This value means that, during the examination of all items not to be included in the random sample, those artifacts observed to have been retouched were extracted, analyzed, and placed into the computer file in order to provide additional data on "formal" artifacts. Such items are listed separately in the tables in Chapter 6.

Field 2: Specimen Number

This number refers to the horizontal provenience of the sample within the site. The grid system used for this project allows an individual item to be assigned a pair of letter-number combinations, with the letter referring to the cardinal compass direction and the number referring to distance (in meters) from the datum. A pair of combinations is utilized, as each represents one of the two axes of the grid; each combination always refers to the southeast corner of the grid square in question. For instance, 12N/10W designates the square for which the southeast corner lies 12 meters north and 10 meters west of datum.

Every horizontal provenience thus designated was assigned a sequential number. Thus, the specimens numbered 1 through 276 refer to site AZ M:7:4 (the first site excavated), 301 through 786 to site AZ M:7:2, 800 through 955 to site AZ M:7:3, 1000 through 1022 to site AZ M:8:2, 1100 through 1238 to site AZ M:8:3, 1300 through 1357 to site AZ M:8:4, and 1400 through 1465 to site AZ M:8:5. For the test excavations, 2001 through 2011 refer to AZ M:8:2, 2012 through 2027 to AZ M:8:3, 2028 through 2051 to AZ M:7:3, 2052 through 2093 to AZ M:7:2, and 2094 through 2116 to AZ M:7:4.

Table 36. Computer card design for project lithic analysis

Field	Content	Columns
1	Analysis type	1
2	Specimen number	3, 4, 5, 6
3	Item number	8, 9, 10
4	Level number	12
5	Material descriptions:	
	A. Type of material	14, 15
	B. Color	16
	C. Variations	17
	D. Light qualities	18
6	Stage of manufacture	20, 21
7	Fragmentation	23
8	Cortex	25
9	Two-dimensional measurements	27, 28, 29
10	Thickness	31, 32, 33
11	Primary utilized portion	35, 36
12	Primary marginal retouch	38
13	Primary use-wear	40, 41
14	Primary edge-angle	43, 44, 45
15	Secondary utilized portion	47, 48
16	Secondary marginal retouch	50
17	Secondary use-wear	52, 53
18	Secondary edge-angle	55, 56, 57
19	Tertiary utilized portion	59, 60
20	Tertiary marginal retouch	62
21	Tertiary use-wear	64, 65
22	Tertiary edge-angle	67, 68, 69
23	Tentative artifact identification	71, 72, 73

NOTE: One column has been left blank between each of the fields (though not between the subfields in the material descriptions).

Secondary and tertiary characteristics (fields 15-22) were coded using the same definitions and codes as used for the primary characteristics. Additional use-wear patterns were described verbally.

This format is largely drawn from Schaafsma 1975, 1976, and 1977.

Table 37. Definitions of codes used in computer card design

Field	Code	Definition
1. Analysis	1	Entire sample analyzed
(Column 1)	2	Selected artifacts taken from artifact bags
2. Specimen number	1	Taken from artifact bag
(Columns 3-6)	through 1500	
3. Item number	1	Assigned during analysis
(Columns 8-10)	through 999	
4. Level number	1	Taken from artifact bag
(Column 12)	through 9	
5. Material descriptions:		
A. Type of material	10	Rhyolite, granular
(Columns 14, 15)	11	Rhyolite, crystalline
	12	Chert
	13	Chalcedony
	14	Obsidian
	15	Floyd Mountain obsidian
	20	Quartz
	21	Quartzite
	30	Basalt
	33	Breccia
	34	Vesicular basalt
	38	Andesite
	39	Granite
	40	Silicified wood
	42	Limestone
	43	Fossils
	90	Other
B. Color	0	White
(Column 16)	1	Clear (transparent)
	2	Gray
	3	Gold
	4	Brown
	5	Red
	6	Purple

Table 37.   (continued)

Field	Code	Definition
5. Material descriptions (continued)		
B. Color (continued)	7	Black
	8	Variegated
	9	Other
C. Variations (Column 17)	0	Light
	1	Dark
	2	Banded
	3	With white inclusions
	4	With gray inclusions
	5	With clear inclusions
	6	With red inclusions
	7	With black inclusions
	8	Plain
	9	Other
D. Light qualities (Column 18)	1	Opaque dull
	2	Opaque glossy
	3	Translucent dull
	4	Translucent glossy
	5	Transparent dull
	6	Transparent glossy
	7	Combinations of above
6. Stage of manufacture (Columns 20, 21)	1	Utilized parent material
	2	Primary core
	3	Secondary core
	4	Core nucleus
	5	Flake, soft-hammer
	6	Flake, hard-hammer
	7	Flake, thinning
	8	Shatter
	9	Uniface, complete
	10	Uniface, partial
	11	Biface, complete
	12	Biface, partial
	13	Other
	14	Resharpening flake
	15	Unidentifiable (usually due to fragmentation)

Table 37. (continued)

Field	Code	Definition
7. Fragmentation (Column 23)	1	Complete
	2	Nearly complete, distal end present
	3	Nearly complete, proximal end present
	4	Incomplete, distal end present
	5	Incomplete, proximal end present
	6	Incomplete, sheared between faces
	7	Incomplete, one lateral side present
	8	Indeterminate fragment
8. Cortex (Column 25)	1	Not present
	2	Dorsal surface of flake, complete coverage
	3	Dorsal surface of flake, partial coverage
	4	Striking platform of flake
	5	Dorsal surface and striking platform
	6	Traces
	7	Striking platform and distal end
	8	Distal end of flake
	9	Patination after flaking
9. Two-dimensional measurements (Columns 27-29)	1 through 999	Taken by quadrant measurement to next highest 0.5 cm up to 5.0 cm, and to next highest 1.0 cm thereafter
10. Thickness (Columns 31-33)	1 through 999	Taken by direct measurement to nearest 1.0 mm
11. Primary utilized portion (Columns 35, 36) (Secondary = Columns 47, 48) (Tertiary = Columns 59,60)	0	None
	1	Utilized original surface
	2	Proximal end of flake
	3	Distal end of flake
	4	Indeterminate end of flake

Table 37.   (continued)

Field	Code	Definition
11. Primary utilized portion (continued)	5	Lateral edge of flake: left (view from dorsal face, proximal end up)
	6	Lateral edge of flake: left, concave
	7	Lateral edge of flake: right (view from dorsal face, proximal end up)
	8	Lateral edge of flake: right, concave
	9	Indeterminate lateral edge
	10	Perimeter
	11	Convenient edge (usually on shatter)
	12	Notch
	13	Projection
	14	Broken edge
12. Primary marginal retouch (Column 38) (Secondary = Column 50) (Tertiary = Column 62)	0	None, unretouched
	1	Unifacial: ventral surface of flake
	2	Unifacial: dorsal surface of flake
	3	Unifacial: other than flake
	4	Bifacial
13. Primary use-wear (Columns 40, 41) (Secondary = Columns 52, 53) Tertiary = Columns 64, 65)	0	None
	1	Light unifacial step-fracture
	2	Heavy unifacial step-fracture
	3	Unifacial chipping
	4	Light bifacial attrition
	5	Heavy bifacial attrition
	6	Bifacial percussion (on an edge)
	7	Percussion on an original surface
	8	Light rotary chipping
	9	Rotary step-fracture
	10	Attrition on a projection
	11	Polish
	12	Edge damage
	13	Indiscernible
	14	Striations
	15	Crushing

Table 37. (continued)

Field	Code	Definition
14. Primary edge-angle (Columns 43-45) (Secondary = Columns 55-57) (Tertiary = Columns 67-69)	1 through 110	Taken by direct measurement
23. Tentative artifact identification (Columns 71-73)	1	Core, primary
	2	Core, secondary
	3	Core nucleus (expended)
	10	Core/hammerstone
	20	Core/scraper
	30	Core/chopper
	31	Chopper
	40	Core/knife
	100	Unutilized flake
	101	Retouch flake
	110	Hammerstone
	121	Scraper, end
	122	Scraper, side-end
	123	Scraper, single-side
	124	Scraper, double-side
	125	Scraper, convergent-side
	126	Scraper, transverse
	127	Scraper, indeterminate fragment
	128	Spokeshave
	131	Knife/scraper
	132	Knife/gouge
	133	Scraper/gouge
	134	Scraper/graver
	135	Scraper/spokeshave
	141	Knife
	142	Knife-projection
	143	Knife/scraper/gouge
	144	Knife/spokeshave
	150	Gouge
	151	Graver
	156	Drill, type II-B
	158	Drill, type IV
	159	Drill, indeterminate fragment
	160	Drill/scraper

Table 37.   (continued)

Field	Code	Definition
23. Tentative artifact identification (continued)	202	Projectile point, type I-A-2
	203	Projectile point, type I-A-3
	204	Projectile point, type I-A-4
	205	Projectile point, type I-A-5
	206	Projectile point, type I-A-6
	211	Projectile point, type I-B-1
	214	Projectile point, type I-B-4
	221	Projectile point, type II-A-1
	222	Projectile point, type II-A-2
	232	Projectile point, type II-B-2
	241	Projectile point, type II-C-1
	242	Projectile point, type II-C-2
	261	Projectile point, type III-B
	271	Projectile point, fragment
	272	Projectile point, serrated fragment
	281	Projectile point, other varieties
	232	Projectile point, preform
	289	Biface
	290	Bifacial knife
	291	Bifacial resharpening flake
	301	Flaked axe
	303	Unknown
	304	Quartz crystal

Field 3: Item Number

Each item from a given provenience was assigned a sequential number, beginning with 1. To save time, only those artifacts of a formal nature (showing retouch) were actually labelled with their item number; the rest were simply assigned numbers on the IBM data sheets as they were removed from their bag, analyzed, and replaced in their bag. (This later proved to be an expedient of dubious value, and is not recommended to future workers.)

Field 4: Level Number

This number refers to the vertical provenience from which the artifact was recovered, with 0 designating surface finds. All other numbers were indicative of 10 cm levels: level 1 indicates 0 to 10 cm in depth, level 2 indicates 20 to 30 cm in depth, and so forth.

Field 5: Material Description

The raw materials from which the chipped stone items were manufactured comprised one of the essential resources available to the inhabitants of the sites. In order to identify the materials used and to enable site-to-site comparisons, the raw material category has been divided into four subcategories, which when combined allow a fairly detailed description of the material.

A. Type of material

A total of 12 varieties of raw material types were distinguished. Identification was performed with the aid of Dana's Mineralogy and with considerable help from various graduate students and staff of the Department of Geology, University of Arizona.

B. Color

As each material often occurred in more than one color, this criterion was introduced in order to more accurately associate materials with locations. Only nine varieties of color were recognized; a tenth classification ("Other") was set up to accommodate those items which did not fit into any of the other categories. Color determinations were subjective, a fact which may limit the analytical value of this category.

C. Variations

Just as materials varied in color, the colors often varied within themselves. Such criteria enabled further refinement of the material identifications, as distinctions could be made between those materials which, for instance, were light brown as opposed to those which were brown with white inclusions. (Inclusions refer to particles which, though an integral part of the stone itself, do not conform in color or texture to the general composition of the stone.)

D. Light Qualities

These criteria refer to the degree to which an object absorbs or reflects light. In the terminology used here, "dull" refers to the fact that an item scatters light without a reflection. "Glossy" objects reflect light, or "shine." "Opaque" objects are those through which no light passes; the viewer sees only the surface. "Translucent" materials are those through which limited light passes, but through which other objects cannot be seen. "Transparent" objects allow light to pass through unrestricted; thus, a pencil held against the surface of a transparent object can be clearly discerned through the object from the other side.

This classification was developed in the absence of any previous intensive geological studies of this region, such as those Schaafsma (1977) was able to use. However, this system proved to be rather unwieldy, and in the future should be abandoned in favor of one similar to that used by Schaafsma (1977: 180). In the latter approach, a material is not identified by a series of separate observations, but rather each variant of a material is assigned a single identification number.

Field 6: Stage of Manufacture

Fifteen stages of manufacture were recognized in this analysis. The criteria used are largely based on those described by Chapman (1973) and Schaafsma (1977), though some modifications have been made for this report.

Code 1: Utilized Parent Material. When an object was taken from its natural surroundings and utilized in its natural state, with absolutely no modification, and with use so limited that the object could not positively be placed in some other classification, it has been classified here as utilized parent material. Such material would be exemplified by a sharp fragment of rhyolite, produced by natural weathering processes, but exhibiting a relatively sharp edge which shows indications of having been used. The object was not shaped by human agency but was nonetheless used for one purpose or another.

Code 2: Primary Core. A core is a piece of parent material
which exhibits one or more scars evidencing the deliberate removal of
flakes (Chapman 1973: 309-310). A core is thus a portable source of
usable raw material. Schaafsma defines primary cores as "original
pieces of parent material that have been worked down" (1977: 182).

Code 3: Secondary Core. Schaafsma describes these cores as
large flakes from which smaller flakes have been removed (1977: 183).
Besides displaying a large positive bulb of percussion and one or more
smaller negative flake scars, the core must also exhibit evidence that
the smaller flakes were removed after the object had been removed from
the primary core or parent material. Otherwise, the object may represent simply a large flake removed from a core after other, smaller
flakes had been removed, leaving their negative scars on its dorsal
surface. Such evidence can be found in platform preparation or flake
removal affecting the ventral surface of the secondary core.

Code 4: Core Nucleus. A core nucleus is simply a worn-out or
expended core. The specimen will have been worked down to a size and
shape that preclude further flake removal.

Code 5: Flake, Soft-Hammer. This study has attempted to dif-
ferentiate among a number of flake types produced by various techniques.
This first flake type refers to those flakes detached from the core
with a soft hammer or percussion device which, when contacting the
core, yields, thus diffusing its force through a wider area of contact
with the platform. According to Crabtree (1972: 44), this process also
produces a small lip or overhang where the platform meets the ventral
surface, immediately above the bulb of percussion. Soft-hammer flakes
are also generally thinner than hard-hammer flakes, and show more
pronounced rippling or shock waves on the ventral surface. This is in
part supported by Frison (1968: 149), who states that "a soft hammer
technique is indicated by a broad, thin flake, with a definite overhang on the bulbar face." More recent work has been performed by Henry,
Haynes, and Bradley (1976), who have found no significant differences
between hard-hammer and soft-hammer flakes in terms of weight. Nonetheless, it seems advisable for the time being to rely upon the data cited,
and to maintain here a soft-hammer versus hard-hammer flake distinction.

Code 6: Flake, Hard-Hammer. These flakes were detached from
the parent material through use of a harder hammer. All hammerstones
or batons are similar in that their pounding surfaces are convex.
Accordingly, only a small portion of the hammer surface comes into
contact with the platform of the core, thus concentrating the force of
the blow within a very small area. As hard hammers do not yield upon
impact, the applied force is concentrated rather than diffused, producing a much more pronounced bulb of percussion. There is no lipping
on the bulbar surface, and, according to some experimenters, such
flakes are generally thicker than soft-hammer flakes (Frison 1968: 149).

Code 7: Flake, Thinning. These flakes are generally removed from the parent material by pressure (or light percussion) in order to thin the piece for artifact manufacture, and usually show special platform preparation (Crabtree 1972: 94). Thinning flakes are generally associated with the production of unifaces and bifaces. They are thin and flat, with a very small bulb of percussion, and are generally smaller than are other flake types.

Code 8: Shatter. These items are irregular, blocky pieces or splinters of material which lack most of the characteristics of regular flakes (such as bulb of percussion, platform, and ventral and dorsal surfaces). These items are considered not to have been deliberately removed from the core, but to have been produced by the removal of other flakes or through faults in the raw material. They usually lack a thin or usable edge (Linford n.d.a).

Code 9: Uniface, Complete. Any chipped artifact which exhibits thinning flaking on either its dorsal or ventral surface (usually on the former) is considered to be a uniface. (This does not include those implements showing unifacial marginal retouch in the absence of facial or thinning modification.) Unifaces are usually prepared from various flake types, though the original stage of manufacture has been obliterated and is impossible to determine (Schaafsma 1977: 184). The terms "complete" and "partial" in this and the following classifications do not refer to the fragmentation of the artifact, but rather to the state or extent of the facial retouch. Those artifacts displaying such retouch over the entirety of one surface (such as many scraper types exhibit) are considered to be complete, while those exhibiting any portion of the original (unretouched) surface on either face are considered partial unifaces.

Code 10: Uniface, Partial. Those unifaces which exhibit thinning flake scars over only part of one surface are considered partial unifaces (see above). Some scrapers and flake knives fit this category.

Code 11: Biface, Complete. Bifaces are here identified by the same criteria used for unifaces, except that the retouch (thinning) is seen on both surfaces rather than on just one.

Code 12: Biface, Partial. These items resemble complete bifaces, except for the fact that retouch is visible over only a portion of both surfaces (or possibly over all of one surface, and part of the other). The area modified is usually the area intended for use (Schaafsma 1977: 183).

Code 13: Other. This category was created in order to classify those implements not assignable to any of the above categories (or to the two additions below). Generally such artifacts are few in number, each usually being unique and representing a new stage of manufacture.

Code 14: Flake, Resharpening. This special variety of flake is created through the resharpening of a uniface or biface (or less often, of a previously unretouched implement) after a certain amount of wear has dictated the need for a sharper edge. A resharpening flake generally shows wear on its proximal end (above the striking platform), which previously lay on the lateral margin of the larger implement being resharpened. Such wear usually ends abruptly at the flake's sides, where the margins have been newly created (see Schaafsma's [1977] discussion of retouch flakes, pp. 181-182).

Code 15: Unidentifiable. A fairly large selection of items was unidentifiable, usually due to fragmentation. Items thus classified differ from those known to belong to some other category not included in this report, which were tabulated under Code 13: Other.

Field 7: Fragmentation

This report has primarily concerned itself simply with whether or not a recovered item was complete. However, more detailed data can be helpful in discerning specific activities undertaken at a site. For instance, a locus exhibiting a number of projectile point bases (proximal ends) may well have been a point where returning hunters removed from weapon foreshafts points broken in the hunt; a locus exhibiting a number of point tips (distal ends) may have been the scene of butchering, the broken tips having been removed from the carcass of a slain animal. On the other hand, a locus exhibiting a large number of both fragment types might indicate the presence of a manufacturing station, the points having been broken during manufacture.

The eight categories for this criterion are self-explanatory. Thus, Code 2: Nearly Complete, distal end present, indicates that the item is broken, with more than half of the item represented by the fragment, and that the item's distal end is present and its proximal end is missing.

Field 8: Cortex

According to Chapman (1973: 310), "parent material prior to its use or preparation as a core exhibits a cortex on its outer surface. This cortex is of a different color and texture than the material composing the interior of the parent material and is produced as a function of weathering through geologic time." The cortex is usually softer and more granular than the material within the core's interior, and is thus much inferior to it in terms of chipping quality. Cortex was generally removed before use or preparation, and is considered waste. It has been suggested that the presence of a large number of flakes exhibiting cortex (decortication flakes) indicates a high incidence of initial core reduction, a process which might well take place at the location of recovery in an effort to reduce the bulk and weight of the cores taken back to the camp or village (Spain 1975; Linford n.d.a, n.d.b).

The presence of cortex is identified on the basis of the criteria of flake morphology discussed at length by Chapman (1973), with the exception of patination after flaking (Code 9). Presence of this particular attribute is indicative of considerable antiquity of a piece of chipped stone, in that a new cortex is being formed. However, patination does not provide a measure of age, as different materials will react differently, some more swiftly, others less so, to the effects of weathering; even in comparing similar materials from relatively widely spaced loci, artifacts of similar age may have been exposed to various weathering elements to different degrees.

Field 9: Two-dimensional Measurements

After microscopic examination, each artifact was measured according to two sets of criteria. The first measurement ascertained artifact length and width, and was obtained by placing the item on a sheet of metric grid paper, with the item's longest axis perpendicular to one axis of the grid. The axis of the artifact was then measured to the next higher half-centimeter (5 mm) up to 5 centimeters (50 mm), and to the next higher centimeter thereafter, thus allowing better control in measuring the numerous smaller flakes; most of the larger implements did not require such precise control. This method, though not as desirable as that involving the taking of two separate and precise measurements, saved considerable time, an important consideration for this project.

Field 10: Thickness

This measurement was obtained with stainless steel, vernier calipers to the nearest one-tenth of a centimeter (1 mm).

In defining use-wear on an artifact, four criteria were considered: 1) the portion of the artifact which exhibited the use-wear, 2) presence or absence of retouch, 3) the type of use-wear exhibited (after Crabtree 1972, Chapman 1973, and Tringham and others 1974), and 4) the angle of the utilized edge (after Wilmsen 1970). A great many lithic artifacts exhibit more than one used edge, each edge often indicating a different function (Linford n.d.b; Schaafsma 1977). For this reason, the analysis was designed to accommodate more than one working edge. Space was made available on the computer cards to record results of the examination of the above criteria for three different utilized edges, with the criteria remaining universal from one edge to the next. It was expected that a few artifacts would exhibit more than three working edges, in which cases the additional edges would be described verbally on separate forms; this situation, however, never arose.

As the criteria were universal and were applicable to all three working edges, they will be described only once below.

Field 11: Utilized Portion (also Fields 15 and 19)

The terms used relative to this field refer to various portions of the morphology of the flake or other item, and are generally self-explanatory. Chapman (1973) and Crabtree (1972) provide more extensive, illustrated discussions of these terms.

Field 12: Marginal Retouch (also Fields 16 and 20)

As opposed to the facial or surfacial retouch examined in discerning stage of manufacture (see Field 6, Codes 9 through 12), this criterion refers to the deliberate alteration of a particular margin or edge of an implement. Such retouch parallels the edge, thus forming a uniform border along it. Marginal retouch is generally not more than three to four millimeters wide, though its extent will vary considerably with the size of the artifact.

The different terms listed refer to morphological characteristics of the flake (if the original morphology is still discernible), and are self-explanatory.

Field 13: Use-Wear (also Fields 17 and 21)

The alteration of an edge through use is usually easily distinguishable from the deliberate alteration created through retouch. The former is usually represented by flake scars smaller than those characterizing the latter, which generally are more irregular both in size and distribution. Among use-wear patterns, a number of varieties are recognized as produced by different kinds of wear; analysts are still unable to associate some patterns with specific edge uses. Fifteen types of use-wear pattern were recognized during the analysis of the Cyprus-Bagdad materials.

With a few exceptions, these terms follow those defined by Schaafsma (1977: 188-194) who, in developing these descriptive criteria, relied heavily on previous works by Tringham and others (1974) and especially by Chapman (1973).

Following Schaafsma's example, the terms "unifacial" and "bifacial" are used here in place of Chapman's "unidirectional" and "bidirectional," since the former terms are more commonly used today. These terms refer to the fact that use-wear was observed <u>predominantly</u> on one or both faces of an edge.

<u>Code 0: None</u>. This classification refers to those instances when wear was observed on the edge examined. Such observations are generally interpreted as indicating that no use-wear occurred. However, on items exhibiting extensive marginal retouch (particularly on bifacial items), use-wear, though expected, was often indiscernible. Edges assigned to this latter category are included in Code 13: Indiscernible.

<u>Code 1: Light Unifacial Step-Fracture; and Code 2: Heavy Unifacial Step-Fracture</u>. Step-fracture nearly always occurs on only one edge face, and is created by the applying of a vector of force perpendicularly to the longitudinal axis of the edge. Minute flakes hinge-fracture in being detached from the surface of the edge opposite the vector of force (Chapman 1973). Researchers agree that this type of use-wear pattern is caused by scraping activities.

Schaafsma (1977: 190-191) uses Code 1 and Code 2 to distinguish between wear caused by use on soft substances, like wood (Code 1), from that caused by use on hard substances, like bone and antler (Code 2). In this respect, he subscribes to interpretations presented by Tringham and others (1974: 191). However, the author feels that Tringham's work was not extensive enough to warrant such assertions without some caution. Therefore, where Schaafsma uses sizes of flake scars to distinguish between Code 1 and Code 2, this report distinguishes between the two merely on the basis of the amount of wear. Thus, Code 1 indicates that the examined items exhibit limited to moderate wear, while Code 2 indicates the presence of extensive wear.

<u>Code 3: Unifacial Chipping</u>. Scraping activities, like step-fracture, produce a type of flaking which results in "scalar-shaped scars" (Tringham and others 1974: 188) which lack hinges at the distal end, but which also occur primarily on one surface of the edge. It has been suggested that these scars are indicative of work with soft materials such as hides and skins (Tringham and others 1974: 189). However, for the purposes of this report, unifacial chipping is considered merely as additional evidence of scraping activity.

<u>Code 4: Light Bifacial Attrition; and Code 5: Heavy Bifacial Attrition</u>. Attrition is evidenced by scalar scars (Tringham and others 1974) or "feathering scars" (Chapman 1973) on both faces of an edge. These scars may or may not show fractures or hinges at their distal ends. Tringham and others (1974: 187) have shown that this type of wear results from moving the edge in a longitudinal manner, holding the

cutting edge parallel to the direction of motion. Chapman (1973) refers to this as "sawing motion." Thus, attrition is associated with cutting activity.

According to Tringham and others (1974), the lighter attrition scars generally lack hinges, and indicate the cutting of soft materials such as skins and hides. On the other hand, the heavy attrition scars are larger, often exhibit hinges, and are indicative of the cutting of harder materials such as wood or bone (1974: 189-191).

However, for the present report, distinctions were made only on the basis of the extent of use present, which was considered a measure of the intensity or the extent of artifact use; thus, the less the use-wear on a particular artifact, the less that artifact was used.

Code 6: Bifacial Percussion (on an edge). According to Schaafsma (1977: 193), this wear is indicative of "chopper" wear. It consists of massive attrition-like scars exhibiting splintering and crushing along the proximal ends (on the apex of the use-edge), accom-panied by other types of wear, such as large step-fractures. These result from direct blows on some unyielding surface, as in the case of chopping on a hard surface such as wood or bone. These edges have generally been prepared by the removal of large retouch flakes, as opposed to those artifacts classified within the next code.

Code 7: Percussion on an Original Surface. Unlike bifacial percussion on an edge (Code 6), no retouch or other preparation is reflected within this criterion. According to Schaafsma (1977: 194), this wear appears as crushed and splintered areas similar to those seen on the edges of choppers or on the surfaces or faces of objects such as hammerstones.

Code 8: Light Rotary Chipping; and Code 9: Rotary Step-Fracture. Items with projections emanating from the main body often exhibit a pattern of chipping or step-fracture on the edges of the projection. Such wear is unidirectional and perpendicular to the longitudinal axis of the edges. Chapman (1973) and Schaafsma (1977: 194) interpret such wear as produced by turning the item in the manner of a drill. Presum-ably, different materials would produce the chipping, while others would produce the step-fracture. However, for the purposes of this report, both were simply interpreted as reflecting drilling activity.

Code 10: Attrition on a Projection. An angular projection with a sharp tip could be utilized in more precise cutting activities. In such cases, attrition would be found on the edges of the projection. The presence of attrition perpendicular to the tip of the projection has been interpreted within the present report as evidence of some sort of "engraving" activity. In cases where the wear parallels the tip, such wear has been interpreted as evidencing "gouging."

Code 11: Polish. Polish was generally difficult to identify under the minimal magnifications available with the microscopes used in conjunction with this project. For this reason, project analysts followed the example of Schaafsma (1977: 194) and recorded the presence of polish only when it was clearly distinct and was the only type of wear observed.

Code 12: Edge Damage. This classification was developed to accommodate those artifacts exhibiting damage to a thin edge, but for which the causes of the damage were not certain. Tringham and others (1974: 181-183) have claimed an ability to distinguish between those patterns resulting from natural forces (water, sand) and those created by use. In most cases, these patterns are discernible. However, when working with a surface collection from an area of desert pavement, where it is often impossible to determine the relative ages of the arti-facts collected, the author feels that such distinctions should not be attempted for artifacts difficult to analyze. Thus, the edges classified within this category are those which may or may not exhibit some use-wear.

Code 13: Indiscernible. This classification includes most bifacially retouched implements, whose wear patterns are often diffi-cult to distinguish from the crushing patterns and striations created in the preparation of each striking platform for each retouch flake (Sheets 1973: 215-218; Hester and Heizer 1973: 220-221).

Code 14: Striations. Semenov (1964) identifies striations as the minute scratches or abrasions which occur along the working edge of an artifact in conjunction with other wear patterns. Chapman (1973) recognized three types of striations: 1) those parallel to the long axis of the edge, 2) those perpendicular to the long axis of the edge, and 3) those occurring at an angle to the long axis of the edge. Each indicates operations using a different angle of the edge to the surface being worked.

Code 15: Crushing. This classification refers to the massive fracturing and flaking produced by percussion. However, crushing was occasionally discovered on edges too thin to have been used for chopping. In these cases, such wear was commonly interpreted as reflecting "backing" or intentional dulling, such as occurs on the basal edges of projectile points to prevent the point from cutting its own binding.

Field 14: Edge-Angle (also Field 18 and Field 22)

Wilmsen (1970) has suggested that edge-angle may be a direct function of the use of an artifact, different uses requiring different angles for optimal performance.

Three measurable types of angle were noted in the course of the project's analysis phase. The first of these is the "spine angle" measured by Tringham and others (1974: Figure 1), which is reflected in the cross section of the flake. The second is the angle which has been deliberately altered by means of retouch, reflecting a desire for a specific degree of slope. The third is that angle created by the micro-spalling and detachment of use flakes, which occurs during use of the implement.

Since the use of an edge alters its original angle, and since it cannot be determined whether or not a tool was considered usable by the user at the time of discard, this latter angle (used by Schaafsma) was avoided. Such an angle may well have been exhausted by use and thus no longer functional in its intended capacity. Instead, on unretouched edges, the spine angle of the edge or the apex angle was measured, thus providing a better idea of the original angle before worn down by use. On those edges showing retouch, the new angle created by the deliberate alterations was measured, taking care to distinguish deliberate alterations from those caused by wear.

All angles were measured carefully to the nearest degree with a stainless steel goniometer or carpenter's protractor.

Field 23: Tentative Artifact Identification

Code 1: Core, Primary. See Field 6, Stage of Manufacture, Code 2, Primary Core.

Code 2: Core, Secondary. See Field 6, Stage of Manufacture, Code 3, Secondary Core.

Code 3: Core Nucleus (Expended). See Field 6, Stage of Manufacture, Code 4, Core Nucleus.

Code 10: Core/Hammerstone. This classification includes items showing deliberate platform preparation and flake removal, as well as additional pounding and battering on their convex surfaces, a character-istic common to hammerstones.

Code 20: Core/Scraper. In the process of reducing a core to obtain workable flakes, flake removal often produces edges of proper dimension and angle to function in a variety of ways, including scraping. If the edge was used, the implement had multiple uses, at least for a limited time (see scraper terminology below).

Code 30: Core/Chopper. This class of items exhibits deliberate flake removal, independent of a use-edge showing massive percussion (see Chopper, Code 31 below).

Code 31: Chopper. This item exhibits at least one utilized edge, usually with bifacial retouch, and massive percussion on the apex of the edge (see Field 13, Code 7). Such wear was produced by pounding the edge on a hard, resistant surface, such as bone or wood.

Code 40: Core/Knife. An item which was a source of usable debitage and which also exhibits cutting wear (bifacial attrition) is referred to as a core/knife.

Code 100: Unutilized Flake. The majority of debitage, including nearly all shatter, showed no alteration through retouch or use. Some of these items displayed thin edges which, though capable of use for a number of purposes, were not so used. Other items plainly could not have been used due to their morphology. All such artifacts have been grouped within this category, as have those implements observed to exhibit edge damage (Field 13, Code 12) and for whose edges it was impossible to determine the cause of the minute wear patterns.

Code 101: Retouch Flake. The process of thinning, straightening, sharpening, or smoothing an artifact to make it more regular in form (Crabtree 1972: 89) produces a distinctive flake, generally thin in cross section, and exhibiting no true striking platform, as the platform was once the apex of an edge. The bulb of percussion is very low and dissipated. Ripples are scarce and quite small.

Code 110: Hammerstone. Hammerstones are generally made of hard, dense materials, and are usually somewhat spherical in shape (except for the "baton" varieties, which are elongated). All or most of the convex surfaces of the stone evidence a great deal of battering and crushing.

A hammerstone was usually used for the removal of flakes from a core, and for the initial stages of manufacture in chipping an implement. Since the hammerstone was usually no harder than the material being chipped, and since accuracy was desired in removing flakes, wear was limited to the most convex surfaces, where the most force could be applied to the material being worked.

Hammerstones were also used to soften hides, and to roughen or "sharpen" ground stone items.

Codes 121 through 127: Scrapers. Items exhibiting step-fracture and/or unifacial chipping are considered to have been used in scraping activities (Chapman 1973; Schaafsma 1977: 190-192). Honea (1965: 36-39) delineates a number of scraper types, some of which were adopted for this report. All are based on the location and number of edges on the item, as well as on the morphology of the flake.

Code 121: Scraper, End. This implement shows wear on the distal end of the flake (although a single specimen was found to exhibit wear on the flake's proximal edge).

Code 122: Scraper, Side-end. Such an item possesses at least two edges, one on the distal end of the flake, one on one lateral side. These use-edges may intersect at a corner. (Note: The use-wear does not always take up the entire length of the utilized edge.)

Code 123: Scraper, Single-side. This scraper type exhibits a single scraping edge along one lateral side of the item.

Code 124: Scraper, Double-side. This scraper type exhibits at least two scraping edges, one on each lateral side of the tool. If there are more than two scraping edges, there will be more than one such edge on one of the lateral sides.

Code 125: Scraper, Convergent-side. On such an implement, at least two scraper edges are found, each on a lateral side. This scraper type differs from the double-side scraper in that the two edges come together at one end of the implement.

Code 126: Scraper, Transverse. This is a type of end-scraper, but the end on which the wear occurs is greater in length than the longitudinal axis of the item. In other words, the tool is wider than it is long.

Code 127: Scraper, Indeterminate Fragment. A number of scraper edges were discovered on fragmentary items, the original shapes of which (and the original location of the edges on which) were impossible to determine. These items were classified as indeterminate scraper fragments.

Code 128: Spokeshave. A different kind of scraper wear was noted on some implements. These showed a concave use-edge, and in many cases the wear seemed to be bifacial. The concavity was nearly semi-circular, a characteristic resembling that of Honea's indented scrapers (1965: 38). It has been suggested that these items were used in shaving irregularities off arrow shafts and other small-diameter, cylindrical objects.

Code 131: Knife/ Scraper. The single most common combination or multiuse tool found by this project exhibited both scraping wear (unifacial step-fracture and chipping) and cutting wear (bifacial attrition). These tools might exhibit either a single edge showing each wear pattern (though never on the same side of the edge) or two edges, each showing a different pattern.

Code 132: Knife/Gouge. Items exhibiting a cutting edge as well as a projection with unifacial step-fracture along its apex and parallel to its long axis reflect another kind of multiple use: cutting and gouging. This gouging wear may have been produced by chiseling or planing, but most likely by the former, due to the size of the projections examined.

Code 133: Scraper/Gouge. Specimens of this implement type show the gouging wear described above, as well as at least one edge exhibiting unifacial step-fracture.

Code 134: Scraper/Graver. Items showing scraper wear on at least one edge, as well as rotary step-fracture, rotary chipping, and/or rotary striations on a projection, indicate combinations of scraper and graver use. The term "gravers" generally refers to tools used for engraving rather than drilling, although it is likely that most of these implements were utilized most often as light-duty drills or punches.

Code 135: Scraper/Spokeshave. These tools exhibit combinations of scraping and "shaving" usages.

Code 141: Knife. Any item which exhibited bifacial attrition, either light or heavy, along one or more thin edges has been classified as a knife. This was the most common form of use-wear found on items recovered by this project. Many of the knives were simple utilized flakes (as were many scrapers), although a large portion also exhibited retouch along the utilized edges. It is quite common to find a specimen with a combination of retouched and unretouched edges.

Code 142: Knife-Projection. This category includes those implements which exhibited attrition on a projection or protuberance. Such an edge would afford the user more accuracy in making small incisions, though it cannot be conclusively stated that this was the primary function of such implements.

Code 143: Knife/Scraper/Gouge. This tool type consists of the only triple-use artifacts identified in conjunction with this project. The tools possess edges exhibiting bifacial attrition and unifacial step-fracture, as well as a projection with step-fracture on its end.

Code 144: Knife/Spokeshave. Tools of this type exhibit bifacial attrition on at least one edge, and a concave edge with unifacial (occasionally bifacial) step-fracture on another portion.

Code 150: Gouge. These tools exhibit at least one projection from a margin. The projection exhibits unifacial step-fracture along its distal end, the step-fracture running parallel to the long axis of the projection. Such wear can be caused by "planing" action or by "chiseling" action, depending on the direction of movement of the tool.

Code 151: <u>Graver</u>. Gravers resemble miniature drills. Their projections are quite small and rarely produced through retouch, being instead accidentally produced. These projections exhibit rotary wear along the shafts in the form of step-fracture or chipping, and occasionally striations. The tips of the projections may be polished or crushed, depending on the intensity of use and the material upon which they were used. Although the term "graver" infers that these tools were used for engraving, it is just as likely that they were utilized as light-duty drills, to punch holes through thin, relatively soft materials.

<u>Codes 156 through 160: Drills</u>. A number of different drills were analyzed and classified according to the criteria set up by Linford (n.d.b). Therefore, there are gaps in the classification numbering system where types expected were not found.

<u>Code 156: Drill, Type II-B</u>. This type of drill is characterized by a rounded base which flares out from the proximal end of the drill shaft, while the shaft of the drill is at least twice the length of the base or longer. The base has been modified to a desired shape.

<u>Code 158: Drill, Type IV</u>. This drill shows very little alteration except for the shaft. The base retains the original, amorphous shape of the flake from which the drill was produced.

<u>Code 159: Drill, Indeterminate Fragment</u>. Those fragments of drill shafts whose original shape or length was impossible to determine were included within this category.

<u>Code 160: Drill/Scraper</u>. This category includes those implements with at least one edge exhibiting unifacial step-fracture and a projection showing heavy rotary step-fracture and rotary chipping.

<u>Codes 202 through 282: Projectile Points</u>. As with the drills, the types utilized in these categories were derived from previous works, and a list considered to be inclusive of all expected types was developed. As not all of the types expected were identified, there are gaps in the classification numbering system.

<u>Code 202: Projectile Point, Type I-A-2</u>. Type I-A points are lanceolate, or long and narrow, with no basal notching. Type I-A-2 points particularly exhibit a rounded base.

<u>Code 203: Projectile Point, Type I-A-3</u>. These points are similar to Type I-A-2 points except that their bases are either flat or concave.

<u>Code 204: Projectile Point, Type I-A-4</u>. Type I-A-4 points are similar to Type I-A-2 points, being lanceolate with rounded bases, but are serrated along both lateral margins.

Code 205: Projectile Point, Type I-A-5. These points are lanceolate, with a concave base (similar to Type I-A-3), but are serrated along both lateral margins like points of Type I-A-4.

Code 206: Projectile Point, Type I-A-6. These points are also lanceolate, exhibit a flat base (like Type I-A-3), and are serrated, like the Type I-A-4 and I-A-5 points.

Code 211: Projectile Point, Type I-B-1. Type I-B points are broad, triangular points, lacking hafting notches. Type I-B-1 points have excurvate or convex lateral margins. The bases are flat or concave.

Code 214: Projectile Point, Type I-B-4. This point type is also triangular, but the lateral margins and the base are incurvate or concave. There also seems to be an attempt to produce hafting notches about three-quarters of the length from the tip or distal end. The notches are shallow and broad.

Code 221: Projectile Point, Type II-A-1. Type II points are stemmed, side-notched, triangular varieties. The Type II-A-1 variety exhibits notches situated at a 45-degree angle to the base of the point; in some studies, such points have been termed "corner-notched." The stem expands, but is not wider than the shoulders.

Code 222: Projectile Point, Type II-A-2. Points of this type have deep, broad side-notches about two-thirds the length from the tip, thus producing a rounded "knob" of a base. The base is not wider than the shoulder.

Code 232: Projectile Point, Type II-B-2. This type of point is characterized by narrow side-notches about two-thirds the length of the lateral sides from the distal end (tip). The shoulder lies above the notch at the broadest point of the item, as the stem below the notch retracts, producing a base narrower than the shoulder. The base is concave. These points are serrated along both lateral margins.

Code 241: Projectile Point, Type II-C-1. Like the Type II-B-2 points, these specimens have small, narrow notches about two-thirds the length from the tip. However, the stem expands below the notches, and the base is wider than the shoulder. The base is flat.

Code 242: Projectile Point, Type II-C-2. Points of this type are identical to the Type II-C-1 points, except that they are serrated along the lateral sides.

Code 261: Projectile Point, Type III-B. Type III points are very large. Type III-B points are triangular and side-notched, very similar to those of Type II-C-1 except in size.

Code 271: Projectile Point, Fragment. This category includes any portion of a point (tip, base, or midsection) whose original shape (and type) is indiscernible.

Code 272: Projectile Point, Serrated Fragment. This category is similar to Code 271 (Projectile Point, Fragment), with the difference that these points show evidence of having been serrated.

Code 281: Projectile Point, Other Varieties. Those points not assignable to any of the above classifications (and those classes which were included in the list of expected types) were placed into this category. Each is unique, and constitutes a type unto itself.

Code 282: Projectile Point Preform. Included within this category are those artifacts suspected of being unfinished points or blanks for points. Such items are usually bifacially retouched and lack the refinements of secondary marginal retouch and final shaping.

Code 289: Biface. This category refers to bifacially flaked items of unknown function, although traditionally they might be called either "knives" or "points." They are too large to have been arrow points, and their primary use-wear, if any, is not bifacial attrition. It is possible that some of them are Archaic points.

Code 290: Bifacial Knife. This class of items is characterized by long, broad-bladed, bifacially retouched artifacts exhibiting secondary marginal retouch as well as frequently showing bifacial attrition. No notching or stemming is evidenced.

Code 291: Bifacial Resharpening Flake. Within this category have been included those flakes which Schaafsma has termed "retouch flakes" (1977: 181-182). These are characterized by use-wear on the proximal end (near the bulb of percussion), ending abruptly at the lateral margins. Generally, on the resharpening flakes recovered by this project, the original use-edge, formed by bifacial retouch, is clearly discernible above the bulb of percussion.

Code 301: Flaked Axe. A single large, relatively flat object made of chert and bifacially retouched was recovered. This item showed facial retouch as well as secondary marginal retouch, both on a much larger scale than appeared with the knives and scrapers. Both ends tapered to a wedge-like point in cross section, and were slightly rounded in outline. The item may have been hafted.

Code 303: Unknown. Those items which were entirely impossible to identify and assign to a distinct category were included within this classification. All exhibit at least some retouch; most are bifaces, but show little or no use-wear.

Code 204: Quartz Crystal. Quartz crystals have sometimes been found in prehistoric medicine bundles or in association with ceremonial activities. Therefore, the quartz crystals found by the Cyprus-Bagdad Project have been tabulated, although it is impossible to determine their actual function.

APPENDIX B

TERMINOLOGY FOR POTTERY AND GROUND STONE

Pottery Types

In identifying pottery types recovered in the course of the project, the following criteria were used:

Prescott Gray Ware

This category includes all previously recognized subtypes: Verde Gray, Verde Black-on-gray, Prescott Black-on-brown, Aquarius Black-on-gray, Aquarius Gray, Aquarius Black-on-orange, and Aquarius Orange. These ceramics can be viewed as representing either a single type or two types, if one distinguishes between painted and unpainted varieties (Euler and Dobyns 1962: 76-77).

Temper. Large amounts of large, angular (ground, crushed?), quartzitic temper (including feldspars and white opaque quartz). On orange specimens, temper tends to show through wash.

Paste. Better fired than in Tizon wares; walls tend to be fired through; more uniform coloration.

Mica Inclusions. Large amounts (usually muscovite, occasionally biotite), though this feature is not truly diagnostic in distinguishing between Prescott and Tizon wares, as all ceramic types in the area may contain mica.

Sherd Walls. Interior face worn off.

Exterior Colors. Orange, gray, brown, or black (often on same specimen).

Exterior Decoration. Wiping striations on both interior and exterior surfaces. Black painted designs on Prescott Black-on-gray, generally broad lines in geometric patterns. Organic paint.

(Colton 1958; Euler and Dobyns 1962; Dobyns, personal communication)

Tizon Brown Ware

Cerbat Brown

Temper. Clear to opaque, rounded (alluvial?) quartz sand temper, coarser than that found in Sandy Brown, finer than that found in Aquarius Brown (thus usually finer than that found in Prescott Gray).

Paste. Finely textured, with more temper than Sandy Brown, less than Aquarius Brown.

Mica Inclusions. Often in considerable quantity (usually muscovite, occasionally biotite), though this feature is not truly diagnostic in distinguishing between Prescott and Tizon wares, as all ceramic types in the area may contain mica.

Sherd Walls. Generally thinner than in the Prescott types.

Exterior Colors. Usually oxidized brown, can include grays, even oranges, though not as warm as in the Prescott wares. Surface scumming present.

Exterior Decoration. Occasional red paint (broad lines) or black paint (thin lines) in geometric patterns. Iron-based paint.

Aquarius Brown

Temper. Clear to opaque, rounded (alluvial?) quartz sand temper, coarser than that found in Cerbat Brown, generally nearly as coarse as that found in the Prescott wares.

Paste. Finely textured (though not as fine as Sandy Brown), with more temper content than Cerbat Brown; generally not as much temper as in the Prescott wares.

Mica Inclusions. Often in considerable quantity (usually muscovite, occasionally biotite), though this feature is not truly diagnostic in distinguishing between the Prescott and Tizon wares, as all ceramic types in the area may contain mica.

Sherd Walls. Generally thinner than in the Prescott types.

Exterior Colors. Oxidized browns, with reduced centers. Other colors include grays and reddish browns; not as warm as the Prescott colors. Surface scumming present.

Exterior Decoration. Black paint, exceedingly rare. Thin lines, patterns not well known.

(Dobyns and Euler 1958; Dobyns, personal communication)

Sandy Brown

Temper. Clear to opaque, rounded (alluvial?) temper, finer than in any other Tizon ware, much finer than in the Prescott types.

Paste. Finely textured, finer than in the other varieties of Tizon ware, with less temper content.

Mica Inclusions. Often in considerable quantity (usually muscovite, occasionally biotite), in generally finer particles than in the other Tizon wares, though this factor is not truly diagnostic in distinguishing between the Prescott and Tizon wares, as all ceramic types in the area may contain mica.

Sherd Walls. Generally thinner than in the Prescott types, and often thinner than in most Cerbat Brown or Aquarius Brown.

Exterior Colors. Generally oxidized browns, usually lighter than in the other Tizon wares, approaching a light tan. No scumming present.

Exterior Decoration. None.

(Dobyns and Euler 1958; Dobyns, personal communication)

Tizon Wiped (also called Cerbat Wiped)

Temper. Clear to opaque, rounded (alluvial?) quartz sand temper, about the same texture as that found in Cerbat Brown (in this particular sample).

Paste. Finely textured, with approximately the same amount of temper as in Cerbat Brown.

Mica Inclusions. Often in considerable quantity (usually muscovite, occasionally biotite), though this feature is not truly diagnostic in distinguishing between the Prescott and Tizon wares, as all ceramic types in the area may contain mica.

Sherd Walls. Generally thinner than in the Prescott wares.

Exterior Colors. Generally oxidized brown to gray, not as warm as in the Prescott wares.

Exterior Decoration. Exterior and/or interior intentionally
striated. No patterns; not painted.

(Dobyns and Euler 1958; Dobyns, personal communication)

Transitional Types

This term was applied to those specimens which exhibited
unmistakable characteristics of both Prescott and Tizon wares. For
instance, a sherd with large, angular temper (Prescott-like), but
exhibiting scumming (Tizon-like), would be placed in this category.
Similarly, a sherd with fine paste texture and medium-sized, rounded
quartz temper (Tizon-like), but with the interior surface eroded off
(Prescott-like), would also be included in this category.

Unidentifiable

This category includes primarily those sherds which were too
small in size or too poorly preserved to enable positive identifications through the analytical procedures utilized.

Exotic Types

The sherds tabulated within this classification included those
identified as definitely not of the Prescott or Tizon types, but of
some variety not indigenous to the area.

Rim Sherds

Sherds exhibiting a portion of the rim of the vessel have in
some cases been utilized to estimate vessel shape and number of vessels
(McGuire 1977). Those recovered from these seven sites proved to be
of insufficient size and quantity for this procedure.

Glossary of Ceramic Terms

The following glossary lists definitions applying to the ceramic
terms used in the above descriptions and in the text. The terms are
commonly used and accepted in the literature, but in many cases have
been assigned different meanings in different contexts. Thus, the
precise meanings used in this particular volume are presented here to
prevent any confusion.

Alluvial: Referring to materials originating from water-washed, unconsolidated sediments; river beds; floodplains; lake beds; and alluvial fans at the feet of mountains (American Geological Institute 1962: 12-13). Sand grains from such deposits have been generally rounded and smoothed by water action.

Bentonite: A clay formed from the decomposition of volcanic ash and largely composed of the minerals montmorillonite and beidellite (American Geological Institute 1962: 49). Generally has excessive shrinkage and cannot be used alone for pottery, but can be used mixed with kaolinite clay (Shepard 1956: 376-377).

Ground (or crushed): Refers to temper materials which, due to their sharp edges and angular fragmentation (as opposed to the rounded, smooth qualities of the alluvial materials), seem to have been purposely reduced in size by manual grinding or crushing with mano and metate or mortar and pestle.

Inclusions: Refers to any foreign matter in the clay, including impurities or natural inclusions (Shepard 1956: 18) or temper. In many cases, such as with the Cyprus-Bagdad Project ceramics, it is quite difficult to distinguish one from the other; hence, the term as used in this report combines the two.

Scumming: A natural occurrence of a thin, shiny layer which forms on the surface of fired clay vessels. This may be due to high sulphur content in the clay (Shepard 1956: 21), or may possibly be caused by the crystallizing of alkali salts (from the water used to moisten the clay) on the surface of the vessel as it dries prior to firing; the salts then fuse during the firing (Colton 1953: 36; Shepard 1956: 193). Scumming may be confused with slipping the surface of the vessel (Shepard 1956: 193).

Temper: Includes only those nonplastic materials added to the clay to reduce shrinkage and insure its even drying, thus lessening the risk of cracking (Shepard 1956: 25). Unfortunately, this material cannot always be identified as temper (see Inclusions).

Ground Stone Artifacts

The following list provides definitions of the types of ground stone artifacts discovered at the seven sites investigated by the Cyprus-Bagdad Project.

Mano: Small, deliberately shaped stone held in the hand and passed back and forth over a nether stone, thus grinding or crushing any material placed between them. The grinding surfaces are generally flat to slightly convex; there are usually two of them on opposite faces of the tabular stone.

Type I: Smallest variety, generally rounded-rectangular in outline, with a thickness about one-fourth the item's width, and the width about one-half the length.

Type II: Larger variety, round in outline, with a thickness approximately one-half the diameter.

Grinding Stone: Stone collected and used with little or no modification (other than perhaps roughening of the grinding surfaces). Usually smaller than a mano, and having a smoother surface texture. May have one or two flat grinding surfaces. Used in the same manner as the mano.

Metate: One type of nether stone, which is placed upon the ground or floor and remains stationary as the mano or grinding stone passes over it, grinding any materials placed between them. The lateral margins show signs of having been deliberately shaped, and usually have only a single flat or concave grinding surface.

Type I: Trough metate, with a deep groove or trough pecked and ground through the surface of the stone, often to a depth of three-fourths or more of the thickness of the stone. Usually open at one end, closed at the other, with vertical sides.

Type II: Basin metate, with a shallow, oval depression pecked and ground into the surface of the stone, generally not more than a few centimeters deep. Closed at both ends, with sloping walls.

Mortar: Circular to oval stone, smaller than a metate, and with a thickness generally exceeding the diameter, with a deep, round depression pecked and ground into the top surface, which is generally rounded or somewhat conical toward the bottom. Materials are placed into this closed hole and beaten with a pestle to reduce or crush them.

Pestle: Cylindrical, hand-held stone or wooden object used to pound the contents of a mortar. Only the ends of these objects show use-wear, as opposed to manos, on which the flattest surfaces show such wear.

Hammerstone: Cobble of varying size, generally fist-sized and spherical, and usually composed of dense, hard, cryptocrystalline materials. Used for removing flakes from cores and preforms in the production of chipped stone artifacts; also used for manufacturing and maintaining ground stone implements, and occasionally for other tasks, such as the softening of hides for leather (Lange and Riley 1966). Exhibits considerable battering over all convex surfaces.

Slab: Flat sheet of rock (volcanic or sandstone) utilized (with little or no shaping or modification) as nether stone in a manner similar to that of a metate. The slab remains stationary while the mano or grinding stone is passed back and forth over it, grinding the material placed between them. Note: Those items listed as fragmentary for this class of artifacts undoubtedly include fragments of nearly all other classes of ground stone artifacts. Due to their size and incompleteness, a number of these objects were impossible to identify.

Fragmentary items: All those items which seemed to be represented by less than one-half of their original size and shape. In many cases the item's original size and shape could be estimated from the recovered fragment; in other cases, the fragments were "unidentifiable," and were tentatively included in the category of slab fragments.

APPENDIX C

ABIOTIC RESOURCES, by Ben Foose

Geology encompasses many areas of significance to the archaeologist. Geological studies enable the archaeologist to determine the stratigraphy of a site, help reconstruct ancient environments, and can even help interpret the past and present life patterns of cultural groups as they relate to the environment in which they live (Augustithis 1974). Intercultural relations can also be established by tracing origins of materials and relating them to possible trade routes. This paper focuses on determining mineral resource loci of those raw materials used in the manufacture of lithic tools by the inhabitants of the Cyprus-Bagdad Project area.

This overview of the geological history of the area will focus on the Tertiary and Quarternary periods because of their significance in terms of mineral resources used by the inhabitants of the area. A description of the present physiography and the identification of minerals examined in a walk-over survey of two of the excavated sites will provide a greater understanding of the processes leading to the occupation of the area by prehistoric groups. The types, density, distribution, and relation of mineral resources to site location will enable the researcher to better understand human adaptations to the environment.

In Archeozoic and Proterozoic times, the project area, located about 32 km (20 miles) west of Bagdad, Arizona, was part of a large oceanic basin. Large, initially igneous bodies (impossible to interpret because of constant metamorphic alteration) make up the majority of these deposits and represent more than half of all geologic time represented.

The Paleozoic is best characterized by a series of transgressing and regressing seas (Effinger 1936) that left deposits of sandstone, conglomerates, shale, and limestone over the existing granite/gneiss, schist, and diorite porphyry deposits of the Precambrian. The Mesozoic era was basically an era of erosion and deformation of the Paleozoic deposits, exposing some of the older Precambrian deposits (Eardley 1951).

The Cenozoic was the last major geologic era leading to the present. Broken down into two periods, the Tertiary and Quaternary, this era witnessed the production or exposure of almost all the mineral

197

resources used in the manufacture of lithic tools in the Cyprus-Bagdad
Project area. The Tertiary Period was a time of prolonged volcanic
activity throughout the western part of what is now Arizona (Lee 1908),
and was the time of origin of the volcanic deposits in the project area
today. Widespread block-faulting was also prevalent at this time,
creating low-relief, mountainous topography. During the late Cretaceous
to early Tertiary transition, the Laramide orogeny began with an uplift
during the Paleocene Epoch that resulted in erosion and deposition of
early Eocene Epoch beds of conglomerates, arkose, limestone, and sandstone (Effinger 1936), with limestone the dominant depositional feature
in the project area. This limestone later precipitated chert nodules
that were used much later by inhabitants of the area for the manufacture
of tools. The uplift was followed by a thrust fault that placed Precambrian to early Paleozoic beds of granite/gneiss on top of the
Eocene limestone bed during the Oligocene Epoch. At this point, there
occurred a period of erosion that terminated with an overlap of volcanics, probably of Miocene age (Eardley 1951). These volcanic
deposits include tuff, breccia, and rhyolitic to andesitic lava flows,
the latter providing more material for lithic manufacture and the tuff
constituting a possible source for ceramic temper. During this time,
the thrusting and high-angle faulting in progress was responsible for
the development of the Basin and Range physiographic province in which
the Cyprus-Bagdad Project area is located.

The early Pliocene was characterized by massive basalt flows
followed by folding and then erosion that produced conglomerates,
sandstone, siltstone, mudstone, and limestone deposits in the lower
elevations (Eardley 1951). Late Pliocene deposits consist mostly of
poorly sorted conglomerates. By the end of the Tertiary Period, the
Laramide orogeny had ceased its major activity, but volcanic activity
continued, producing fine-grained basalt overlying the earlier folded
beds of the Pliocene.

The Quaternary was chiefly a period of extensive pediment
development around the mountains (Wilson 1962). Basalt flows continued
into the early Pleistocene, with late Pleistocene erosional activity
producing pediment gravels of coarse clastics making up the valley and
basin fill, in many areas thousands of feet thick. During this erosional process, the Precambrian deposits of granite/gneiss, schist, and
diorite porphyry were exposed, along with other archaeologically
significant deposits of quartzite, limestone, chert, chalcedony, basalt,
rhyolite, and possibly obsidian. This process has continued to the
present, producing talus slopes and drainage systems containing clastics
ranging in size from fine-grained silts and sands to coarse cobbles of
igneous and metamorphic material. Burro Creek is the major drainage
system responsible for the removal of clastic materials from the
immediate project area. This watercourse in turn empties into the Big
Sandy River; this river and the Bill Williams River make up the major
drainage systems of the region. The present physiography of the

project area is essentially the same throughout, with mountains of Precambrian mineral composition capped by Tertiary volcanic deposits of basalt, rhyolite, and andesite. Extensive wash cutting and erosion of earlier (Tertiary) deposited sediments is also prevalent (Wilson 1962).

Because of the limited time available for a walk-over geological survey of the area, this report will deal with only two of the seven sites excavated. The sites chosen, AZ M:7:2 and AZ M:7:3, were selected because of their proximity and the potential for intersite correlation of activity. AZ M:7:2 has also produced firm evidence of habitation.

After viewing the geology of the project area and the sites contained therein, it was found that a study of sites AZ M:7:2 and AZ M:7:3 would be representative of the other sites from a geological standpoint due to the lack of variation in mineral resource availability. The present geology of the sites under study is indicative of the late Tertiary volcanics common to this region.

AZ M:7:2 is located on a terrace at the confluence of Burro Creek and Cornwall Wash. Burro Creek, which generally flows in a southwesterly direction, flows due south at this point to the east of the terrace on which AZ M:7:2 is located. The entire creek bed consists of coarse clastic material transported from the surrounding relief, and includes granite, quartzite, gneiss, schist, and basalt. These materials are mixed with fine-grained silt, sand, and gravel, and date to the late Tertiary and Quaternary periods.

Along Cornwall Wash (which forms the northern boundary of the terrace on which AZ M:7:2 is located) are large Precambrian granite/gneiss outcrops exposed by the erosional activity of the wash. On the north side of and beyond Cornwall Wash is a large basalt deposit; rising out of this relief are the Aquarius Cliffs, composed of granite/gneiss and capped by a rhyolitic to andesitic layer (Lee 1908). Following Cornwall Wash westward for about 200 meters, a fork is encountered. Here, a large deposit of Eocene limestone sandwiched between layers of granite/gneiss dips to the southeast and is in the process of decomposing and altering to chert. Following the left fork of the wash about 50 meters in a southwesterly direction, one encounters a large deposit of volcanic tuff, reddish-white to white in color, on the left bank of the wash. This deposit continues over the bank to the southeast, borders the south side of the terrace on which AZ M:7:2 is located, and terminates at Burro Creek.

To the south and southwest of AZ M:7:2 are large outcrops of Precambrian to early Cambrian granite/gneiss capped by a basalt flow that is also late Tertiary to Quaternary in age. Downslope from the granite/gneiss outcrop is an extensive bed of chert lenses. Above and below the chert bed, a tuff slope falls off and is littered with chunks of basalt, granite, gneiss, and chert. There appears to be a correlation between this chert bed and the limestone altering to chert bed found at the first fork of Cornwall Wash. The fact that this bed has fully altered chert lenses, is situated at a higher elevation, and does not have a visible granite/gneiss deposit underlying it does not alter the possibility of this association. Evidence supporting their association is derived from the fact that the dip of both beds is in the same direction; a fault line runs between the two beds, accounting for their displacement; and the granite/gneiss bed that should be underlying the chert bed is probably present, but covered by the tuff deposit on the hillside. The fully altered chert bed could be due to differing pressures resulting from the fault that displaced the bed. It should be mentioned that this deposit of chert nodules is in association with a very decomposed limestone bed that has almost completely disappeared. There are numerous chert nodules on the ground in the area, thus facilitating collection for lithic manufacture, and the deposit itself could be easily quarried, though there is no evidence of such past activity. Evidence of quarrying, however, could have easily been obliterated by weathering in this case.

The entire area northwest to southwest of AZ M:7:2 is littered with chunks of basalt, rhyolite, chert, and chalcedony, with some quartzite in association. To the south, about 200 meters from the site and along the west bank of Burro Creek, is a deposit of large, tabular, basalt slabs, suitable for metates, which have become detached from the existing basalt beds through weathering processes.

From 0.75 km to 1.25 km east of AZ M:7:2 and beyond Burro Creek, the third of three terraces spreads out to the foot of Centipede Mesa. This terrace is covered with a basalt cobble pavement mixed with sand, tuff, and agglomerate, probably of Miocene age. In the middle of this terrace and directly east of AZ M:7:2 lies site AZ M:7:3. In association with AZ M:7:3 and its deposits of basalt, tuff, and agglomerate are large cobbles and boulders of a granular, grayish-white chert; many have been utilized as cores. This chert does not resemble that from any of the deposits found near AZ M:7:2; its origin is unknown. The mesas beyond AZ M:7:3 are made up entirely of basalt that is late Tertiary to Quarternary in age.

The archaeological record at AZ M:7:2 and AZ M:7:3 (as well as at all other sites investigated during the project) shows that the minerals used for toolmaking were chert, chalcedony, rhyolite, quartzite, basalt, and obsidian. As has been shown, all of these materials are readily available in the surrounding area, with the possible exception of obsidian. Obsidian is an extrusive igneous lava that cools so rapidly that it fails to crystallize, giving it a glassy appearance. It is high in silica content and is the uncrystallized equivalent of rhyolite and granite (Pough 1960). The walk-over survey of sites AZ M:7:2 and AZ M:7:3 failed to locate any obsidian deposits, but it is entirely possible that such deposits do occur in the area because of their close structural association to that of rhyolite. However, the small ratio of obsidian to rhyolite and other mineral specimens recovered from archaeological context is a good indication of a lack of obsidian deposits in the area. Obsidian is highly valued because of its excellent fracturing properties; if deposits did occur naturally in the area, it is probable that a far greater number of obsidian artifacts and debitage would have been uncovered. Walter Duering (Arizona Department of Transportation) has stated that small "Apache tears" can be found in Burro Creek where it crosses Highway 93, about 24 km (15 miles) south of sites AZ M:7:2 and AZ M:7:3. However, obsidian in this form is rarely of value in tool manufacture, due to the small size of the specimens. With a notable exception, most of the obsidian found in archaeological context was of a black color with no impurities, much like the obsidian described in the western area of the San Francisco volcanic field (Schreiber and Breed 1971). If the obsidian recovered from the seven project sites is not found in geological context in the project area, it could possibly have been derived from the above-mentioned area.

Thirty-eight pieces of obsidian were found in archaeological context at AZ M:7:2, while none were found at AZ M:7:3. Thirty-one are of a pure black color, five are banded, one has red inclusions, and one is of a dull gray and black color. The obsidian sample makes up three percent of the total lithic assemblage at AZ M:7:2, indicating its scarcity in the area. Ken Austin has informed Laurance Linford that an obsidian deposit does occur in a bed on the south side of Pine Canyon where it joins Burro Creek near the Harper Ranch, about 8 km (5 miles) upstream from AZ M:7:2. Why the site's inhabitants did not use these sources more is unknown, unless they were simply unaware of the presence of these deposits. Due to a lack of time to study the project area, the author was unable to look for this deposit in order to verify its presence and any cultural activity associated with it. The previously mentioned variety of obsidian characterized by dull gray and black coloration due to impurities within its structure has been traced to Floyd Mountain in the San Francisco volcanic field. Its presence at AZ M:7:2, then, indicates contact with groups from that area.

Rhyolite is another extrusive igneous lava that crystallizes to produce a fine-grained, felsitic texture. The presence of quartz is necessary for a felsite to be classified as a rhyolite (Hurlbut 1971); materials found in both natural and archaeological contexts exhibit this characteristic. Rhyolite occurring in archaeological context displays shades varying from light red to reddish purple and dark brown, and sometimes exhibits whitish or grayish flow lines or "banding." Rhyolite outcrops were not discovered at AZ M:7:2 and AZ M:7:3, but the surrounding areas were littered with large chunks of rhyolite and rhyolite-welded tuffs of the same coloration as those found in archaeological context, indicating local collecting activity to obtain this material. Although the origin of these rhyolite chunks is uncertain, they must have been transported from some local source (dikes, plugs, or the rhyolitic cap on the Aquarius Cliffs) by erosional processes. The only other known deposit of rhyolite in the area is a large out-crop about 19 km (12 miles) southeast of both sites near a third site, AZ M:7:4 (see Arizona Bureau of Mines Map of Yavapai County, 1958). Use of these deposits for quarrying or collecting is doubtful because of the distance required for transportation, and because of the ready availability of this material in its raw form in the vicinity of AZ M:7:2 and AZ M:7:3. Although its fracturing qualities do not equal those of obsidian, chert, or chalcedony, rhyolite is readily formed into usable shapes and can present a relatively sharp edge. It is also softer and more easily worked than quartzite.

Rhyolite was used sparingly at AZ M:7:2 and AZ M:7:3, accounting for only 6.4 percent of the total lithic sample at the former and 1.1 percent of the total lithic sample at the latter site. Rhyolite is found closer to AZ M:7:2 than AZ M:7:3, and the specimens found archaeo-logically at AZ M:7:3 were apparently derived from the source near AZ M:7:2. Also, since there are large quantities of chert and quartzite at AZ M:7:3, it would seem likely that these materials would have been utilized far more readily than would effort have been spent to obtain other materials at a greater distance. It has even been hypothesized that the primary function of AZ M:7:3 was the extraction of the cherts and quartzites, further reducing the likelihood that other raw materials would appear at the site. This hypothesis is further substantiated by the extremely low incidence of chalcedony (1.1 percent) at the site and the absence of any other lithic raw materials.

Basalt is a fine-grained, black, dark brown, or reddish brown extrusive lava of the gabbro family that is composed mostly of plagio-clase, feldspars, pyroxene, and olivine (Pearl 1960). There is no quartz in association with basalts. The basalts of the project area are partially altered on the surface by weathering processes, thus producing a vesicular appearance. Although some debitage flakes of basalt were recovered, basalt was used almost exclusively for the manu-facture of ground stone implements, as evidenced by the large number of basalt manos and metates found. The most likely place of basalt pro-curement for AZ M:7:2 is the late Tertiary to Quarternary deposit located about 200 m south (downstream) along Burro Creek, where basalt is available in already detached slabs of convenient size for making metates. Burro Creek and the surrounding hills are an excellent source for manos, and an occasional slab suitable for making a metate can be found. No basalt was found at AZ M:7:3, while only 21 pieces of worked basalt were found at AZ M:7:2, most of those (18) being unutilized flakes.

Quartzite is formed by the metamorphism of sandstone, and is among the hardest and most resistant to wear of all rocks (Pough 1960).

Although this hardness could result in a longer use-life of a tool manufactured from it, quartzite exhibits poorer fracturing properties than do other available materials. Nonetheless, a large number of quartzite artifacts and debitage were recovered from both sites. Quartzite found in geological context in the area of AZ M:7:2 and AZ M:7:3 and in archaeological context was mostly grayish or white, with some reddish stains from iron oxide impurities. The occurrence of quartzite in the area is confined mostly to washes and to Burro Creek, with some material scattered on the hillsides around AZ M:7:2 and on the terrace around AZ M:7:3. The source deposits of this quartzite are unkown, but could have been produced by the metamorphism of Precambrian or Devonian beds of sandstone which have since been eroded away. Quartzite is the second most utilized lithic material found in archaeological context at AZ M:7:2 and AZ M:7:3, accounting for 18.2 percent of the entire lithic sample at the former and 38.6 percent of the entire sample at the latter site. The incidence of quartzite seems unexpectedly high if one considers the fact that there are better materials available for manufacture of stone tools. This high rate of use probably results from the ready availability of the material and its durability.

The preference for a gray-colored quartzite by the inhabitants of both sites seems to reflect the availability of this material, by far the most plentiful of the quartzites geologically available. This gray quartzite accounts for 58.8 percent of the quartzite sample at AZ M:7:2 and 75.6 percent of the sample at AZ M:7:3. White quartzite was the second most utilized, accounting for 27 percent of the quartzite at AZ M:7:2 and 21.5 percent at AZ M:7:3. Brown and gold-colored quartzites account for the remainder of the sample.

It should be noted at this point that some of the material here classified as quartzite was very fine-grained and could possibly be a grainy chert. The fracture lines were much smoother than in the coarse-grained quartzites, but still were not as smooth as those observed in chert. These materials were classified as quartzites because their fracture planes appeared to exhibit fractures through the crystalline grains, a characteristic common to quartzites.

Chalcedony is a microscopically crystallized quartz mineral whose individual crystals are slender fibers arranged in parallel bands (Hurlbut 1971). The surface tends to be botryoidal, smooth, and translucent. The agate variety of chalcedony, grayish white in color, is the only variety found in the project area; its occurrences were restricted mostly to the hillsides west and southwest of AZ M:7:2. Such material occurs much less frequently than do the rhyolite, chert, and basalt associated with it. This circumstance, coupled with the fact that all of the chalcedony was structured with hollow pockets, makes it less desirable for lithic manufacture. Most of the chalcedony cobbles were too thin to work with, which probably accounts for the small number of tools made from this material, even though its fracturing properties are good. Although no chalcedony deposits were found in the vicinity of AZ M:7:3, some chalcedony was found in the archaeological context at that site, indicating that the sources near AZ M:7:2 were probably used for the procurement of this mineral.

Chalcedony accounts for 10 percent of the entire lithic sample at AZ M:7:2 and 1.1 percent of the sample at AZ M:7:3. Although chalcedony is superior to quartzite and even to chert in its fracturing properties and in producing sharper edges, the low quality of the chalcedony available in the area of these two sites most likely accounts for its relatively seldom occurrence in the archaeological record.

Two varieties of chalcedony were common to both sites archaeologically. At AZ M:7:3, only three pieces of chalcedony were found, one of a white color and the other two of a gray color. This small sample size reflects the low quality of the chalcedony and hence its infrequent use. Since the chalcedony from AZ M:7:3 is not available in the vicinity of that site, but matches the types found around AZ M:7:2, it was probably obtained from the vicinity of the latter site. The white and gray chalcedonies account for almost 60 percent of the chalcedony sample at AZ M:7:2; the remaining 40 percent consists of chalcedony of various other colors and inclusions. In all cases, the chalcedony utilized by the inhabitants of both sites was available in the vicinity of AZ M:7:2.

Chert is also a microscopically grained quartz, but without the banding and translucence common to chalcedony (Pough 1960), although some of the chert does possess a translucent quality. Chert usually contains more impurities and occurs in a wider variety of colors than does chalcedony. The archaeological record shows chert to be the most common mineral for the manufacture of lithic tools at AZ M:7:2 and AZ M:7:3. Chert in fact possesses better fracturing properties and is fairly abundant in the region surrounding these two sites. Chert occurs in large chunks in association with rhyolite, chalcedony, and basalt to the west and southwest of AZ M:7:2, and in a large deposit of lenses to the southwest. Red, gray, white, brown, and gold-colored cherts appear in both geological and archaeological contexts. The limestone altering to chert deposit in Cornwall Wash was utilized sparingly for raw materials for lithic manufacture by the inhabitants of AZ M:7:2; the brittleness of this material renders its usefulness doubtful. A gray chert differing from that found near AZ M:7:2 appears in both geological and archaeological contexts in the vicinity of AZ M:7:3, and was used considerably. The presence of cherts of varying shades of brown to reddish brown at AZ M:7:3 indicates the use of alternate sources such as those found around AZ M:7:2, since no such deposits occur in the vicinity of AZ M:7:3.

Chert is by far the mineral most commonly used for lithic tool production, accounting for 60.2 percent of the total lithic sample at AZ M:7:2 and 56.3 percent of the total lithic sample at AZ M:7:3. The chert assemblage from AZ M:7:2 includes all the chert types available in the area, except for a gray variety with white inclusions and a gray variety with gray inclusions found in the vicinity of AZ M:7:3. Gray cherts alone account for 85.3 percent of the chert at AZ M:7:3, with the remainder of the sample composed of white chert (9 percent), brown chert (5.1 percent), and gold chert (0.6 percent). At AZ M:7:2, gray chert accounts for 63.4 percent of the total chert recovered, with the remainder comprised of brown chert (14.2 percent), white chert (12.7 percent), gold chert (5.4 percent), and other varieties (4.3 percent). This last 4.3 percent of the sample from AZ M:7:2 includes cherts not found at AZ M:7:3.

The gray chert with white inclusions and the gray variety with gray inclusions occur geologically only in the vicinity of AZ M:7:3 and account for 68 percent of the gray cherts and over 50 percent of the total chert sample from this site. All other chert varieties found in archaeological context at this site are not available there geologically and were probably obtained from the vicinity of AZ M:7:2. Studies of trace element compositions of these minerals would prove or disprove this hypothesis. The gray chert with white inclusions accounts for approximately 32 percent of the entire chert sample found in archaeological context at AZ M:7:2, indicating a considerable preference for the use of this particular variety at this site, since the inhabitants had to travel farther to obtain this chert than they would have had to for any other chert available to them. This preference may reflect the fact that this type of chert occurs in larger cobbles than do any of the other varieties, thus enabling the detachment of larger flakes so that larger tools could be manufactured. This particular type of chert does not seem of any better quality than the others.

The deposits of tuff west to south of AZ M:7:2 are loosely packed and crush easily. The tuff, along with the sandy deposits in the washes and creek bed, could have been ready sources of temper for ceramic manufacture, although there is no evidence that the tuff was thus utilized at this site.

In all cases, minerals were identified using the basic methods available to the geologist for mineral identification, including both testing and visual inspection of physical characteristics for color, patterns, luster, hardness, scratch color, cleavage, fracture, reaction to dilute (1:10) hydrochloric acid, and inspection under the hand lens and binocular microscope. These characteristics were then compared to those listed in several manuals on the identification of rocks and minerals. Findings were later confirmed by the Department of Geology at the University of Arizona.

Correlation of minerals used for lithic tool manufacture at AZ M:7:2 and AZ M:7:3 with factors of workability and availability indicates that the inhabitants of those sites utilized the minerals locally available to them in accordance with those two factors. The table below lists various lithic raw materials in descending order of most to least used material, and compares them on the basis of workability and availability.

Table 38. Comparison of lithic raw material types

Material Type	Workability	Availability
Chert	Very good	Common
Quartzite	Good	Common
Chalcedony	Very good	Moderately common
Rhyolite	Good	Moderately common
Obsidian	Excellent	Rare

With the exception of obsidian, it can be safely stated that all lithic materials found in archaeological context at AZ M:7:2 and AZ M:7:3 were procured in the immediate vicinity of those sites. This conclusion is based on a positive correlation of stone recovered in archaeological context as compared to mineral resources found in geological context. The Floyd Mountain obsidian recovered from AZ M:7:2 indicates direct or indirect contact with groups in the area encompassing the San Francisco volcanic field. The other obsidian recovered could also have originated from this same region, or it could be traced to Pine Canyon or to some other source. The "Apache tears" located in Burro Creek at Highway 93 are small, and it is unlikely that they were used. The archaeological record of the project area in fact produces no indication of their use.

In order to confirm the hypothesis regarding mineral resource procurement for the Cyprus-Bagdad Project area and to clear up the confusion surrounding the procurement of obsidian, further investigation is needed. Several methods of analyzing the trace elements within a mineral can be used to trace the origin of obsidian found in archaeological context. Neutron activation (Griffin, Gordus, and Wright 1969; Frison and others 1968), emission spectroscopy (Green and associates

1967), X-ray spectroscopy (Parks and Tieh 1966), and optical spectrography (Renfrew, Cann, and Dixon 1965) have all been successfully used in analyzing the trace elements of obsidian samples. By comparing the trace elements of obsidian artifacts with trace elements in obsidian samples from a known geological context, it can be determined whether the two samples originate from the same source or not. Any one of these processes could also be used in identifying sources of other lithic materials such as chert, chalcedony, basalt, and quartzite. Using one of the above-mentioned methods for analyzing trace elements of lithic samples would put to rest any doubt as to the origins of these lithic materials.

REFERENCES

American Geological Institute
   1962   Dictionary of geological terms. Garden City, New York:
             Anchor Books.

Andrews, Tracy J.
   1975   The archaeological resources of the Harquvar, Aquarius,
             and Hualapai Planning Units of the Bureau of Land Manage-
             ment. Arizona State Museum Archaeological Series 73.

Asch, David L.
   1975   On sample size problems and the uses of nonprobabilistic
             sampling. In Sampling in Archaeology, edited by James W.
             Mueller, pp. 170-191. Tucson: University of Arizona
             Press.

Augustithis, S. S.
   1974   On the role of geology in tribal life patterns. Bulletin
             of the Geological Society of Greece.

Baldwin, Gordon C.
   1950   Archaeological survey of the Lake Mead area. In For the
             Dean: essays in anthropology in honor of Byron Cummings,
             edited by Eric K. Reed and D. S. King, pp. 41-49. Tucson
             and Santa Fe: Hohokam Museum Association and Southwest
             Monuments Association.

Barnett, Franklin
   1970   Matli Ranch Ruins: a report of excavation of five small
             prehistoric Indian ruins of the Prescott Culture in Arizona.
             Museum of Northern Arizona Technical Series 10.

Binford, Lewis R.
   1964   Some considerations of archaeological research design.
             American Antiquity 29: 423-441.

   1968   Post-Pleistocene adaptations. In New perspectives in
             archaeology, edited by Sally R. Binford and Lewis R.
             Binford, pp. 313-341. Chicago: Aldine.

Bolton, Herbert E.
   1950   Pageant in the wilderness: the story of the Escalante
             expedition to the Interior Basin, 1776. Salt Lake City:
             Utah Historical Society.

Bolton, Herbert E. (editor)
    1916   Spanish exploration in the Southwest, 1542-1706. New York: Charles Scribner's Sons.

Carter, Harvey L.
    1971   Jedediah Smith. In The mountain men and the fur trade of the Far West (Vol. 8), edited by LeRoy R. Hafen, pp. 331-348. Glendale, California: Arthur H. Clark.

Caywood, Louis P.
    1936   Fitzmaurice Ruin. In Spicer and Caywood, pp. 87-115.

Chapman, Richard M.
    1973   Lithic analysis techniques. In Human systems research: technical manual. 1973 survey of the Tularosa Basin. Albuquerque.

Collins, Michael B.
    1975   Lithic technology as a means of processual inference. In Lithic technology: making and using stone tools, edited by Earl Swanson, pp. 15-34. The Hague: Moulton Publishers.

Colton, Harold S.
    1939   Prehistoric culture units and their relationships in northern Arizona. Museum of Northern Arizona Bulletin 17.

    1945   The Patayan problem in the Colorado River Valley. Southwestern Journal of Anthropology 1: 114-121.

    1953   Potsherds: an introduction to the study of prehistoric Southwestern ceramics and their use in historic reconstruction. Museum of Northern Arizona Bulletin 25.

Colton, Harold S. (editor)
    1958   Pottery types of the Southwest. Museum of Northern Arizona Ceramic Series 3D.

Coues, Elliot
    1900   On the trail of a Spanish pioneer: the diary and itinerary of Francisco Garcés. New York: Francis P. Harper.

Crabtree, Don E.
    1972   An introduction to flintworking. Occasional Papers of the Idaho State University Museum 28.

Davis, Emma Lou
    1963   The Desert Culture of the western Great Basin: a lifeway of seasonal transhumance. American Antiquity 29: 202-212.

Davis, E. L., C. W. Brott, and D. L. Weide
　　1969　　The Western Lithic Co-Tradition. San Diego Museum Papers 6.

Deetz, James F.
　　1967　　Invitation to Archaeology. Garden City, New York: Natural
　　　　　　History Press.

Dobyns, Henry F.
　　1956　　Prehistoric Indian occupation within the eastern area of
　　　　　　the Yuman Complex. MS. Master's Thesis, Department of
　　　　　　Anthropology, University of Arizona, Tucson.

　　1957　　The Yavapai fighters: kinship structure and territorial
　　　　　　range of a Hualapai congery. A report sent to Marks and
　　　　　　Marks of Phoenix, and to Strasser, Spiegleberg, Fried, and
　　　　　　Frank of Washington, D.C. MS. Arizona State Museum
　　　　　　Library, Tucson.

Dobyns, Henry F., and Robert C. Euler
　　1956　　Ethnographic and archaeological identification of Walapai
　　　　　　pottery. Paper presented at the 32nd Annual Meeting of
　　　　　　the Southwestern and Rocky Mountain Division, American
　　　　　　Association for the Advancement of Science, Las Cruces,
　　　　　　N.M.

　　1958　　Tizon Brown Ware: a descriptive revision. In Colton
　　　　　　(editor).

　　1960a　　Aboriginal socio-psychological structure and the ethnic
　　　　　　group concept of the Pai of northwestern Arizona. MS.
　　　　　　Museum of Northern Arizona.

　　1960b　　A brief history of the Northeastern Pai. Plateau 32: 49-57.

Doelle, William H.
　　1975　　Desert resources and Hohokam subsistence: the Conoco
　　　　　　Florence Project. Arizona State Museum Archaeological Series
　　　　　　103.

Drucker, Philip
　　1941　　Culture element distributions: XVII Yuman-Piman. Anthropo-
　　　　　　logical Records 6(3). Berkeley: University of California
　　　　　　Press.

Eardley, A. J.
　　1951　　Structural geology of North America. New York: Harper &
　　　　　　Row.

Effinger, William L.
1936   Geology of the southwestern United States. United States
        Department of the Interior, National Park Service,
        Berkeley, California.

Euler, Robert C.
1958   Walapai culture-history. Ph.D. dissertation, University of
        New Mexico. Ann Arbor: Microfilms Press.

1963   Archaeological problems in western and northwestern Arizona,
        1962. Plateau 35: 78-85.

1968   An archaeological survey of a portion of the proposed Granite
        Reef Aqueduct, central Arizona. MS. Center for Archaeological
        Studies, Prescott College, Prescott, Arizona.

Euler, Robert C., and Henry F. Dobyns
1956   Tentative correlations of Arizona Upland ceramics. Paper
        presented at the 32nd Annual Meeting of the Southwestern
        and Rocky Mountain Division, American Association for the
        Advancement of Science, Las Cruces, N.M.

1962   Excavations west of Prescott, Arizona. Plateau 34: 69-84.

Favour, Alpheus H.
1936   Old Bill Williams, mountain man. Chapel Hill: University
        of North Carolina Press.

Frison, George C.
1968   A functional analysis of certain chipped stone tools.
        American Antiquity 33: 149-155.

Frison, G., G. Wright, J. Griffin, and A. Gordus
1968   Neutron activation analysis of obsidian: an example of its
        relevance to northwestern Plains archaeology. Plains
        Anthropologist 13(41): 209-217.

Fuller, Steven L.
1975   The archaeological resources of the Black Mountains Planning
        Unit and the Cerbat Mountains Planning Unit of the Bureau of
        Land Management. Arizona State Museum Archaeological Series
        70.

Gifford, E. W.
1932   The Southeastern Yavapai. University of California Publica-
        tions in American Archaeology and Ethnology 29(3): 177-252.

1936   The Northeastern and Western Yavapai. University of Cali-
        fornia Publications in American Archaeology and Ethnology
        34(4): 247-354.

Gladwin, Harold S.
1957   A history of the ancient Southwest. Portland, Maine: Bond
        Wheelwright.

Gladwin, Winifred, and Harold S. Gladwin
1930   The western range of the Red-on-buff Culture. Medallion
        Papers 5. Globe: Gila Pueblo.

1934   A method for designation of cultures and their variances.
        Medallion Papers 15. Globe: Gila Pueblo.

Goodyear, Albert C.
1975   A general research design for highway archeology in South
        Carolina. The Institute of Archeology and Anthropology
        Notebook 7(1). University of South Carolina, Columbia.

Gould, Richard A.
1978   The anthropology of human residues. American Anthropologist
        80: 815-835.

Granger, Byrd H.
1960   Will C. Barne's Arizona place names. Tucson: University of
        Arizona Press.

Green, R.C., R. R. Brooks, and R. D. Reeves
1967   Characterization of New Zealand obsidians by emission
        spectroscopy. New Zealand Journal of Science 10: 675-682.

Griffin, James B., A.A. Gordus, and G. A. Wright
1969   Identification of the sources of Hopewellian obsidian in
        the Middlewest. American Antiquity 34: 1-14.

Hackett, Charles W. (editor)
1926   Historical documents relating to New Mexico, etc. (Vol. 2),
        collected by Adolph Bandelier. Washington, D.C.: Carnegie
        Institution of Washington.

Hammack, Nancy S.
1975   An archaeological survey of the Cyprus-Bagdad Copper Company
        pipeline right-of-way. Arizona State Museum Archaeological
        Series 90.

Hammond, George P.
1926   Don Juan de Oñate and the founding of New Mexico. New
        Mexico Historical Review 1(4).

Hammond, George P., and Agapito Rey
1929   Expedition into New Mexico made by Antonio de Espejo 1582-
        1583, as revealed in the journal of Diego Perez de Luxan,
        a member of the party. The Quivira Society, University of
        Southern California.

Hargrave, Lyndon L.
1938   Results of a study of the Cohonina Branch of the Patayan
        Culture in 1938. <u>Museum of Northern Arizona Notes</u>,
        Flagstaff.

Haury, Emil W.
1950   <u>The stratigraphy and archaeology of Ventana Cave, Arizona.</u>
        Tucson: University of Arizona Press.

1976   <u>The Hohokam: desert farmers and craftsmen. Excavations at
        Snaketown, 1964-1965.</u> Tucson: University of Arizona Press.

Henry, Don O., C. Vance Haynes, and Bruce Bradley
1976   Quantitative variations in flaked stone debitage. <u>Plains
        Anthropologist</u> 21: 57-61.

Hester, Thomas R., and Robert F. Heizer
1973   Arrow points or knives? Comments on the proposed function
        of "Stockton points." <u>American Antiquity</u> 38: 220-221.

Honea, K. M.
1965   A morphology of scrapers and their production. <u>Southwestern
        Lore</u> 31(2).

Hurlbut, Cornelius S.
1971   <u>Dana's manual of mineralogy.</u> New York: John Wiley and Sons.

Ives, Joseph C.
1861   <u>Report on the Colorado River of the West, explored in 1857 and
        1858 by Lt. Joseph C. Ives.</u> House Executive Document, No. 90,
        36th Congress, 1st Session. Washington: Government
        Printing Office.

Jelinek, Arthur J.
1976   Form, function and style in lithic analysis. In <u>Cultural
        change and continuity: essays in honor of James Bennett
        Griffin</u>, edited by Charles E. Cleland, pp. 19-33. New York:
        Academic Press.

Jennings, Calvin H.
1971   <u>Early prehistory of the Coconino Plateau, northwestern
        Arizona.</u> Ph.D. dissertation, University of Colorado. Ann
        Arbor: Microfilms Press.

Jennings, Jesse D.
1957   Danger Cave. <u>Memoirs of the Society for American Archaeology</u>
        14.

Jeter, Marvin D.
  1977   Archaeology in Copper Basin, Yavapai County, Arizona: model
           building for the prehistory of the Prescott region. Arizona
           State University Anthropological Research Paper 11.

Kemrer, Sandra, Sandra Schultz, and William Dodge
  1972   An archaeological survey of the Granite-Reef aqueduct.
           Arizona State Museum Archaeological Series 12.

Kniffen, Fred B.
  1935   Geography. In Kroeber (editor), pp. 27-47.

Kroeber, A. L. (editor)
  1935   Walapai ethnography. Memoirs of the American Anthropologi-
           cal Association 42.

Lange, Charles H., and Carroll L. Riley (editors)
  1966   The southwestern journals of Adolph F. Bandelier, 1880-1882.
           Albuquerque: University of New Mexico Press.

Lavender, David
  1954   Bent's Fort. Garden City, New York: Doubleday and Company.

Lee, Willis T.
  1908   Geological reconnaissance of a part of western Arizona.
           Washington, D.C.: Government Printing Office.

Leslie, Lewis Burt (editor)
  1929   Uncle Sam's camels: the journal of May Humphreys Stacy
           supplemented by the report of Edward Fitzgerald Beale, 1857-
           1858. Cambridge: Harvard University Press.

Linford, Laurance D.
  n.d.a   An assessment of the research potential of six archaeological
           sites within the Cyprus-Bagdad Copper Mining Company Wickiup
           to Bagdad pipeline corridor. MS. Cultural Resource Manage-
           ment Section, Arizona State Museum, Tucson.

  n.d.b   Archaeological interpretation through lithic analysis:
           Arizona AA:15:11. Arizona State Museum Archaeological
           Series.

Lowe, Charles H.
  1964   The vertebrates of Arizona. Tucson: University of Arizona
           Press.

MacGregor, Gordon
  1935   Houses. In Kroeber (editor), pp. 76-78.

Matson, Richard G.
　　1971　Adaptation and environment in the Cerbat Mountains, Arizona. Ph.D. dissertation, University of California, Davis. Ann Arbor: Microfilms Press.

　　1974　The determination of archaeological structure: an example from the Cerbat Mountains, Arizona. Plateau 47: 26-40.

McGimsey, Charles R. III
　　1972　Public archaeology. New York: Seminar Press.

McGregor, John C.
　　1941　Winona and Ridge Ruin. Museum of Northern Arizona Bulletin 18, 19.

McGuire, Randall H.
　　1977　The Copper Canyon-McGuireville Project: archaeological investigations in the middle Verde Valley, Arizona. Contribution to Highway Salvage Archeology in Arizona 45.

McKennan, Robert
　　1935　Marriage and sex. In Kroeber (editor), pp. 61-70.

McPherson, Gale M., and Peter J. Pilles
　　1975　Archaeological investigations, Cyprus-Bagdad Copper Corporation Bagdad Mine expansion, Yavapai County, Arizona: final report, for Phase I archaeological and ethnohistorical investigations. MS. Museum of Northern Arizona.

Mekeel, Scudder
　　1935　Subsistence. In Kroeber (editor), pp. 48-57.

Morgan, Dale
　　1953　Jedediah Smith and the opening of the West. Indianapolis: Bobbs Merrill.

Parks, G.A., and T. T. Tieh
　　1966　Identifying the geographical source of artifact obsidian. Nature 211(5046): 289-290.

Pattie, James D.
　　1930　The personal narrative of James O. Pattie of Kentucky, edited by Timothy Flint. Chicago: Lakeside Press.

Pearl, Richard M.
　　1960　Rocks and minerals. New York: Barnes and Noble.

Phillips, David A., Jr.
    1974   A limited testing program for Arizona T:11:31 (ASM), AA:10:3 (ASM), and AA:14:14. In An Archaeological Survey of the Tucson Gas and Electric El Sol-Vail transmission line, by James McDonald, David A. Phillips, Jr., Yvonne Stewart, and Ric Windmiller, pp. 135-142. Arizona State Museum Archaeological Series 53.

Pough, Frederick H.
    1960   A field guide to rocks and minerals. Boston: Houghton Mifflin.

Ransome, F. L.
    1903   Geology of the Globe copper district, Arizona. USGS Professional Paper 12.

Redman, Charles L.
    1973   Multistage fieldwork and analytical techniques. American Antiquity 38: 61-79.

    1975   Productive sampling strategies for archaeological sites. In Sampling in Archaeology, edited by James W. Mueller, pp. 147-154. Tucson: University of Arizona Press.

Renfrew, C., J. R. Cann, and J. E. Dixon
    1965   Obsidian in the Aegean. Annual of the British School of Archaeology at Athens 60: 225.

Rogers, Malcolm J.
    1939   Early lithic industries of the lower basin of the Colorado River and adjacent desert areas. San Diego Museum Papers 3.

    1945   An outline of Yuman prehistory. Southwestern Journal of Anthropology 1: 167-198.

    1966   Ancient hunters of the Far West. San Diego: Union Tribune Publishing Company.

Schaafsma, Curtis F.
    1975   Archaeological survey and excavations at Abiquiu Reservoir, Rio Arriba County, New Mexico. School of American Research, Santa Fe. Report submitted to U.S. Army Corps of Engineers.

    1976   Archaeological survey of maximum pool and Navajo excavations at Abiquiu Reservoir, Rio Arriba County, New Mexico. School of American Research, Santa Fe. Report submitted to U.S. Army Corps of Engineers.

Schaafsma, Curtis F.
1977   <u>Archaeological excavation and lithic analysis in the Abiquiu Reservoir District, New Mexico</u>. School of American Research, Santa Fe. Report submitted to City of Albuquerque.

Schiffer, Michael B.
1972   Archaeological context and systemic context. <u>American Antiquity</u> 37: 156-165.

1975a   Archaeology as behavioral science. <u>American Anthropologist</u> 77: 836-848.

1975b   Archeological research and contract archeology. In The Cache River Archeological Project: an experiment in contract archeology, assembled by Michael B. Schiffer and John H. House, pp. 1-7. <u>Arkansas Archeological Survey, Publications in Archeology, Research Series</u> 8.

1975c   Behavioral chain analysis: activities, organization, and the use of space. In Chapters in the prehistory of eastern Arizona, IV, by Paul S. Martin, Ezra B. Zubrow, Daniel C. Bowman, David A. Gregory, John A. Hanson, Michael B. Schiffer, and David Wilcox, pp. 103-119. <u>Fieldiana: Anthropology</u> 65.

1976   <u>Behavioral archeology</u>. New York: Academic Press.

Schiffer, Michael B., and George J. Gumerman (editors)
1977   <u>Conservation archaeology: a guide for cultural resource management studies</u>. New York: Academic Press.

Schreiber, John P., and William J. Breed
1971   Obsidian localities in the San Francisco volcanic field, Arizona. <u>Plateau</u> 43: 115-119.

Schroeder, Albert H.
1952   A brief history of the Yavapai of the middle Verde Valley. <u>Plateau</u> 24: 111-118.

1957   The Hakataya cultural tradition. <u>American Antiquity</u> 23: 176-178.

1960   The Hohokam, Sinagua and Hakataya. <u>Archives of Archaeology</u> 5. Madison: Society for American Archaeology and the University of Wisconsin Press.

1961   The archeological excavations at Willow Beach, Arizona, 1950. <u>University of Utah Anthropological Papers</u> 50.

1974   <u>A study of Yavapai history</u>. New York: Garland.

Schwartz, Douglas W.
  1956   The Havasupai 600 A.D. - 1955 A.D.: a short culture history.
          Plateau 28: 77-85.

Sellers, William D., and Richard H. Hill (editors)
  1974   Arizona climate 1931-1972 (2nd revised edition). Tucson:
          University of Arizona Press.

Semenov, S. A.
  1964   Prehistoric technology. New York: Barnes and Noble.

Service, Elman R.
  1962   Primitive social organization: an evolutionary perspective.
          New York: Random House.

Sheets, Payson D.
  1973   Edge abrasion during biface manufacture. American Antiquity
          38: 215-218.

Shepard, Anna O.
  1956   Ceramics for the archaeologist. Carnegie Institution of
          Washington Publication 609, Washington.

Smith, Charline G.
  1973   Selé, a major vegetal component of the aboriginal Hualapai
          diet. Plateau 45: 102-110.

Spain, James N.
  1975   Lithic analysis: AZ T:11:31 (ASM) and AZ AA:10:3 (ASM).
          Arizona State Museum Archaeological Series 86.

Spicer, Edward H.
  1936   King's Ruin. In Spicer and Caywood, pp. 5-85.

Spicer, Edward H., and Louis P. Caywood
  1936   Two pueblo ruins in west central Arizona. University of
          Arizona Bulletin, Social Sciences Bulletin 10.

Spier, Leslie
  1928   Havasupai ethnography. American Museum of Natural History
          Anthropological Papers 29: 81-392.

Steward, Julian H.
  1955   Theory and culture change. Urbana: University of Illinois
          Press.

Tringham, Ruth, Glenn Cooper, George Odell, Barbara Voytek, and
  Anne Whitman
  1974   Experimentation in the formation of edge damage: a new
          approach to lithic analysis. Journal of Field Archaeology
          1: 171-196.

220

U.S. Bureau of Land Management
  1974   Proposed Big Sandy-Bagdad water pipeline. EAR No. 02020-6-1:
          final environment analysis record. Phoenix District Office.
          MS. Cultural Resource Management Section, Arizona State
          Museum, Tucson.

  1976   BLM unit resource analysis, Aquarius Planning Unit. MS.
          Cultural Resource Management Section, Arizona State Museum,
          Tucson.

Voelker, Frederic E.
  1971   William Sherley (Old Bill) Williams. In The mountain men
          and the fur trade of the Far West (Vol. 8), edited by
          LeRoy R. Hafen, pp. 365-394. Glendale, California: Arthur H.
          Clark.

Warren, Claude N.
  1967   The San Dieguito Complex: a review and hypothesis. American
          Antiquity 32: 168-185.

Wasley, William W., and R. Gwinn Vivian
  1965   Report of surveys conducted by the Arizona State Museum for
          the National Park Service under Contract 14-10-0333-995.
          MS. Arizona State Museum, Tucson.

Weed, Carol S., and Albert E. Ward
  1970   The Henderson Site: Colonial Hohokam in north central
          Arizona: a preliminary report. The Kiva 36(2): 1-12.

Wilmsen, Edwin N.
  1968   Functional analysis of flaked stone artifacts. American
          Antiquity 33: 156-161.

  1970   Lithic analysis and cultural inference: a Paleo-Indian case
          study. University of Arizona Anthropological Papers 16.

Wilson, Eldred D.
  1962   A résumé of the geology of Arizona. Arizona Bureau of Mines
          Bulletin 171.